AF600652

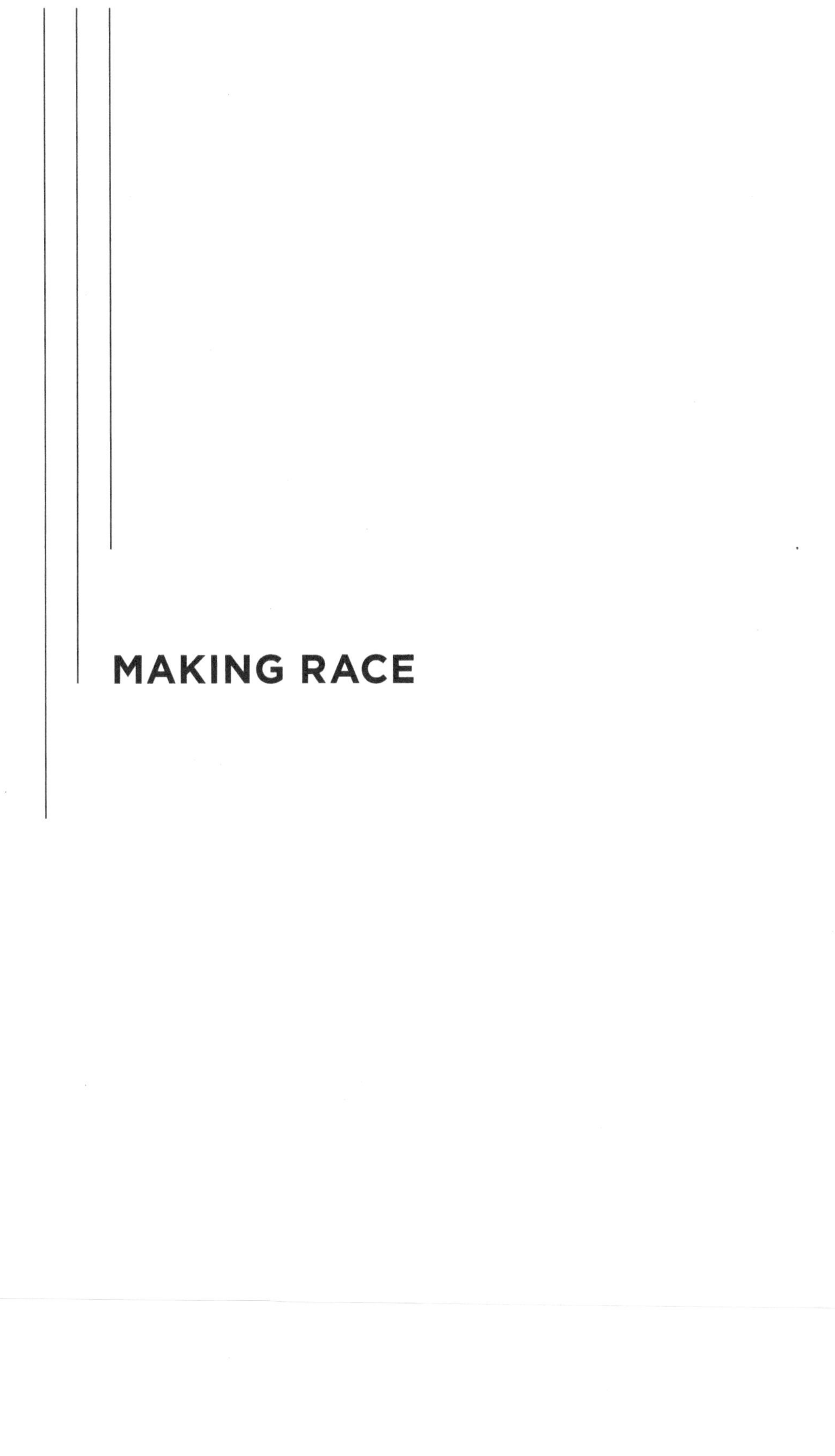

MAKING RACE

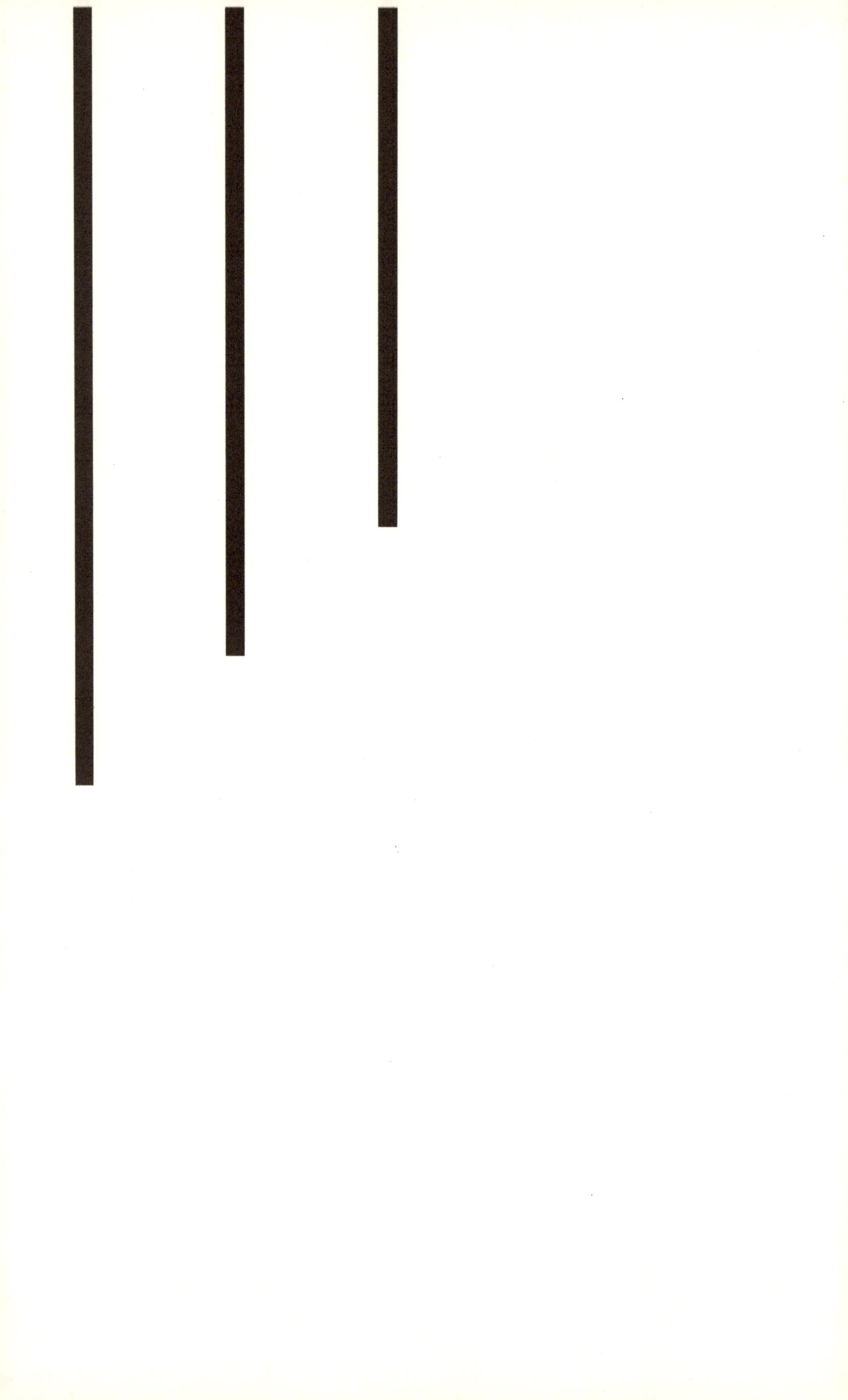

MAKING RACE

MODERNISM AND "RACIAL ART" IN AMERICA

Jacqueline Francis

A MCLELLAN BOOK

UNIVERSITY OF WASHINGTON PRESS
Seattle & London

Making Race: Modernism and "Racial Art" in America is published with the assistance of a grant from the McLellan Endowed Series Fund, established through the generosity of Martha McCleary McLellan and Mary McLellan Williams.

The book also received generous support from the Wyeth Foundation for American Art.

Printed in the United States of America
Design by Thomas Eykemans
16 15 14 13 12 5 4 3 2 1

UNIVERSITY OF WASHINGTON PRESS
P.O. Box 50096, Seattle, WA 98145, U.S.A.
www.washington.edu/uwpress

LIBRARY OF CONGRESS CATALOGING-IN-PUBLICATION DATA
Francis, Jacqueline.
Making race : modernism and "racial art" in America / Jacqueline Francis.
p. cm.
Summary: "A comparative history of New York expressionist painters Malvin Gray Johnson (1896–1934), Yasuo Kuniyoshi (1893–1953), and Max Weber (1881–1961)"—Provided by publisher.
Includes bibliographical references and index.
ISBN 978-0-295-99145-0 (pbk.)
1. Modernism (Art)—United States. 2. Painting, American—20th century. 3. Johnson, Malvin Gray, 1896–1934—Criticism and interpretation. 4. Kuniyoshi, Yasuo, 1889–1953—Criticism and interpretation. 5. Weber, Max, 1881–1961—Criticism and interpretation. 6. Art criticism—United States—History—20th century. 7. Art and race. I. Title.
ND212.5.M63F73 2012 759.13—dc23 2011017782

The paper used in this publication is acid free and meets the minimum requirements of American National Standard for Information Sciences—Permanence of Paper for Printed Library Materials, ANSI Z39.48-1984.∞

For Malvin Gray Johnson, Yasuo Kuniyoshi, and Max Weber

CONTENTS

ACKNOWLEDGMENTS

There are many people who have encouraged me in my career and, in doing so, helped make this book possible. I am indebted to David H. Brown, my dissertation advisor, who modeled ways of asking good questions and rethinking easy assumptions. I also thank Richard A. Long and Clark V. Poling, now professors emeriti at Emory University, who served on my committee and remain committed supporters of my work.

At the University of Michigan, the Center for African and African American Studies organized a forum in which this book was read in manuscript form: thanks to Paul A. Anderson, Kevin Carr, Erica Doss, and Rebecca Zurier for their constructive comments and suggestions. Jorella Andrews, Sussan Babaie, Celeste Brusati, Megan Holmes, James S. Jackson, Martha Jones, Arlene Keizer, Ifeoma C. Kiddoe Nwankwo, Alka Patel, Alex Potts, Julius Scott, M. Sarita See, Patricia Simons, and Susan Siegfried are all friends in word and in deed. My research assistant Kathy Zarur worked hard to track down and procure images and handle correspondence with collectors and institutions; she served beyond the call of duty. The Department of the History of Art provided subvention funds for illustration costs and the Japanese translation services of Yasuo Watanabe. The Visual Resource Collections and Media Services staff of the Department of the History of Art also provided key support as I wrote this book.

I owe considerable debt to other academic colleagues and those who work in museums, for they have heard this book's arguments in talks I have given at their institutions, on panels at conferences and symposia, and in spirited conversations with them. Among these individuals are Jasmine Alinder, Scott Anderson, Renée Ater, Judith Bettelheim, John P. Bowles, Jacqueline Nassy Brown, Mary Ann Calo, Floyd Coleman, Bridget R. Cooks, Shiree Dyson, Gwendolyn H. Everett, Ruth Fine, Tuliza Fleming, Bill Gaskins, Stephen Hall, Camara Dia Holloway, Nicole Gilpin Hood, Ben Jones, Steven Loring Jones, Linda Kim, Tirza True Latimer, Julie McGee, Valerie J. Mercer, Amy Mooney, Stacy I. Morgan, Richard J. Powell, Jordana Moore Saggese, Eric J. Segal, Helen Shannon, Gwendolyn DuBois Shaw, Cherise Smith, Krista A. Thompson, James Tottis, Margaret R. Vendryes, Jonathan Walz, Shi-Pu Wang, Susan Weiner, and Judith Wilson. I also must acknowledge students in my classes at Kenyon College, the University of Michigan, the California College of the Arts, California State University at San Francisco, and Stanford University who asked me good questions about the arguments presented in this book, which, in turn, prompted me to better articulate its claims.

I am grateful for the expertise of librarians and visual resource professionals who helped me find important documents and artworks at the Amistad Research Center at Tulane University, the Archives of American Art, the Archives of the National Academy of Art, the California College of the Arts, California State University at San Francisco, Emory University, the John S. Guggenheim Foundation, Kenyon College, the Library of Congress, the National Archives, the Oakland Museum of California, the New York Public Library, the San Francisco Public Library, the Smithsonian Institution's Archives of American Art, the University of Michigan, and the Whitney Museum of American Art.

I greatly appreciate the generosity of the individual collectors and administrators of private and public collections and estates who granted me permission to reproduce artworks from their holdings. At the University of Washington Press it has been my honor to work with the director Pat Soden, acquiring editor Jacqueline Ettinger, managing editor Marilyn Trueblood, editor Kerrie Maynes, and members of the design and marketing departments. I am extremely privileged to have received additional support from the Wyeth Foundation for American Art, administered by the Center for Advanced Study in the Visual Arts, Washington, D.C.

The encouraging words of friends outside of academia and from family have sustained me during this project. I thank Roy Bogle, Una Cambrige, Sam Gilliam, Gladys House, Katya M. May-Wilson, Muriel Morgan, Ingrid Pollard, Dr. Quintin and Mrs. Beulah Richmond, Cathy Richmond Robinson, Myrtle M. Robinson, Jessica Rykken, and John P. Sawyer. My parents, Grace Francis Heslop and the late Guy A. Francis, raised me to be an independent thinker. By sparing no expense in the funding of my education, they made it possible for me to live the life of the mind.

Finally, Pamela R. Franco, Regina R. Graham, Lance T. McCready, and my partner, Carla Richmond, are my best friends. I cannot adequately thank them for their affection, humor, and balanced perspective on everything that matters. To Carla, in particular, I must say, this book would never have been finished without your unwavering love and support.

ILLUSTRATIONS

PLATES FOLLOW PAGE 2

FIGURES

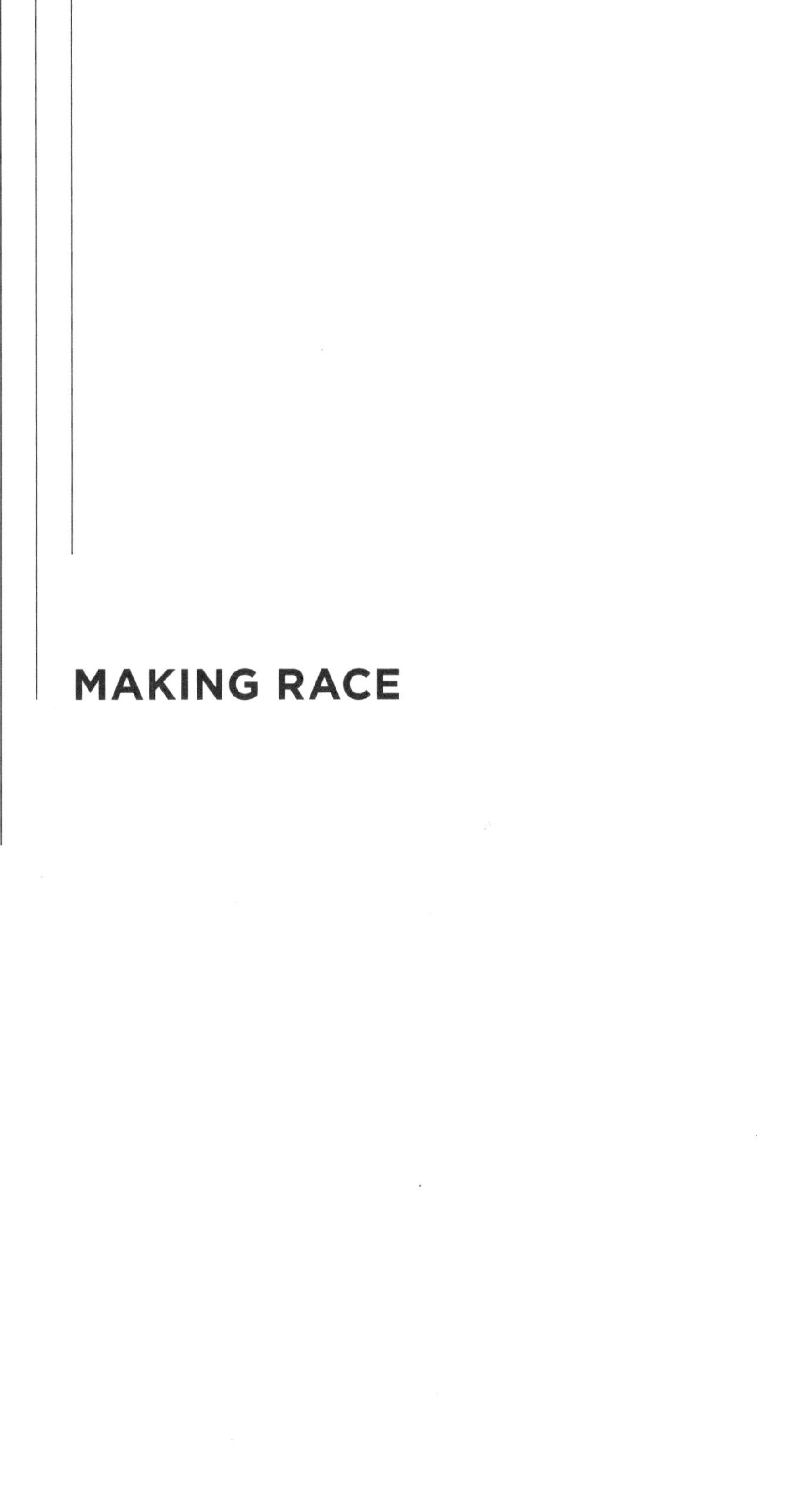

MAKING RACE

1

Malvin Gray Johnson, *Self-Portrait (Myself at Work)*, 1934
Oil on canvas, 38 1/8 x 30 in.
Smithsonian American Art Museum, Washington, D.C./Art Resource, New York

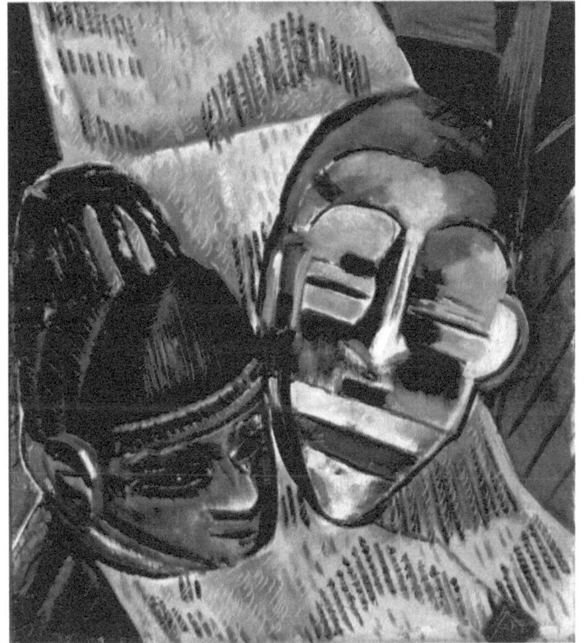

2

Malvin Gray Johnson, *Negro Masks*, 1932
Oil on canvas, 20 x 18 in.
Hampton University Museum, Hampton, Virginia

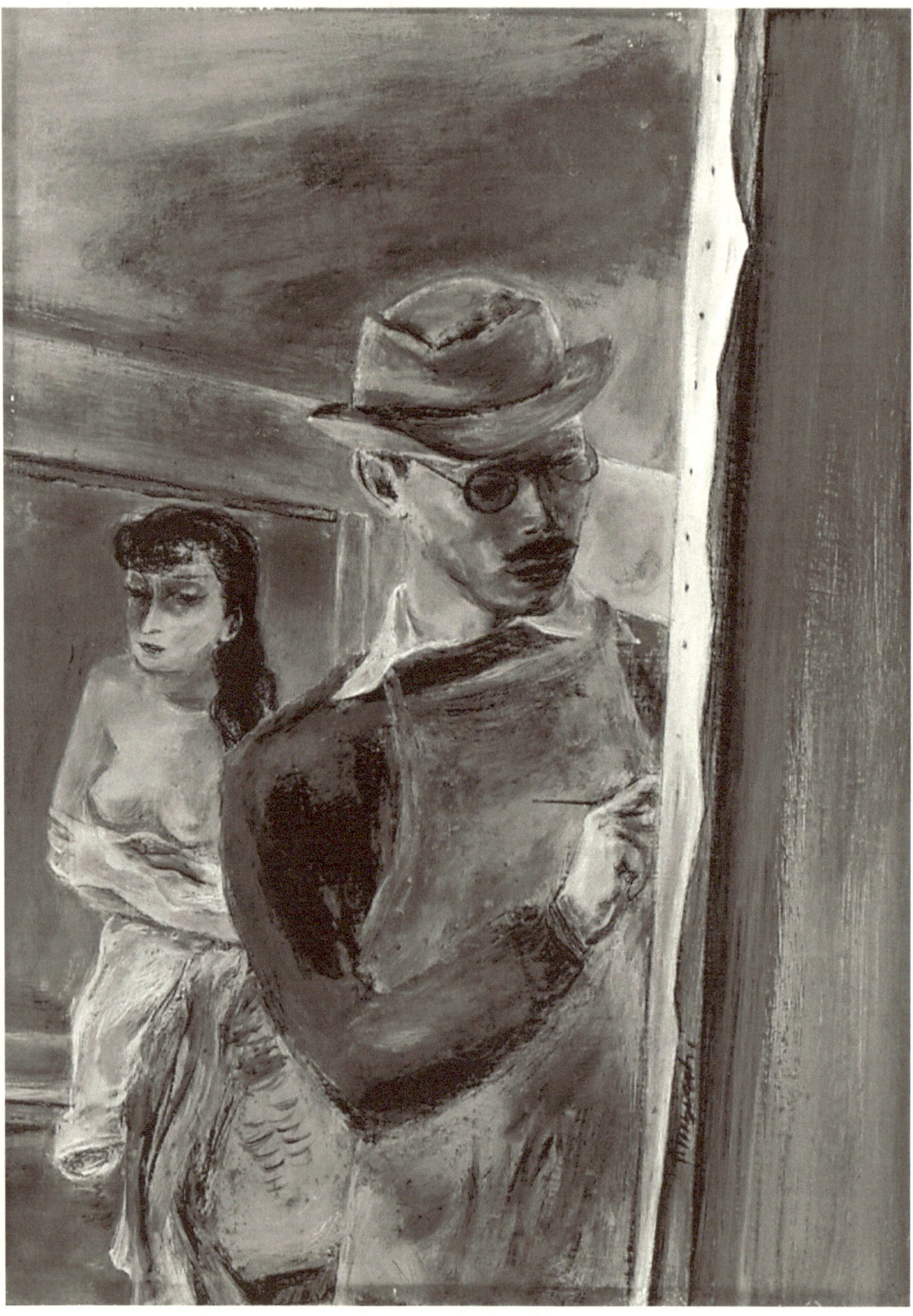

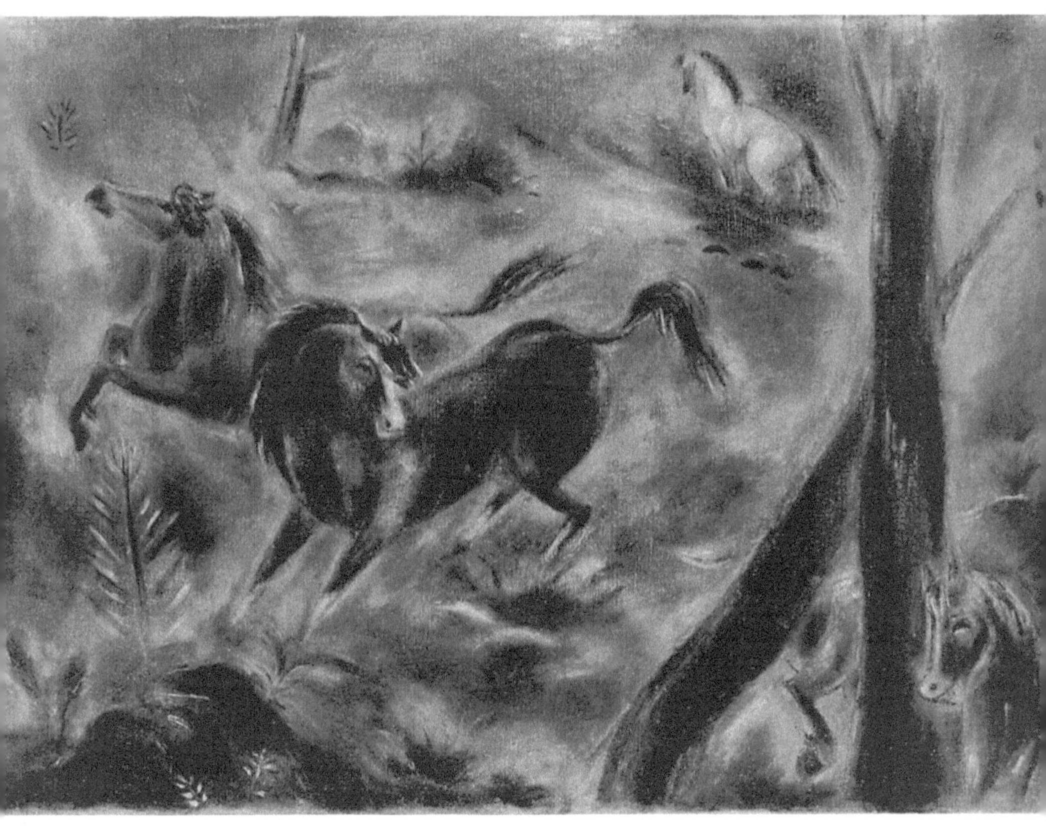

3

Yasuo Kuniyoshi, *At Work*, 1943

Casein on gesso panel, 19 1/8 x 14 1/8 in.

Fukutake Collection, Okayama, Japan

4

Yasuo Kuniyoshi, *Wild Horses*, 1921

Oil on canvas, 20 x 30 in.

Fukutake Collection, Okayama, Japan

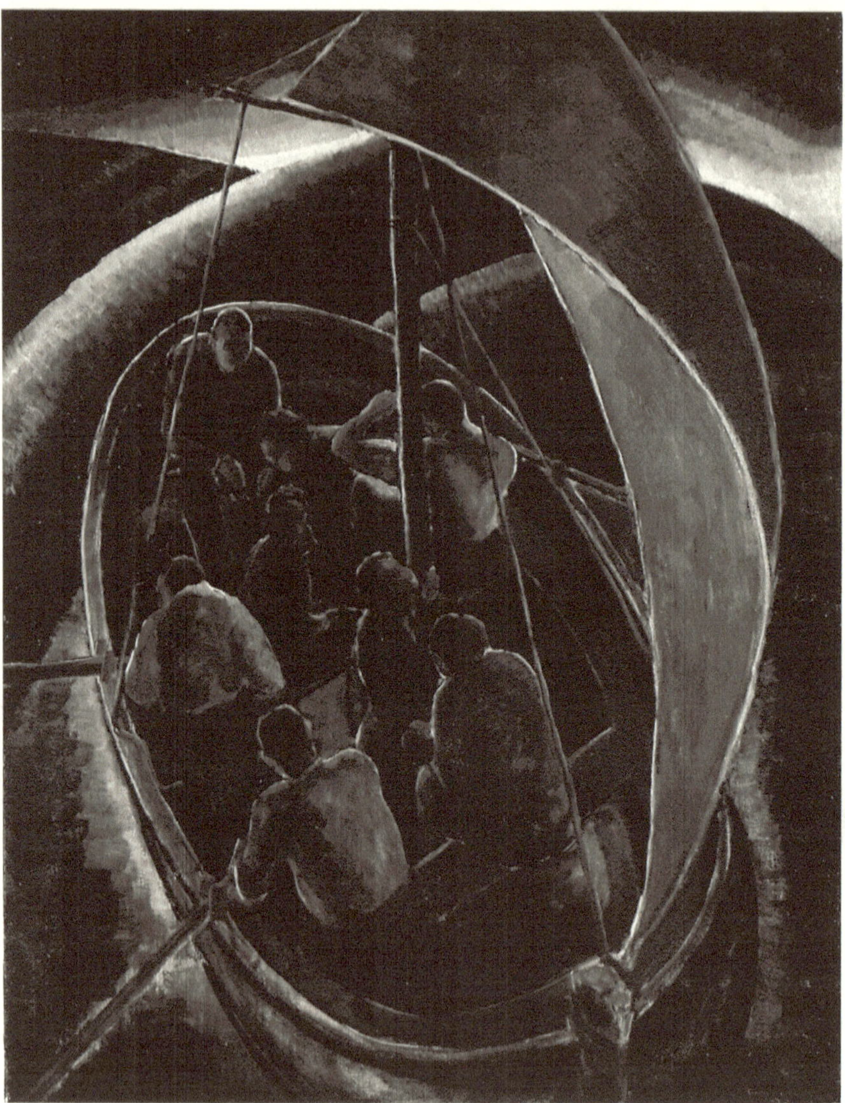

5

Malvin Gray Johnson, *Roll Jordan, Roll*, 1930

Oil on canvas, 36 x 29 in.

Courtesy Steve Turner Gallery, Los Angeles, California

6

George Bellows, *Paddy Flannigan*, 1908

Oil on canvas, 30 x 25 in.

Erving and Joyce Wolf, New York, New York

7

Mark Gertler, *The Rabbi and His Grandchild*, 1913

Oil on canvas, 20 x 18 in.

© Southampton City Art Gallery, Hampshire, UK/ The Bridgeman Art Library

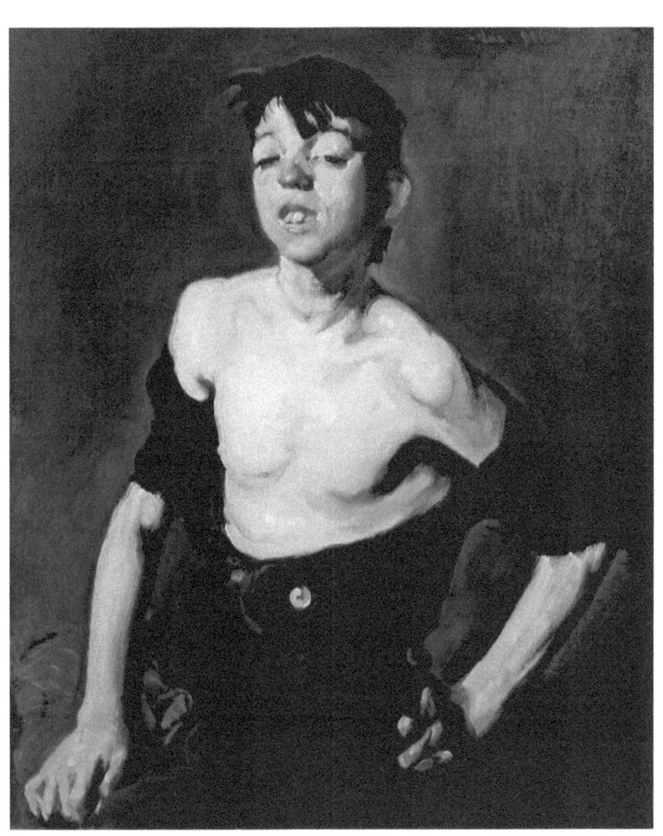

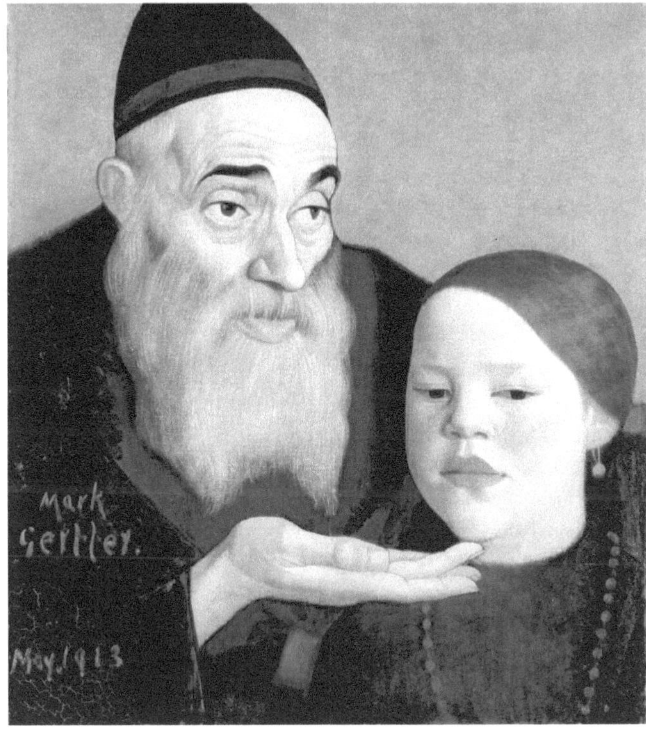
Mark
Gertler.
May. 1913

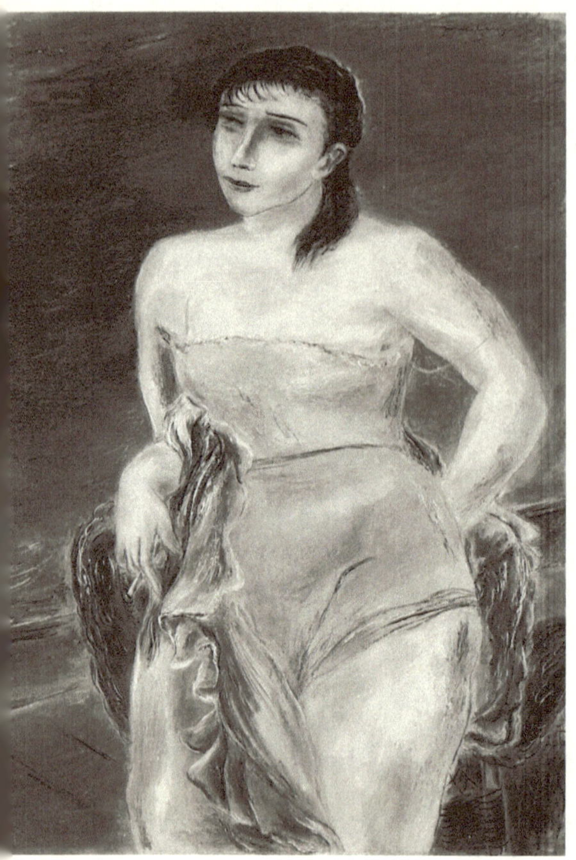

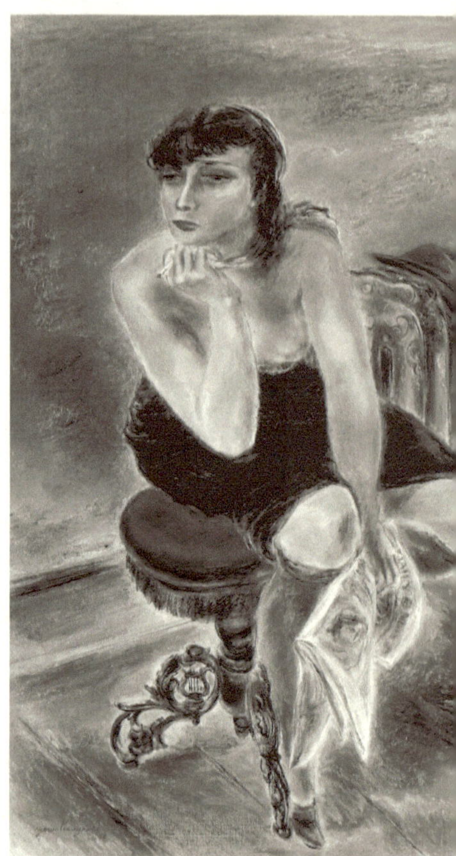

8

Yasuo Kuniyoshi, *Girl in a Pink Slip*, 1932

Oil on canvas, 40 3/10 x 30 1/5 in.

Menard Art Museum Collection, Aichi, Japan

9

Yasuo Kuniyoshi, *Daily News*, 1935

Oil on canvas, 50 x 33 in.

Cincinnati Art Museum, Edwin and Virginia Irwin Memorial, acc. # 1949.48

10

Yasuo Kuniyoshi, *Daily News*, 1935

Oil on canvas, 50 x 33 in.

Cincinnati Art Museum, Edwin and Virginia Irwin Memorial, acc. # 1949.48

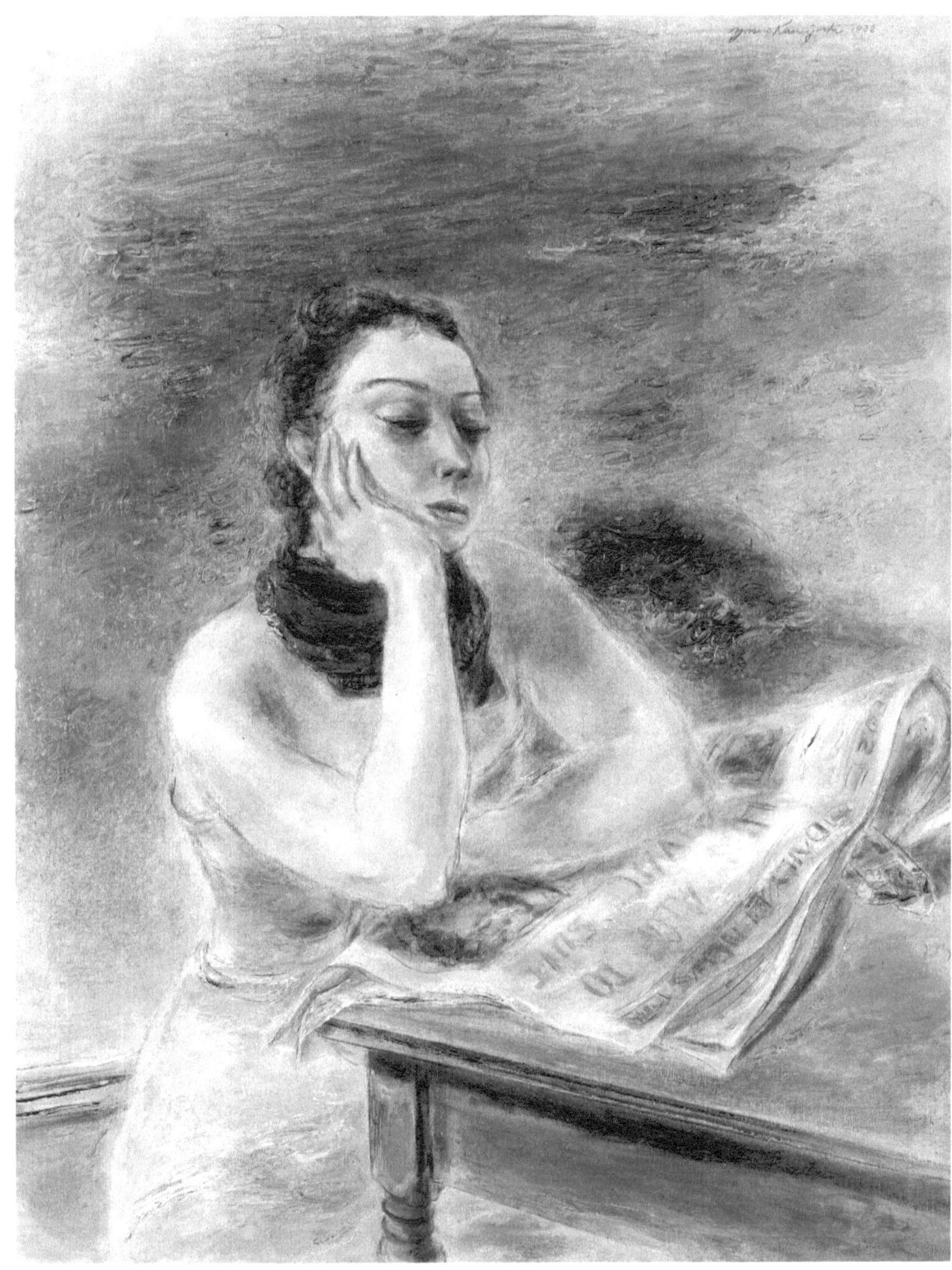

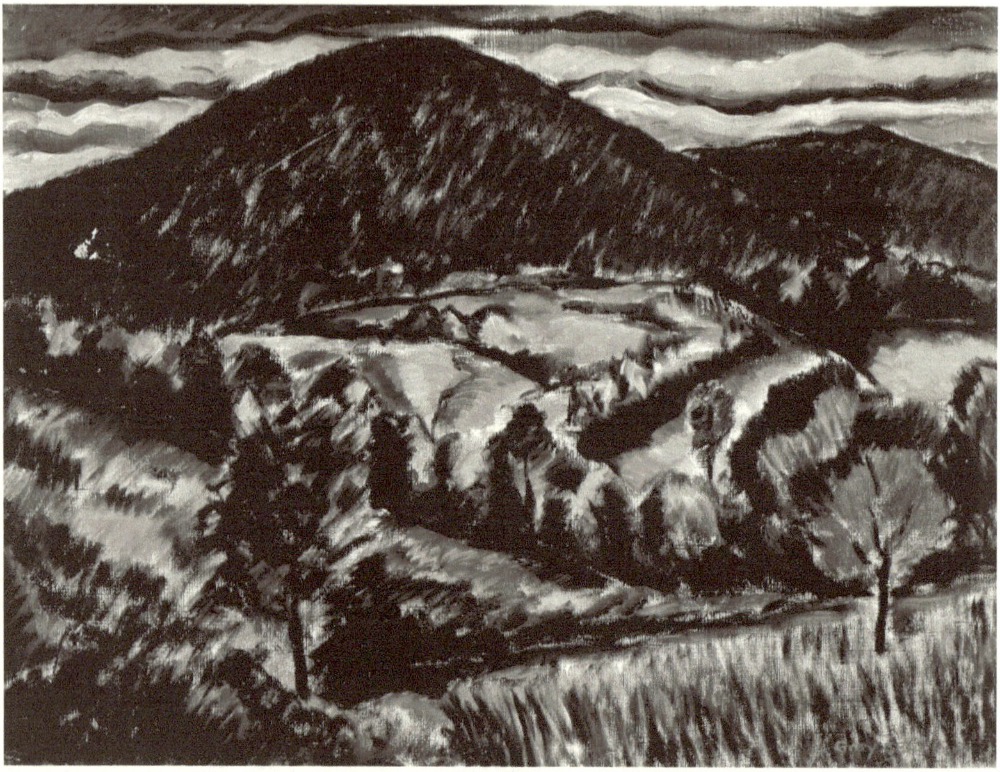

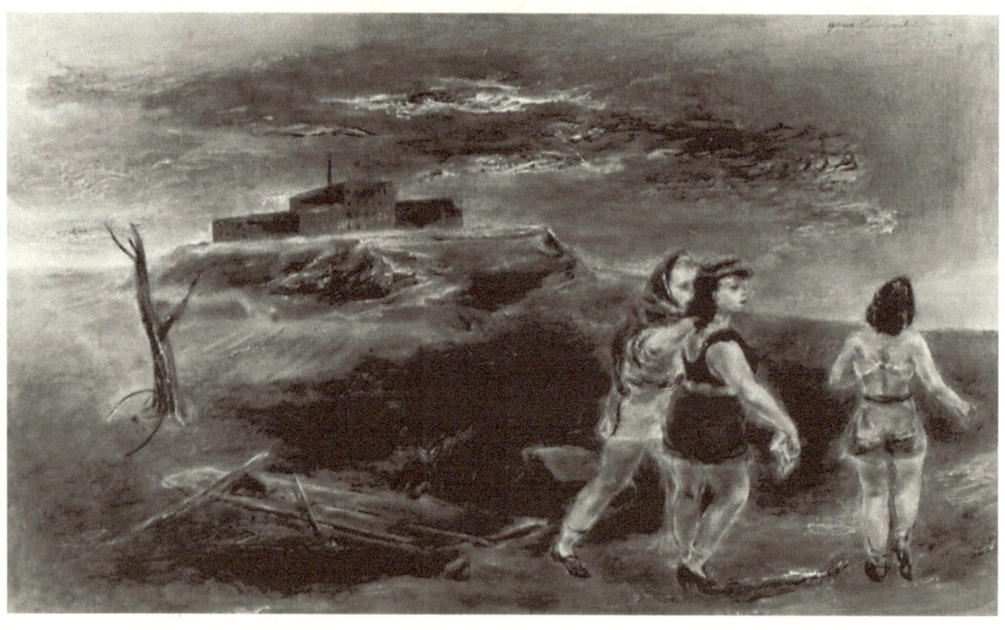

11

Malvin Gray Johnson, *Southern Landscape*, 193

Oil on canvas, 20 x 24 in.

Fisk University Galleries, Nashville, Tennessee

12

Yasuo Kuniyoshi, *Between Two Worlds*, 1939

Oil on canvas, 23 3/4 x 39 3/4 in.

Private collection

ONE

INTRODUCTION

THIS BOOK IS A COMPARATIVE HISTORY OF THREE NEW YORK PAINTERS—Malvin Gray Johnson (1896–1934), Yasuo Kuniyoshi (1893–1953), and Max Weber (1881–1961)—and of the discussions of their works in the early twentieth century. In their images and in their forms, these artists struck a balance between academic naturalism and School of Paris modernism. Johnson, Kuniyoshi, and Weber similarly distorted and exaggerated figures and space while presenting readable imagery of the ethnic and racial "other," a category to which the artists themselves were assigned. Such affinities have gone unnoticed, and by mapping their parallel paths, I provide evidence of American modernism's overlapping, intersecting, and interwoven histories. Operating in this complex matrix, Johnson, Kuniyoshi, and Weber faced challenges quite typical of their era, when Americans clamored for distinctively ethnoracial and national cultural production and simultaneously expressed deep commitment to figural conventions valued in Europe. Having examined the interwar art of

Johnson, Kuniyoshi, and Weber, I find that it was situated in a modernist current particular to the American context, namely, the interwar rhetoric of "racial art."

From the outset, it should be noted that the careers of Johnson, Kuniyoshi, and Weber were dissimilar. Weber is a well-known figure to scholars and students of American modernism. In the twentieth century's first two decades, he developed a cubist style that was admired by progressive audiences but widely denigrated by antimodernist critics. In the 1930s writers rushed to praise his Jewish genre painting and realist landscapes; by the 1950s he was considered "the pioneer in modern American art."[1] Johnson's fortunes were quite different. While active in New York's African American art circles during his brief career, this part-time painter earned less than half the press notices that Weber did because his work was seen primarily in "Negro exhibitions." Still, in those venues and in integrated settings as well, Johnson's painting and drawing generated critical comments, and today several of his figurally abstract genre portraits are mainstays in retrospective Harlem Renaissance exhibitions. As for Kuniyoshi, he, too, was more successful and more famous than Johnson. A sometime romantic realist artist, Kuniyoshi rose to prominence in the 1920s when his whimsical painting and colorful drawing were displayed in New York galleries. Like Weber, Kuniyoshi participated in the Museum of Modern Art's "Paintings by Nineteen Living Americans" of 1929, although Kuniyoshi's inclusion—as a Japan-born immigrant—was widely debated in a way that the Russian-born Weber's was not. Nonetheless, Kuniyoshi's standing as an American artist was firmly established toward the end of his career by two measures: a 1948 retrospective exhibition of his work at the Whitney Museum of American Art and his presence at the 1952 Venice Biennale as a U.S. representative.[2]

As different as the fortunes of Johnson, Kuniyoshi, and Weber were, the three artists are rich subjects for comparative study because they wrote and spoke about their projects in the contemporaneous context of "racial art." They also formed identities, as we all do, around race, ethnicity, nationality, sexuality, gender, and class, subjectivities they constructed and that were simultaneously informed by the society in which they lived. My approach in this book is not strictly biographical, for there are useful exhibition catalogues and monographs that address all three artists' lives. I am interested, nonetheless, in their works as efforts to realize their ideas and in their statements about their art and its reception. Specifically, I examine their modernist practices, which were received as racial art, and their strategies of defining and negotiating their identity positions as they coincided with their ethnoracial and sociocultural heritages. In their era, as in ours, race mattered, and it was deployed to describe Johnson as a Negro, Weber as a Jew, and Kuniyoshi as an Oriental—and such nominations superseded all others. That these characterizations of minority Americans do not square with the present-day's lexicon and perceptions reminds us that race is not a trans-historical category but, more accurately, a sociopolitical and cultural designation that is constantly shored up for differently motivated reasons.[3]

My use of the term "race" warrants explanation. This book examines race as a historic appellation that was applied across the board to many groups—economic, cultural, ethnic, national, and social. Used somewhat more narrowly in the present, "race" is a signal term of nonwhite difference. Yet the history of racialization necessarily includes the formation of whiteness and such precedents as the eighteenth-century invention of "Caucasian" as a racial designation.[4] "White," in fact, is, as sociologist Min Zhou has succinctly stated, "an arbitrary label that has more to do with privilege than biology."[5] Hence, this study's concerns are not only with the deployment of racial terms and their boundaries but also with their meanings and mobility over time. However tempered these terms are by more positive valences—for in the United States, the noun "Negro" has been replaced by "black" and "African American"; "Oriental" by "Asian American," "Asian Pacific Islander," and, more desirably, specific identity designations that index cultural, ethnic, and national heritage tied to the vast and disparate regions of Asia—all of these terms, as well as the designation "Jewish," remain bloc identities that undergo refinement while maintaining their legitimacy. Citing both nineteenth-century legal rulings that prohibited Chinese, black, Native American, and mixed-race persons' testimonies in U.S. trials and the twentieth-century stereotype of Asian Americans as the "model minority," legal scholar Janine Young Kim has argued that Asian Americans' "racial status has shifted from basically 'black' to almost 'white' over the last two centuries.[6] Likewise, "Jewish" is not presently considered a nonwhite, American racial category: in the twenty-first century, Jews, irrespective of their national origins, are generally assigned to the heterogeneous group of white, ethnic minorities in the United States, joining Irish Americans and Italian Americans.[7] As was the case in the nineteenth and twentieth centuries for these European immigrants to the United States, both Jewish émigrés and Jewish Americans faced racialized discrimination that was linked with religious prejudice. Because of anti-Semitism and autoracialization, Jewish Americans were not categorized as Caucasians until late in the twentieth century.[8] Jewish American self-representations as cultural, ethnic, and religious communities are current, contemporary rhetorical stances that are, for good reason, numerous and complex.[9]

It is significant that Weber, like Johnson and Kuniyoshi, considered himself a racialized subject.[10] Today there are those who refute this history, such as the executor of the Weber estate, who refused to grant the rights to reproduce the artist's work in this publication.[11]

Certainly, critics saw Weber's work as "racial art." New York critic Forbes Watson (1880–1960) confidently asserted in 1930, "It is when Mr. Weber paints woeful racial pictures that belong to his own race and are evolved from the sadness of that race that his art comes closest to the sense of life as contrasted with a mental art born out of art."[12] In this study, I am considering the history of the word "Jew," alongside "Negro" and "Oriental," as racial assignment and perceived essence in the twentieth century. Of Weber's *Draped Head* (1926), which was part of his own collection, Duncan Phillips wrote, "The tormented Soul of a Race speaks through this portrait which carries on the Byzantine and El Greco traditions."[13] Images of Jews and images produced by Jewish artists were once placed outside of whiteness and "American-ness" and into the precincts devoted to aberration, deficiency, and anomaly.[14] Early twentieth-century viewers looked for the vibrant color they associated with melancholy Russian Jewish folk culture in Weber's work, much as they looked for Oriental delicacy and African rhythms in Kuniyoshi's and Johnson's, respectively.

Yet however similar Johnson's, Kuniyoshi's, and Weber's solutions to expectations for racial art were, their individual histories were distinct, as were their objectives and each man's experience of race and racism. As well-established, professional artists, Kuniyoshi and Weber were regarded as modernists and they exhibited in emergent spaces for the "new" painting. By contrast, Johnson, a part-time painter, most often exhibited in the "all-Negro" group exhibition, a format that generated race-preoccupied reviews and the search for exotic modes. The question "What is Negro art?" drew audiences to exhibitions, for it was urgently posed in the 1920s and 1930s, and similar discussions took place around the works of artists who were Jewish or of Asian heritage.[15] Of course, viewers who looked for something different in the work of minority artists were determined to find it and held fast to stereotypes that filled the visual field and survived alongside new and occasionally revisionist representation.[16]

"Racial art" was a term often used in the decades between the world wars in the context of Johnson's, Kuniyoshi's, and Weber's practices, and yet it was never explicitly defined by those who summoned it. The modern origins of racial art arose from nineteenth-century European and European American demands for pure painting and original and individual expression. In the subsequent century, racial art's parameters expanded to incorporate the primitivist desires of Westerners dissatisfied with their industrialized societies and keenly interested in peoples they located outside of them. This epistemological shift fortified already potent essentialisms: the work of artists who belonged to religious, ethnic, and racial minorities in the United States was contrasted with that of the national majority. With the latter's avant-garde pursuit and development of art as intuitive performance and emotional release translated into an unmediated practice, the perception was that minority artists had atavistic access to such visual expression. In liberal quarters, racial art was welcomed as the translation of exotic heritage.

Hence modernism was a doubled designation for Johnson, Kuniyoshi, and Weber, one generated by audiences' approbation of their compositions and their bodies as well. In many ways, the three were typical American modernists whose ambitious art is evidence that cultural production is always a contested site, a struggle between producers and consumers. In an era when most Americans disapproved of figural abstraction and held modernism in contempt, these artists gained some appreciation for measured artistic experimentation that departed from naturalism and realism and carried great risks. The critics who first praised their bright palettes and energetic pictures applied similar phrases to the artists' races, nationalities, ethnicities, and cultures. Indeed, many exhibition reviewers—white and nonwhite alike—confidently asserted that the artists' racial positions were self-evident in their themes and practices.

Since style, the outcome of an artist's strategy, is also shaped by critical reception and patronage, in this book I treat criticism seriously. Indeed, exhibition catalogue essays and reviews comprise the principal historical record of styles at a time when American art generated little scholarly attention.[17] In the cases of Johnson, Kuniyoshi, and Weber, the knowable and proclaimed aspects of their ethnoracial identity positions drove discussion of what racial art was and ought to be, and undoubtedly influenced their decisions about what and how to paint. In examining the critical discussions of their work, I am trying to recover the period's sense of racial art as a modernism local and particular to the New York context.

The second chapter, "The Meanings of Modernism," contextualizes this unwieldy category in terms most relevant to Johnson, Kuniyoshi, and Weber. Nonwhites, non-Westerners, and ethnicized non-Christians were emblems of modernity: they were subjects accessible principally to artists living in expanding cities and able to travel to far-flung places in search of new content they hoped would invigorate artistic conventions considered moribund. Modernism, as a diverse suite of formal artistic practices that generally veered away from naturalism, depended on embodied identities that operated around essentializing ideas of the foreign and the primitive. That is to say, these categories have always been defined in both positive and negative terms. They are what they are not. While Johnson, Kuniyoshi, and Weber did not invent such binaries, they reinforced them in the forging of their careers. They were modernists, ones who engaged the United States' ambivalently democratizing art schools, museums and galleries, emergent patronage organizations, and the meta-aesthetic of racial art. Their agency, presence, and investment in these spaces—conceptual and real—undermine broad characterizations about the homogeneity of the American art establishment and demonstrate the heterogeneity of the modernist impulse and its outcomes.

In the next three chapters, I study the artists' work in three prevalent genre practices of their era—religious painting, genre portraiture, and landscape—and analyze racial figuration and symbolism within them. In chapter 3, "Making Race in American Religious Painting," I examine Johnson's and Weber's representations of pious black Protestants and Hasidic Jews, respectively, and the positive reception of these projects as successful racial art. Both of these artists in their statements described their religious subjects in romantic terms with the clear intent of ennobling them. Just as important to the artists' framings of their subjects, however, are their abstractions and summarizations of figures and compositional space. I would argue that Johnson and Weber created types that epitomize twentieth-century transformations of the body and yet are also reliant on stereotypes formed decades earlier. I contend that the success of their modernist forms—often presented as documentary and authentic—was entirely reliant on audience recognition of and familiarity with racial, ethnic, and cultural iconology, including its resilient derogatory symbols. Indeed, the significance and enjoyment of Johnson's and Weber's religious paintings in the era of their making depended on the circulation of past and present signs of difference. These paintings are material evidence of the dialectics inherent to modernism, always regarded as a clean break with the past, and paradoxically, utterly wedded to it. Neither Johnson nor Weber ever stated that these paintings were meant to break from longstanding representational conventions, perhaps because the prospect of doing so was inconceivable.

In chapter 4, "Type/Face/Mask: Racial Portraiture," I survey genre portraiture produced by all three artists, and focus on their depictions of "the other." If the first function of portraits of named sitters is commemoration of specific individuals, genre portraiture willingly lends itself to overarching description of the anonymous, subsequently received as interesting and variably illustrative types. Johnson, Kuniyoshi, and Weber aimed to present the generic and representative racial subject even as they developed formal strategies that disrupt the body's unity. Early in their respective careers, Kuniyoshi and Weber in particular aroused the critics' ire with their antinaturalistic approaches. Yet observers embraced their subsequent expressionist treatment of strangely racialized female nudes and rabbis, as well as Johnson's similar interpretations of African American subjects. Apparently, expressionism was the right means to achieving the promise of racial art, for it offered exuberant color and form, and decorated space; in sum, it was a style that resonated with audiences' internalized ideas about ineffable racial essences. The artists' explanations of their projects sometimes dovetailed with such overdeterminacy, and on other occasions served to distance them from it, illuminating their ambivalence toward racial art, and I suspect, to donning the mask of race.

Chapter 5, "The Race of Landscape," considers the artists' marshalling of resonant and delineative signs for a genre once considered bereft of meaningful subject. In the interwar period, and especially in the Depression era, landscape as a format presented the opportunity to instill American scenes and sights with symbolism. Like many of their contemporaries, Johnson, Kuniyoshi, and Weber subscribed to the myths of the triumphant, American space; inspired by these myths, Johnson traveled to the romanticized region of the South in 1934, and Kuniyoshi to New England and the West during the thirties and forties. While the artists framed their trips as journeys of discovery, their ensuing production—staffed with conventional signs that bind places to affirming narratives and histories—indicates that their journeys began before they left home. What then could landscape mean and do for them? I propose that they turned to landscape as a traditional artistic convention through which they could continue their modernist experimentation minus the specter of identity politics; landscape, moreover, was a marketable format during the lean years of the economic downturn. Lastly, for Johnson, Kuniyoshi, and Weber, variably situated outside of the centralized and privileged American identity of white, native Anglo-Saxonism, representing place was a chance to assert their belonging and commitment to the national body.

This book's guiding purpose is to investigate racial art as a concept that was significant to New York artists and their audiences less than a century ago. This does not mean that I relegate expectations for racial art to the past. In the book's concluding chapter, I argue that if the term "racial art" has fallen into disfavor, the interest in racial aesthetics and spectacle has not. Art critic Harold Rosenberg famously raised the question "Is there a Jewish art?" in an essay of the 1960s, and in subsequent decades many exhibition catalogue writers and survey text authors have taken up the question as well in discussions that answer Rosenberg's query in the negative and simultaneously expand notions of Jewish cultural production.[18]

Where African American artists' production was concerned, the collective Afri-Cobra outlined an artistic program of black aesthetics in the 1960s, and three decades later art historian Richard J. Powell theorized that a black cultural "blues aesthetic" was evident in expressionist painting, realist photography, and mixed media sculpture.[19] Powell has seriously investigated a broad, black cultural particularity, taking on a task not unlike some counterparts who study the production of Asian American artists. Notably, Allan deSouza, the Kenyan-born, Britain-raised artist and critic of Indian descent, has argued that, however anachronistic, problematic container categories such as "Asian American art" are necessary placeholders: they mark the spaces where "there are questions unanswered, exclusionary practices left intact, and vistas yet to be explored that still require some kind of model or platform from which they can be at least addressed if not resolved."[20] My view is less sanguine than Powell's or deSouza's, and closer to that of art historian Margo Machida, author of a survey of contemporary Asian American artists' practices in which she distances herself from any "overarching constructions collectivity that posits the presence of unified Asian subjects."[21] Things may seem radically different in the multicultural present when we celebrate difference and have established customs—political, social, and cultural—designed to institutionalize pluralism. However, in its most cynical and oversimplified manifestations, U.S. multiculturalism often uncritically guarantees the positions on the margin (minority) and at the center (majority), and insures that difference is always the same.[22]

The origins of *Making Race* lie in my intensive research on Johnson, documenting his training at the National Academy of Design, his participation in New York exhibitions, and his relationship with the Harmon Foundation, a philanthropy founded to improve race relations. Racial art rhetoric surrounded Johnson and was advanced by the foundation, which mounted "Negro exhibitions" in the 1920s and 1930s, and by the audiences who attended these shows in search of black expression, which was seen as different from that of whites. Majority nationalist jingoism, articulated loudly and clearly, can be of no surprise to any Americanist researcher, for it was a persistently struck chord among artists and observers from the nation's inception. The book grew out of my surprise at the stark ethnoracial and sociocultural terms used in interwar portrayals of U.S. artists (black and nonblack) and their work. Theodore Roosevelt's melting pot, as a metaphor and ideal, seemed to be utterly unrealized; instead, the descriptive language applied to the national body was unapologetically particularist. I discovered that period sensibilities were accustomed to recognizing difference and manufacturing a justifying logic, a phenomenon that seemed to demand comparative study of the articulations of race and ethnicity.

This study of racial art discourse is built on the foundations laid by historians who charted the arcs of these artists' lives. As I stated above, commentaries that appeared during their lifetimes are valuable records, ones that I will discuss in subsequent chapters. In addition, much of the literature produced about Johnson, Kuniyoshi, and Weber has been published in exhibition catalogues and brochures, and in reviews in periodicals. Cultural historian Yoshi Ozawa's book-length biography of Kuniyoshi in the 1970s and the revised and reissued 1991 version offer ardent readings of an artistic life informed by English-language sources and interviews with the artist's friends and family.[23] Prior to Ozawa's efforts, one-time Whitney Museum of American Art director Lloyd Goodrich authored an exhibition catalogue on Kuniyoshi in 1948 and contributed to the museum's 1986 exhibition catalogue, along with Susan Lubowsky and Tom Wolf.[24] Lubowsky, Alexandra Munroe, Takeo Uchiyama, and Bert Winther collaborated on a Japanese celebration of the one hundredth anniversary of Kuniyoshi's birth, and published a data-rich catalogue whose essays chart his career.[25] Wolf's interest in Kuniyoshi kept the artist in public view in the 1980s and 1990s with the monograph *Yasuo Kuniyoshi's Women* and with an exhibition catalogue with Jane Myers, *The Shores of a Dream: The Early Work of Yasuo Kuniyoshi*.[26] In the same way, Percy North has dedicated herself to Weber studies: her essays for the Jewish Museum of New York and Atlanta's High Museum of Art exhibition catalogues usefully organize and thematize the artist's oeuvre.[27] Daryl R. Rubinstein also has offered rigorous scholarship in his catalogue raisonné of Weber's graphic work.[28] North's and Rubinstein's efforts significantly build upon preceding exhibition catalogues by Goodrich, Ala Story, and Alfred Werner.[29]

In the twentieth century, Johnson was posthumously featured in catalogues accompanying group exhibitions, including those surveying the highlights of the Harlem Renaissance of the 1920s. In my dissertation, the first extensive consideration of his career, I position him as a key figure of a middle period in African American history bracketed by the Harlem Renaissance and the Federal Art Project (1935–1943), and dominated by the Harmon Foundation exhibitions (1928–1931, 1933, 1935).[30] This research subsequently informed a 2002 retrospective exhibition and a catalogue to which I contributed an essay on Johnson's aspirations to join the American art mainstream.[31] He features in two more essays I have published, the first on government-sponsored art projects in the 1930s and the second on visual representations of the South in that decade focusing on the historical conventions of symbolizing that region.[32]

Two prominent art historians have recently investigated Weber's and Kuniyoshi's stories through the prism of identity. Matthew Baigell's 2000 essay "Max Weber's Jewish Paintings" takes on the topic squarely, eschewing sentimental readings of the work, and these arguments are restated in his 2007 survey *Jewish Art in America: An Introduction*. Baigell's self-assigned charge is to find out why the artist decided to work "within a very circumscribed range of genre themes" of the Jewish past.[33] Baigell researches the question assiduously, as did Sheila B. Braufman for her 1981 master's thesis "Max Weber's Judaic Themes," and yet neither finds the answers they seek.[34] Both inventory this aspect of Weber's work with care, and successfully establish that it is a rare example of Jewish visibility in American art. Gail Levin pays similar attention to Kuniyoshi in her 2004 article "Between Two Worlds: Folk Culture, Identity, and the American Art of Yasuo Kuniyoshi."[35] As Josephine Bloodgood did in the 2003 exhibition catalogue *At Woodstock: Kuniyoshi*, Levin investigates Kuniyoshi's incorporation of Japanese toys in his still lifes.[36] Although Levin initially argues that the artist's "work exemplifies cultural hybridity and cross-fertilization" and cites his own statements about his feeling of alienation during a 1931 visit to Japan, she ultimately characterizes Kuniyoshi's sensibilities as thoroughly Japanese.[37] Other scholars, namely, Masanori Ichikawa, Alexandra Munroe, and Shi-Pu Wang, have judged Kuniyoshi's position to be more fluid and have freshly considered his self-awareness, whimsicality, and cosmopolitan art.[38] Munroe's conclusions mirror my own when she writes that his "art and training and stylistic lineage were thoroughly based in the modern European tradition. . . . He neither denied nor exaggerated his Japanese sensibilities in his natural and genuine embrace of modernism. . . . He painted his personal reality, which he saw and experienced as a paradox."[39]

Making Race is a critical race art history, a comparative investigation and analysis of the central role that visual representation has played in the construction of race, a category that has and continues to matter. In name and in intellectual formation, critical race art history is obliged to Frankfurt School critical theory and Critical Race Theory ideated in the 1970s to study and redress American racialization and racism as a historical and continuing norm. Criticalists, as Critical Race Theory proponents are called, develop counternarratives—biography, autobiography, and creative nonfiction—to highlight the inadequacy of U.S. civil rights laws and legal scholarship. Like Critical Legal Studies (another reformist movement of the seventies), Critical Race Theory starts from the premise that American courts, run by living subjects shaped by our society, history, and culture, are unavoidably political, far from neutral, and never objective.[40] While art history is not the disciplinary equivalent of either legislation or legal history, the critical race theorists' stance toward bodies of knowledge and their construction is usefully applicable to productive examinations of artists' agendas, scholarly assessments, and reception. Critical race art historians aspire to the standard of self-reflective inquiry set by the Frankfurt School toward generating awareness of the ways that art—and even art history and art criticism as interpretive writing and discursive representation—makes race real.[41] Furthermore, if "race is social value become perception," as historian Matthew Frye Jacobson has asserted,[42] who better than art historians—trained in visual analysis and research methodologies—to consider this phenomenon?

I have written *Making Race* to draw us closer to the "critical multiculturalism" that Lauren Berlant and Michael Warner envisioned more than a decade ago. Berlant and Warner, who write in the fields of cultural and queer studies, recognized that identities often have been put forth as "generic and iconizing sources of ethnicity, of political validity, and of authenticity."[43] When survey texts add American minorities to art history, the profiles of these cultural producers improve, and yet they remain sidebar items because they are not integrated into the main story. "The normalization of multiculturalism," in cultural critic Kobena Mercer's diagnosis, rarely generates radical reconsideration of dominant narratives, much less sincere reconsideration of how narratives sometimes run parallel to and intersect with each other to create complex, multiple, and layered histories.[44] Yet Ann Eden Gibson's *Abstract Expressionism: Other Politics* demonstrates that such projects can be done.[45] *Making Race* follows Gibson's polemical model of mapping the dynamic construction of identities and situating them as knowledge production—artistic, cultural, and social—with a powerful legacy. As my title indicates, I have also been influenced by

Kymberly N. Pinder's anthology *Race-ing Art History* and sociologist Roderick A. Ferguson's essay "Race-ing Homonormativity," both of which actively challenge the status quo in their disciplines and the stability of identity categories.[46] All of these cited texts inform the antiracist politics of critical race art history, which not only examines race as concept but means to unsettle it by scrutinizing its function in myriad relations of power and privilege.[47]

As an Americanist, one who focuses on the modernist period and has been trained in the history of African American artistic production, I have long worried about what literary critic Gerald Early has termed "the conceptual bind" of African American Studies. Early has suggested that our inquiries "institutionalize the very thing [we] wish to destroy, the act of imposing a unified identity upon a huge population of disparate people."[48] Early's assessment, I believe, is broadly applicable to the fields of gender, national, race, cultural, ethnic, and visual studies in the United States. Our attention to the status of women and minority Americans' cultures and histories is understandable because they have been understudied. Nonetheless, I fear that we are concretizing the margins, and, in the case of African American Studies, we are looking for race only in the precincts of nonwhite difference.[49] Critical race art history emerges from these concerns; it is a push to better theorize the social-cultural and historical approaches that are so central to African American studies and that have been influential outside of it.

The comparative nature of critical race art history promises a sharper analysis of identity positions and their formations. Beyond my primary archive of African American art, I have researched Asian American and Jewish American art histories in search of similarities and contrasts in narrative experience. I have found that the questions raised in the twentieth century about the qualities of racial art had corollaries that formed an ongoing discourse.[50] Triangulation has been a useful approach, and not only because it breaks from the binary analytic that centralizes whiteness, and ultimately, fails to consider its construction.[51] Studying race comparatively also removes minority studies from the niche they occupy in most scholarly fields that reify difference.

Throughout the twentieth century and at the start of this twenty-first one, difference has been a draw, even as it has vexed and guided our determination to classify and organize our bodies, our cultural production, and our spaces.

Among the spate of publications in the last two decades that focus on difference, there are invaluable art histories that demonstrate that modernism must be a pluralized nomination, that is, modernisms. Alejandro Anreus's *Orozco in Gringoland: The New York Years*; Samantha Baskind's *Raphael Soyer and the Search for Modern Jewish Art*; Donna Cassidy's *Marsden Hartley: Race Region and Nation*; Elizabeth Hutchinson's "Modern Native American Art: Angel DeCora's Transcultural Aesthetics"; Anthony W. Lee's *Yun Gee: Poetry, Writing, Art, Memories*; Jonathan Weinberg's *Speaking for Vice: Homosexuality in the Art of Charles Demuth, Marsden Hartley, and the First American Avant-Garde*; and Janet Wolff's *Anglo Modern: Painting and Modernity in Britain and the United States* present artists who were contemporaries of Johnson, Kuniyoshi, and Weber, and who similarly negotiated the tight spaces that minorities are regularly assigned.[52] Significantly, many of these early twentieth-century artists entered the discourse on racial art through the statements they made that alternately supported and rejected the notion. I chose Kuniyoshi and Weber because they were high-profile painters who faced racial art scrutiny, and, like Johnson, had significant responses to it. Furthermore, I find that the works of Johnson, Kuniyoshi, and Weber comprise a concurrent expressionist rejoinder to the challenge of making painting that was modern and au courant.

While known to American art specialists, Johnson, Kuniyoshi, and Weber need to be introduced to most others. I preface summaries of these artists' careers with an analysis of each's self-portraiture, which seems appropriate for this book about socially engaged cultural producers and their projects of representing race.

WEBER

Presented on a modestly sized support of seventeen by fifteen inches, Max Weber's *Self-Portrait* (circa 1926–28) exudes artistic and personal confidence.[53] His centralized body fills the space as a sturdy form built up by oil paint energetically applied with brush and palette knife. Weber's handling of the medium is expert, for, while he chose to limit his palette to related hues of brown, red, and a bit of blue, the painted form solidly occupies the picture's foreground and never threatens to recede into the dark backdrop. To assert the body's primacy,

Weber uses the same sandy colors to describe his hair and his open-necked jacket and then renders his head in higher values of brown. His masklike face is distinguished by the simply rendered dark eyes that register a steady gaze, and by faceted passages and highlights of pink daubs on the nose, chin, and near the roughly approximated right ear. With the pictured body's shoulders sloped and colored in patches like Cézanne's Mount Saint-Victoire and the face interpreted through Fauvist and realist manipulations, *Self-Portrait* is the material evidence of Weber's unwavering commitment to modernism.

Weber, who emigrated from Bialystok (then part of Russia, presently in Poland) in 1891, was an established New York artist by 1928. In the year *Self-Portrait* was made, the conservative Art Institute of Chicago awarded one of Weber's still lifes its Potter Palmer Gold Medal, a distinguishing honor. The following year Weber was included in the Museum of Modern Art's group show, "Paintings by Nineteen Living Americans," and in 1930 MoMA organized a one-artist exhibition of his work, its first for a contemporary American artist. From this juncture Weber was a regular participant in New York and national exhibitions, and considered an elder statesman frequently recognized by art schools, universities, and artists' societies. Weber, Ralph M. Pearson wrote in 1954, "more than any other American, has become our living old master. . . . He is a rock of ages in the history of contemporary art."[54]

Weber's fortunes had decidedly turned at the end of the 1920s, in dramatic contrast to the notoriety of his prior "Cubist Decade."[55] In the earlier period, his figurally abstract modernism gained him prominent admirers, including Alfred Stieglitz, Roger Fry, the Washington, D.C., collector Duncan Phillips (1886–1966), and the New York newspaper critic Henry McBride (1867–1962). Though he was one of the few Americans invited to exhibit in the landmark Armory Show of 1913, Weber declined to do so because the selection committee accepted only two of the nine works he submitted for display.[56] He influenced Stieglitz's modernist sensibility and exhibited in his "291" Gallery and in other progressive avant-garde sites in New York, as well as at the Grafton Gallery in London. But the American and English public and their mainstream presses initially rejected Weber's modernist interpretations of the traditional genres, from his blocky, ritual art-influenced still life *African Sculpture* (*Congo Statuette*; 1910) and his angular proto-cubist nudes to his dynamic views of New

York and its interior spaces, such as *Chinese Restaurant* (*Memory of a Chinese Restaurant*; 1915). Weber fared no better than European modernists with the public, for puzzled and antagonistic critics of the twentieth century's opening decades ridiculed his work just as they had that of Picasso, Matisse, and Duchamp—artists whom Weber revered, and, in the case of Matisse, with whom he had studied in Paris. In 1911 *New York Globe* critic Arthur Hoeber (1854–1915) fumed at Weber's work, "The more the work is strange, crude, awkward, appalling, evidently the more it is in favor with him. . . . Here are travesties of the human form, here are forms that have no justification in nature, but that seem all the world like the emanations of someone not in his right mind, such as one might expect from the inmate of a lunatic asylum."[57] Weber's offense was the willful turn away from naturalism, what *New York Times* critic Elizabeth Luther Cary (1867–1936) in 1911 deemed "the idea of representation as a true function of art."[58] From 1916 to 1922, Weber rarely exhibited, and in the opinion of art historian Susan Krane, the artist "gradually narrowed the scope of his work [toward] . . . anecdotal and religious subjects that gave full play to his lyrical facilities, sentiments, and expressionist bent."[59] While Weber's work of the 1920s has been characterized as abruptly shifting from an avant-garde cubism to a less risky figuration, I would argue that he never abandoned modernism but rather made observable changes in content and format. Weber painted more still lifes and landscapes in the 1920s and 1930s, and more figure groups of recognizably Orthodox Jews. In doing so Weber was searching for a viable modernism, and his moves, like Johnson's and Kuniyoshi's, were driven by artistic ambitions and the fragile and ultimately depressed art market.

JOHNSON

In *Self-Portrait (Myself at Work)* (1934; fig. 1.1, plate 1), Johnson employed the "painting within the painting" conceit, for his 1932 oil painting *Negro Masks* (fig. 1.2, plate 2) is inversely presented in the self-portrait's backdrop.[60] These African masks are deliberately and strategically positioned at the same height as the artist's head, an arrangement that literally aligns the maker with his previously painted subject. Like a totemic African sculpture, the pictured body looks wooden and yet brims with potential energy. And, as is the case with the

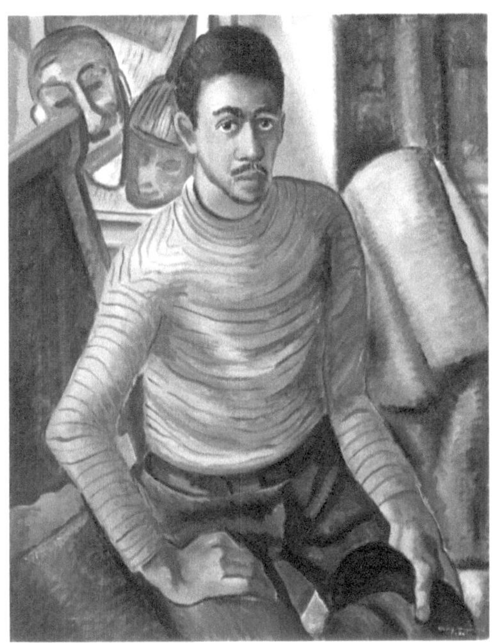

1.1 Malvin Gray Johnson, *Self-Portrait (Myself at Work)*, 1934 (plate 1). Smithsonian American Art Museum, Washington, D.C./Art Resource, New York

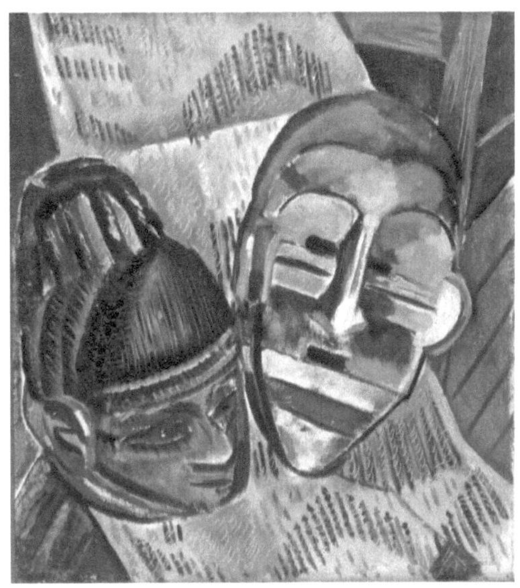

1.2 Malvin Gray Johnson, *Negro Masks*, 1932 (plate 2). Hampton University Museum, Hampton, Virginia

wide range of Western modernist representation spurred by non-Western art, the subject exists in a strangely disjunctive space. How might we understand Johnson's claim that he is "working" in such a cramped setting? By the inclusion of the beautifully painted *Negro Masks* as an achievement in which he took pride? Through the "hat in hand" gesture as oblique entreaty to patrons? Moreover, although this large canvas is subtitled "Myself at Work," why are there few denotative signs of the "artist" and his studio here? Johnson holds no painting tool: indeed, his right hand—his painting hand—rests on his leg. In his left hand, he grips a black Homburg—a symbolic object—against his knee, exactly where a palette might have been placed. With its pregnant silences and suggestive elements, *Self-Portrait* is arguably the central achievement of Johnson's career.

Compared with Weber and Kuniyoshi, Johnson was a lesser-known artist. Johnson, like them, had had formal training. Yet art did not afford him a steady living, and he performed blue-collar and clerical jobs until 1928, when it appears that he devoted himself entirely to painting. He produced almost one hundred oil paintings, watercolors, and ink drawings, working in a careful, realist fashion early in his career.[61] But it was his figurally abstract production from the late 1920s onward that earned Johnson critical attention. A *New York Times* reviewer, "K. G. S.," singled him out for praise in a 1932 group exhibition whose participants included the white American painter Alice Neel (1900–1984): "The best painter in the group . . . is Gray Johnson, a Negro artist plentifully endowed with the conviction that so many of our contemporaries lack. He paints each subject, one feels, because in Corot's words, 'it calls distinctly and insistently upon the eye and heart.' Johnson does not paint light or design or plastic form or psychological intensity. He paints things, and for that reason his canvases have a weight."[62]

Johnson's best press notices followed his participation in all-Negro exhibitions mounted by the Harmon Foundation, a New York charity that supported white, black, and Asian artists and intellectuals.[63] While the foundation's exhibitions in the twenties and thirties provided opportunities for little-known and marginalized artists to display their work, the all-black format facilitated the particularist discourse of racial art.[64] Critics scrutinized the Harmon entries for racial qualities, and, as art historian Mary Ann Calo explained, they "were especially pleased when they discovered evidence of an emotional sensibility rooted in black folk culture and religion. They were in fact looking for the visual equivalents of the Negro spiritual."[65] Significantly, racial art was grounded in the assumption that it was a product of the intuition rather than the intellect. Johnson's darkly rendered, gilded arc painting *Swing Low, Sweet Chariot* (1928; fig. 1.3), the prize-winning painting from the Harmon Foundation's 1929 exhibition of African American art, was favorably compared in *Art Digest* to the work of the white American Albert Pinkham Ryder (1847–1917). This comment and that of another writer who referenced the African American painter Henry Ossawa Tanner's (1859–1937) moody, symbolist religious painting, were rare in their attempts to situate Johnson in an art historical genealogy. Instead, "emotion," "feeling," and "spirit"' resonated in period discussions of *Swing Low,*

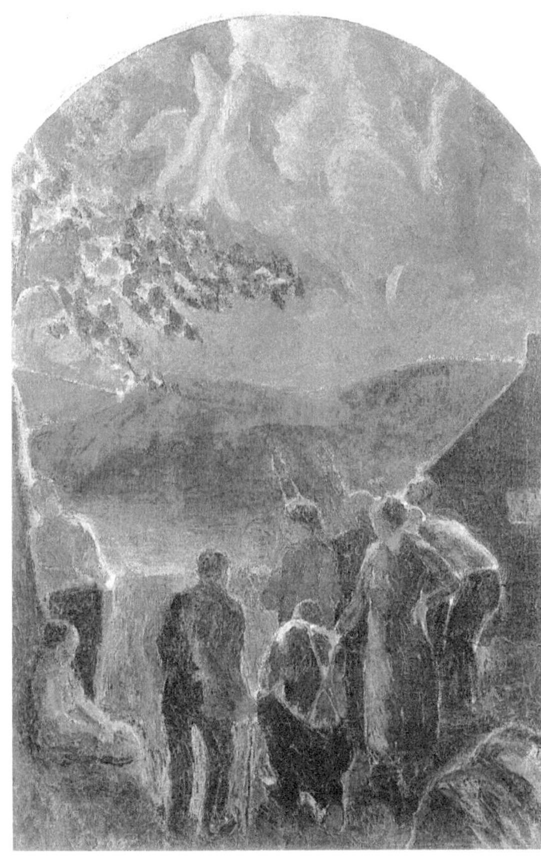

1.3 Malvin Gray Johnson, *Swing Low, Sweet Chariot*, 1928. Oil on canvas, 49 x 29 in. Private collection

Sweet Chariot, and, as we shall see, other works produced by American ethnic, cultural, and racial minorities.

KUNIYOSHI

Kuniyoshi's *At Work* (1943; fig. 1.4, plate 3) is situated in the artist's studio, directing the viewer's attention to the creative métier, the iconic creator, and the female model whose appearance threatens to exceed the accepted parameters of white identity. Curiously, Kuniyoshi depicts himself turned away from this human subject and showing his visage to his audience. It is a dramatic pose, much like the one struck in *Self-Portrait as a Photographer* (1924; fig. 1.5), in

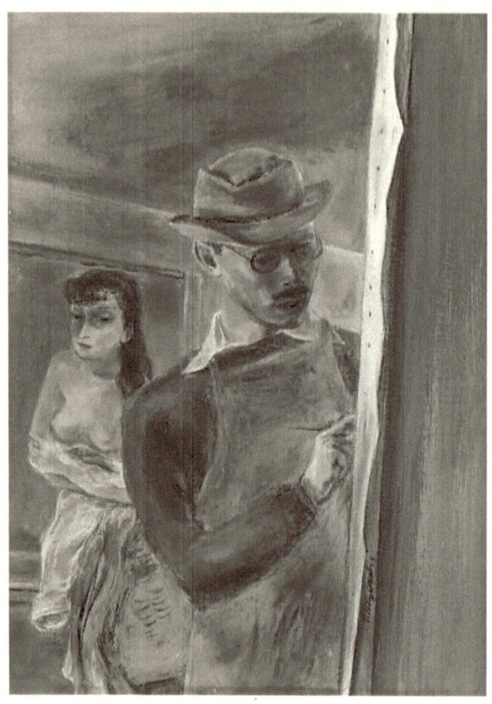

1.4 Yasuo Kuniyoshi, *At Work*, 1943 (plate 3). Casein on gesso panel, 19 1/8 x 14 1/8 in. Fukutake Collection, Okayama, Japan

which the artist wears a bellows camera covering like a cowl and looks over his left shoulder to confront the viewer. The earlier painting's linear and aestheticized personality is indebted to early Italian Renaissance portraiture and communicates Kuniyoshi's knowledge of canonical art as well as an awareness of being seen. Both self-portraits confound because they seem to suggest that representation is not the outcome of close observation but that pictures are made from the imagination. This conclusion is ironic in a painting about photography and one in which the oval shape of the camera eye is evoked in the painting's simplified space and forms, including an East Asian face as it has been historically formulated in the West.

In *At Work* Kuniyoshi offers more information about himself. His grayish face, more shadowy than the model's exposed skin, is heavily worked with paint, as if it is the work of art. He, of course, is tactilely linked to the art object, since his painting hand—a mixed patch of white, brown, and gray hues—abuts the large canvas's surface and his name is signed along its stretcher. Kuniyoshi is also

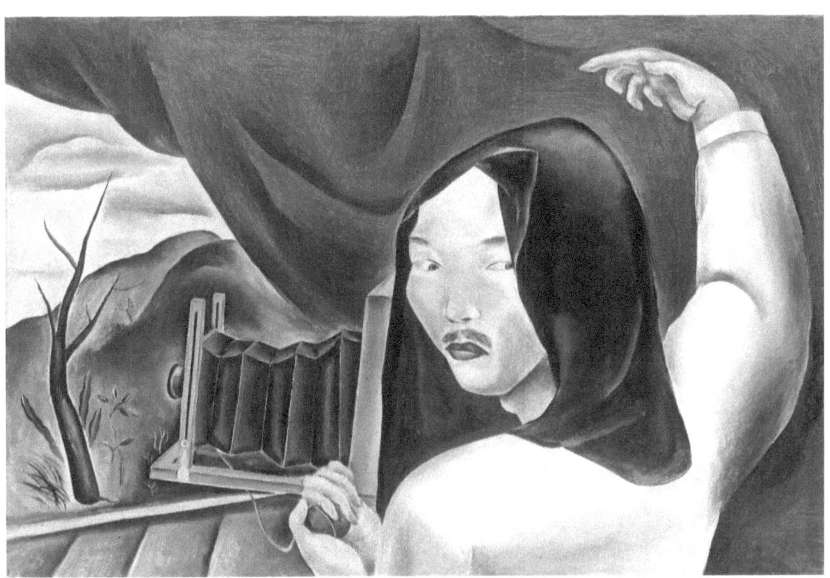

1.5 Yasuo Kuniyoshi, *Self-Portrait as a Photographer*, 1924. Oil on canvas, 20 3/8 x 30 1/4 in. Metropolitan Museum of Art, bequest of Scofield Thayer, 1982 (1984.433.11)

tied to his muse, despite her position in the picture's backdrop.[66] The two facially resemble one another, and yet the possibility of close identification between them is subtended by tensions. His impossibly broad shoulder overlaps one of hers, and the cloth covering her lower half seems to be a man's shirt. Many of Kuniyoshi's female genre portraits of the 1930s, such as *Daily News* (1935), incorporate symbols of a masculine presence, if not a proprietorship of the pictured subject. Beyond this ever-present gender dynamic and the version of it played out between male artists and nude female models in the West, the symbolic measure of national power is germane to *At Work*, which was made during World War II. Considering the era's propaganda images of marauding Japanese soldiers—including those Kuniyoshi produced for the U.S. Office of War Information in 1942–43—*At Work* was provocative, as the fiery hue of the pictured artist's sweater could be associated with the centralized rising sun orb of Japan's national flag.

Kuniyoshi's national loyalties and his place in the discussion of U.S. art were questions debated long before the outbreak of war. Born in Japan in 1893,

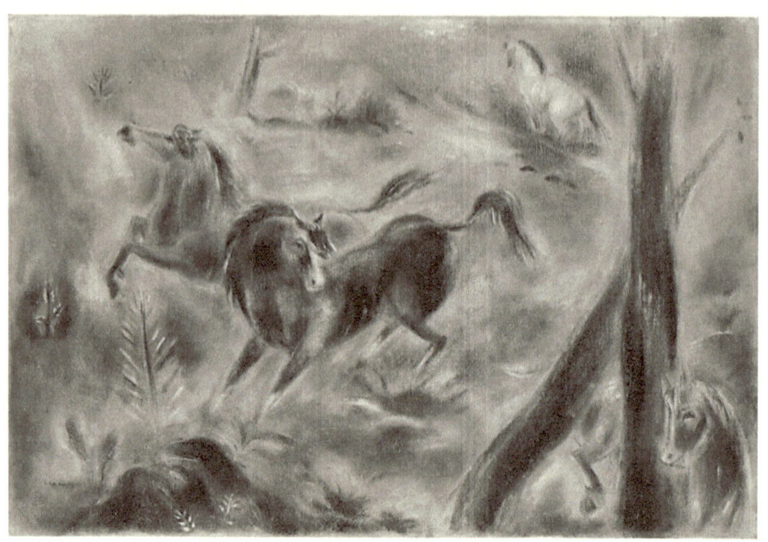

1.6 Yasuo Kuniyoshi, *Wild Horses*, 1921 (plate 4). Fukutake Collection, Okayama, Japan

he lived in the Pacific Northwest, then in Los Angeles, and finally arrived in New York City in 1910. There were other Japan-born painters exhibiting in New York in this era, among them Noboru Foujioka (1896–?), (Léonard Tsugouharu) Foujita (1886–1968), Kyohei Inukai (1886–1954), Kaname Miyamoto (1891–?), Fuji Nakamizo (1889–1950), Chuzo Tamotzu (1888–1975), and Bumpei Usui (1898–1994), but they did not generate the reviews—in number or in tone—that Kuniyoshi did.[67] To assess Kuniyoshi's figurally abstract and whimsical realism in the teens and twenties, American commentators relied upon Orientalist constructions and used his art to reify their essentializing binaries about East and West. Although Kuniyoshi studied at the Los Angeles School of Art and Design, and, ultimately, with Kenneth Hayes Miller (1876–1952) at New York's Art Students League, most critics deemed his skills racial, cultural, and bodily. Kuniyoshi's paintings, wrote the *New York Times* critic in 1922, demonstrated "the genius of his artistically expressive race."[68] According to another anonymous writer, *Wild Horses* (1921; fig. 1.6, plate 4) held the "aloofness of Eastern art influences," with its "bare essentials," and *The Bad Dream* (1924; fig. 1.7) was "very Japanese in spirit . . . a fantasy of demons belaboring the victims

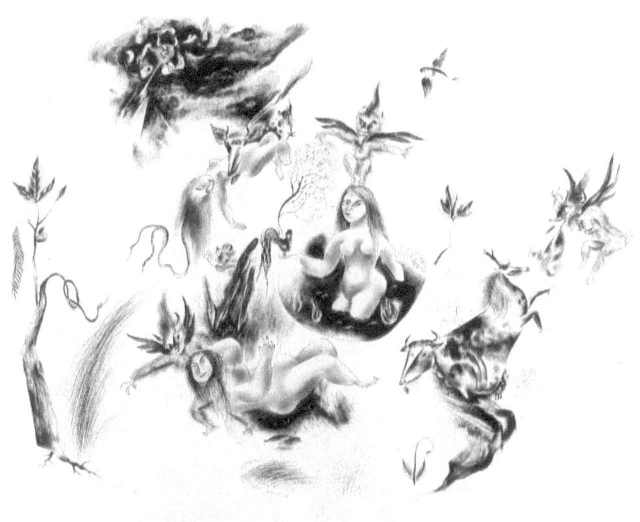

1.7 Yasuo Kuniyoshi, *The Bad Dream*, 1924. Ink on paper, 15 1/2 x 20 1/4 in. Collection of the Ogunquit Museum of American Art (53.12). Gift of Henry Streeter

in a nightmare landscape."[69] Kuniyoshi clearly embodied the idea of "Japanese art" in the United States, which some perceived as a threat.[70]

Simply put, the citing of identity and difference preoccupied early twentieth-century observers who attempted to fix the artist's body and make sense of modernism. As I have shown above, Johnson's race was consistently noted. Weber's and Kuniyoshi's immigrant status were referenced, in turn, throughout their careers, as were their "Oriental" origins.[71] Yet if views about Weber's ethnocultural, religious, and national subjectivity sometimes shifted, Kuniyoshi (like Johnson) remained an insistently "raced" subject. Most critics saw Kuniyoshi's training in U.S. art schools, European travel in the twenties, and activities in New York's progressive art circles as interruptions to the consideration of his perceived Oriental vision, sensibility, and racial art aesthetic. Prominent collectors, curators, and gallerists argued, as did the artist himself, that Kuniyoshi belonged in American exhibitions and museum collections. In 1937 he told Harry Salpeter of *Esquire*, "I can't be very much Oriental. I have spent most of my life here." Yet he added, "I am as much an individual as anyone—except that I have Oriental blood in my veins."[72] Over his lifetime, Kuniyoshi alternately resisted and encouraged singular identity declarations, and claimed to strive toward a unique hybridity. A year before painting *At Work*, he asserted:

> The [Eastern] tendency is toward the spiritual side, while Western art seems to me based on content and forms derived by intellectual analysis. Here is my fist against the light casting a shadow on the table. The fist is the West and the shadow is the East. The fist is actuality—it has form and exists in space, while the shadow is shape, sometimes it has depth and it is diffused with mystery. I try to combine the two kinds of art that I have just mentioned, and to penetrate the meaning, the essence of whatever I'm doing by fully realizing the outer, material aspect.[73]

Kuniyoshi ultimately published this statement in a 1949 essay, "Universality in Art."[74] A commonly articulated ideal after World War II, universality held special significance for the New York School of Abstract Expressionists who characterized nonobjectivity as an accessible visual language. In this climate, Kuniyoshi retained his commitment to figuration, and, apparently, to his humanist principles as well.

As the criticism cited above indicates, contemporary observers freely discussed both artistic and extra-artistic issues they believed relevant to assessment of the works of Johnson, Kuniyoshi, and Weber as American racial minorities. If art historians and critics since the post-modernist period have generally abandoned "the structure of representation," as Rosalind Krauss charged in her 1991 jeremiad "In the Name of Picasso," our predecessors could hardly be accused of the same failure.[75] What we hear in contemporaneous writing about Johnson, Kuniyoshi, and Weber are concerns about pictorial form and subject, and efforts to align the elements of visual expression with the artist's social identity. The rhetoric of identity politics threads through the narratives of American modernity—a diverse array of historical phenomena that included rapid urbanization, migration, industrialization, and social integration—and of American modernisms as well.

TWO

THE MEANINGS OF MODERNISM

In the early twentieth century, modernism broadly referenced a number of art styles and subjects that Americans deemed new. In 1933 New York critic Forbes Watson rightly referred to modern art styles in the plural when he discussed the "development of a series of international painting-fashions" during the first decades of the century.[1] Modernist practices were as numerous as the interpretations of them. Throughout this book, "modernism" connotes the move away from naturalism in painting and toward abstraction—moderate and radical—of figure and ground.[2] Malvin Gray Johnson, Yasuo Kuniyoshi, and Max Weber were variably relegated to, self-identified with, and invested in painting "the other" as new and innovative content, and in writing about them I also locate a reflexive ethnic and racial representation within modernism's boundaries. Before discussing these artists' modernist formal strategies, I will first engage a social aspect of modernism, namely the ways in which bodies were ideologically constructed, understood, and disciplined in its name. Modernism emerged, in part, from a transvaluation of ideas and cultures, and was perfectly tautological: it did not end unequal, historical relationships but instead maintained them and the essentialized identities of all concerned parties. In sum, the modernist framework, defined by negations, required opposition and opposites to establish its authority, meaning, and status.

Race was discursively central to modernity, and "racial art" was a significant inflection of American modernism.[3] The headline of a newspaper review of Weber's 1923 one-artist exhibition at New York's Montross Gallery deemed him a modernist, and, within the review, critic Henry McBride proclaimed, "Jewishness in art, at least of this quality, is new."[4] Nonetheless, in the U.S. press and in art history surveys of the period, modernism was situated as an unwelcome foreign import from Europe that arrived via Ellis Island, "a degenerate new art" and a raging epidemic. Royal Cortissoz, a *New York Tribune* art critic, wrote disparagingly and discouragingly about these new directions in U.S. art:

> There is something in this art situation analogous to what has been so long going on in our racial melting pot. The United States is invaded by aliens, thousands of whom constitute so many acute perils to the health of the body of politic. Modernism is of precisely the same heterogeneous alien origin and is imperiling the republic of art in the same way. . . . These movements have been promoted by the types not yet fitted for their first papers in aesthetic naturalization—the makers of a true Ellis Island art.[5]

The entry of women, the working class, and racial, ethnic, and religious minorities into art academies similarly produced anxiety. Eliot Clark (1883–1980), a white American artist and one-time president of the National Academy of Design (NAD), the institution where Johnson and Kuniyoshi studied, wrote of this period,

> The foreign population in New York had increased immeasurably, each nationality congregating in a separate quarter of the lower city. . . . Writers, artists, adventurers, strays from all parts of the country championed the cause of the underprivileged, of who indeed they were a part. . . . The old New Yorker was passing. Traditional culture was taboo. Reality was equated with the masses.

Squalor was thought more realistic than luxury. This new milieu directly affected the artists' ideology and temperament.[6]

Clark's narrative demonstrates the way that texts can embellish and privilege certain heritages, for this historian did not disguise his allegiance to the powerful collective identity of "the old New Yorker" and its claims to tradition and rarified culture.[7] As a clearly expressed fear that his was the disappearing race at the turn of the nineteenth century, Clark's statement makes content the very basis of style; moreover, the accepted American style that he fears forever lost had been determined and configured by the self-selecting, white Anglo-Saxon bodies in its paintings and sculptures.[8] Yet modernist styles, and the reception of them, were critically inseparable from their content.[9] Neither form nor style explicitly enters Clark's discussion, which tellingly focuses on the consumption of a realism that was newly attractive because its subject matter was foreign-born or foreign-sounding, underprivileged, ghettoized, and squalid. In the experience of Clark's mostly conservative circle of members and defenders of institutions such as the NAD, modernism had battered and then crashed through the doors of their establishments.[10] For some, the very bodies of non-Christian, nonwhite, and immigrant artists such as Johnson, Kuniyoshi, and Weber threatened a naturalized order even as the institutional gatekeepers at the NAD and its more liberal rival school, the Art Students League, and social philanthropies such as the Harmon Foundation presided over their entry into the professional, social, and cultural ranks.

This consideration of racial art deepens the history of modernism in the United States and provides an opportunity to consider modernism's embodied genealogy. So many histories of modernism are accounts of an avant-garde that sits atop a totem pole. The aspirations and productions of modernizers—in Europe, North America, and elsewhere—garner little attention because their efforts are dwarfed by the bold achievements of Picasso and Matisse, individually, and by the School of Paris, collectively. Similarly, in heroic narratives of American modernism, the members of the overlapping Stieglitz, Arensberg, and Dreier circles fill the historical field: these artists are portrayed as lone knights who faced unceasing resistance from a philistine public and a reactionary academy. With this in mind, we should first establish that, like Picasso and

Matisse, the U.S.-based artists of the Stieglitz, Arensberg, and Dreier circles were atypical cultural producers whose visionary work was quite unlike most of their contemporaries' more cautious efforts. Second, our histories of art should consider extraordinary and typical practices alike without downgrading the former or inflating the import of the meaning given by the latter to the notion of the mainstream: such histories would shed brighter light on the limits of experimentation and popular tastes in cultural production. Third, there is no sense in relegating new subjects to the conceptualized margins of modernism or of any particular movement. Johnson, Kuniyoshi, and Weber were successfully raced during their lifetime, and my intention is to draw attention to that historical fact rather than to authorize their racially deictic contextualization in an unraced modernist pantheon. Ultimately, art history will include more examinations of the normalized and neutralized racial subject positions of its canonical figures. I cannot do that work here. My contribution to these inevitable discussions is to narrate and dramatize Johnson's, Kuniyoshi's, and Weber's intersecting and overlapping expressionist interpretations of race as a modernist mode and the sanctioning of their racial art approaches during their careers. Treating them as case studies, I mean to substantiate art historian Janet Wolff's characterization of American modernism as an "open and heterogeneous" set of practices.[11]

"Modernist" was a double designation for Johnson, Kuniyoshi, and Weber, one generated by audiences' approbation of both their compositions and their primitivized bodies. If modernists celebrated and embraced primitive values, they nonetheless maintained a dialectical, sovereign relationship with the primitive other. Johnson's, Kuniyoshi's and Weber's bodies (as opposed to the individuals themselves), set apart from Eliot Clark's conceptualization of the American artist, were realizations of reactionary fears. The conceptual borders surrounding minority artists recognize their ethnic, national, and cultural differences; although these delimitations are often regarded as absolute and impervious—and, indeed, in many cases they were—Johnson, Kuniyoshi, and Weber ably forged and traveled upon the incursive paths of American modernism. All three were fully aware that contemporary critics and patrons focused on their particularity. I believe that, in response to such attention, they alternately resisted and embraced the role of other; they resignedly accepted interstitial positioning as minorities, since it meant having some position—as opposed to none at all—in U.S. art. At the same time, in their creative efforts and passionate statements, they claimed an American identity when not all artists were doing so, for by the 1930s internationalism was part of modernist debates, alternately cast as a virtue and a heresy.[12]

It is no coincidence that racial art's lexicon segues with nationalism's and primitivism's and that the objects it characterized circulated in a market both eager to consume and ambivalent about consuming. So why hasn't the discourse of racial art been positioned closer to the center of the American modernist narrative? This is in part due to American denial of racism and of even less malignant forms of social demarcation.[13] The 1936 comments of philosopher and cultural critic Alain Locke articulate the modernist desire to find essence, difference, and exotic identities in artistic production: "Before too very long, the tang, taste, color and rhythm of our art will have changed irreparably from the purely racial to the universal . . . [and] those who have cried for the sea will doubtless cry for the loss of their river."[14] With this prediction that the particular would eventually become universal, Locke laid bare his pluralist belief that American culture would be made richer by embracing distinctive streams of cultural production. Locke, who exhorted African American artists to investigate School of Paris approaches and the lessons its artists learned from African ritual sculpture, understood the onerous and diverse pressures brought to bear on all U.S. artists.[15] As U.S. intellectual historian Paul Allen Anderson has recognized, Locke hoped that the interest in the racial particular would "embolden a journey outward to an even deeper sea of unrealized and uncharted cosmopolitanism."[16] Modernism depended on the conceptualization of race in ethnocultural, social, and national terms, in art created by the racialized body and informed by the idea of racial art. In turn, racial art and the racial body were organized according to the binary concept of "native and foreigner," with the latter figured as an interloper whose difference from the former was overdrawn. The idea of the essential subject, as a construct, allowed for the preservation of racist and limiting racialized terms used by admirers and detractors. As points of identity, the foreign, the primitive, and the essential subject overlap; they fold in on each other and are not easily detached.[17]

FOREIGN

Assessments of the worth of early twentieth-century American artists closely followed the measure of European influence observed in their works. "Has any American artist created a style which was unique in painting, completely divorced from European models?" artist Stuart Davis (1894–1964) asked Henry McBride in a 1930 letter.[18] In 1920 Chicago-based African American painter Archibald J. Motley Jr. (1891–1981) denounced the imitation of Impressionist and post-Impressionist painting at black artists' exhibitions, "There exists entirely too much imitation and not enough originality. . . . Our artists are entirely too much interested and influenced by the modern school of French painting. In practically all exhibitions of our group, I have 'seen' Renoir, Matisse, Corot, and many other Frenchmen imitated and poorly copied."[19] The shock of the new art from Europe, from the mid-nineteenth century onward, struck many as bizarre, including those who eventually embraced it. African American painter Hale A. Woodruff (1900–1980) was taken aback by the styles and imagery he first saw in Paris during the interwar years. In a column for his hometown paper, the *Indianapolis Star*, he described modernism in the most derogatory terms:

> Bleak, dismal, perspectiveless landscapes; bowls of fruit that do anything but whet your appetite and are only known as such by their titles; corpulent nude ladies who recline in grassy landscapes with turbulent seas in the background; streets of busy improportioned people with the house toppling over them; such are the natures of works found among "the conservatives" . . . and a number of them seem to have said to themselves, "I am going to see just how badly I can paint."[20]

Modernist abstraction and antinaturalist styles were consistently linked to Paris, although its practitioners were an international bunch who did not all hail from the French capital but instead flocked there to pursue the opportunity for creative exchange, inspiration, and professional success. Nonetheless, chauvinist Americans—artists and critics, whites and nonwhites, within the cultural mecca of New York and outside of it—found much to ridicule in U.S.-based painters' references to School of Paris and European avant-garde painting. Hostile commentators charged modernism in general with artistic lawlessness, pointless anomie, and illegibility. Its practitioners—among them Cézanne, Modigliani, Raoul Dufy, and Henri Rousseau—and admirers were roundly condemned by conservative white American critic Thomas Craven (1888–1969) in 1936:

> The Modernists were men of the strongest anti-social propensities. They took pride in their aloofness and gloried in their refusal to traffic in bourgeois sentiments and vulgar emotions. . . . such an atmosphere art turns inward, feeds upon itself, takes refuge in abstractions. It was only natural that men living in a world of metaphysical disputations should have produced an art divorced from its human context; it was expected that the defense of this art should be the hopeless effort to separate social, moral and sentimental activities from what was snobbishly labelled [sic] "pure aesthetics."[21]

Furthermore, artistic association—actual or perceived—with modernist practices was likely to produce contempt, as this *New York Tribune* review of a Kuniyoshi exhibition in 1922 makes clear:

> He has thrown his lot in with the modernists. . . . His drawing is naiveté itself. There is next to no instruction about his figures. In only one of his paintings, the "Wild Horses," which has an inkling of form and of movement, does he seem to concern himself with realistic truth. There are traces of humor in his work. But they are advanced in too halting an idiom to make themselves felt.[22]

Most Americans had no reason to abandon their taste for mimetic figuration and to develop an interest in nonobjective and abstract art. As the *Tribune* piece demonstrates, they believed that there was still too much subject matter to render in already accepted naturalistic and realistic modes, in work to follow the examples set by Thomas Eakins, Winslow Homer, John Singer Sargent, and J. M. Whistler. In the opinions of many cultural commentators—from the conservative Thomas Craven to the liberal Alfred H. Barr Jr. and Holger Cahill—there was a particular white Anglo-Saxon Protestant racial spirit in American art, one firmly established by these nineteenth-century artists. These preceding modes, broadly considered realist, comprised an available and serviceable style for their successors. Sargent (1856–1925), for example, was gifted with "manual dexterity," according to Craven, and had a worthy successor in George Bellows (1882–1925), who had embraced "the riotous and gaudy, the loud and belligerent aspects of native subject matter."[23]

Like modernism, the ideation of a national, U.S. art style—modernist or any other kind—was not a settled matter in the interwar decades. Reviewing the Museum of Modern Art's 1929–1930 exhibition "Paintings by Nineteen Living Americans," the *New York Times*' Edward Alden Jewell (1888–1947) said that this nominally American work left most viewers dumbfounded, for they could not, from a "bird's-eye view," confirm nor deny what was American about it.[24] Samuel M. Kootz (1898–1982), an advertising executive who would open a New York gallery in 1944, was more convinced that there was such a thing, yet he charged that American art was hamstrung by good technique and sorely lacked evidence of its makers' spirit and raw emotion. What was needed, Kootz suggested, was "self-revelatory" national art, infused with "highly sensitized personal emotion."[25] When Kootz articulated these concerns in a 1931 newspaper article, African American painter and art historian James A. Porter (1905–1970) responded in print, charging:

> the art of the American Indian is probably the only purely American art we know. . . . The "new races of America" have had neither sufficient time nor isolation to allow any considerable growth in homogeneity of race being. We can have American art in the collective sense only. Its features must be heterogeneous; but from the standpoint of truth to American modes of being, feeling, acting and appearing, our art must represent a homogenous greatness.[26]

Along with his insistence that indigenous peoples were the first "Americans"—a stance that indicts European colonization and advances a romantic conception of a single, homogeneous, and pure indigenous culture—Porter's national art emerges from pluralist tendencies that triumphantly cohere. Like Kootz, Porter conceptualized American art as not yet extant but rather a project in the making.

When the Museum of Modern Art followed its successful 1929 group exhibition of the work of Cézanne, Gauguin, Seurat, and Van Gogh with Paintings by Nineteen Living Americans, active debates formed around what constituted national and freshly modernist art. Among the exhibition's participants were Kuniyoshi and Weber, and older well-established painters such as Kenneth Hayes Miller and John Sloan (1871–1951). While conceding that the show could not please everyone, especially not the artists who were not included, the *New Yorker*'s conclusion that many of the exhibitors were "men who are in no way modern" was doubtlessly aimed at these older participants.[27] Some critics praised Weber's and Kuniyoshi's paintings, and yet the latter's *Nude (Reclining)* generated both controversy for its languid subject and compliments for its abstraction.[28] Furthermore, adamant objections were raised regarding the inclusion of Kuniyoshi and two other painters: in the minds of many, the Bulgarian-born Jew Jules Pascin (1885–1930) and the German American Catholic Lyonel Feininger (1871–1956) also did not belong in the company of U.S.-born exhibitors.[29] For Henry McBride, a champion of both Kuniyoshi and Weber who often explained their work's modernist qualities through their heritages, the show's biggest failing was its tentativeness: "It had a chance—in fact, it had the obligation—to explain what the word 'modern' in its title meant but it hesitated so painfully over this part of its task that it gave the impression of lacking the courage of modernity."[30] Yet two European observers in the period found neither courage nor fearlessness in American art of the 1920s. "Suppose I were to judge modern American art as it is usually represented abroad, or even in most galleries here," mused Paris-based cultural writer Muriel Ciolkowska in her 1926 essay "Absolutism in Modern American Art." "It would strike me as very pale and 'unexciting' compared with the work of modern English artists like Augustus Johns, the Nashes, Laura Knight, Eric Gill, etc."[31] Another observer, German critic Julius Meier-Graefe (1867–1935), distributed praise differently, generalizing that there were good artists in the United States—more than in England, but fewer than in France and Germany; his American exemplars were cubist-influenced Preston Dickinson (1881–1930) and John Marin (1870–1953).[32] Hence, for its European detractors and admirers, modernism paradoxically started somewhere else and was borne from a sensibility that was radically different from that of the prototypical white American.

Writing to the *New York Sun* in 1919, Weber bemoaned the American artist's predicament and framed the issue between the binaries of the native and the foreign: "Little need we wonder then at Europe's depreciation of American art. Americans and the subnascent academicians themselves are in a large measure responsible for this. Even third rate foreign artists come here and are welcomed and shown preference, while native talent is allowed to struggle and shift for itself. It has become a national custom of this young, wealthy country to neglect and starve its own artists."[33] Weber concluded this letter with a prophecy for modernism: "A new, a vital, inter-racial art is born, destined to become rich and glorious, rivaling the best art-traditions of the past."[34] Like Porter's plural yet cohering modernism, Weber's offers a composite model. Nonetheless, Weber's citation of race connotes more than it denotes. Was interracial art characterized by an inseparable unity that somehow displaced the particularities of identity? Was modernism inherent in the U.S. soil, an ore with latent racial and national constituents? Was it a set of artistic approaches developed in New York, Paris, and other Western sites of modernity?

Although cross-cultural influences and exchanges are, as philosopher Jacob T. Levy has argued, "facts of the world, facts of our condition,"[35] the notion of hybrid art styles and aesthetic approaches, like the mixing of the races, provoked anxiety and resistance in many early twentieth-century American audiences. Anticipation and expectation for the visualization of difference coevally existed with utter dread of change in any tradition. Deep commitment to the authority and reliability about American identity constructions was matched by a desire to be certain about foreign identities as well. For instance, when Ernest Brace asserted that Kuniyoshi's work "has more that is basically Oriental than has the painting of most contemporary Japanese, who have been running away from their own culture to follow the bandwagon of modern French Art,"[36] the critic sought to preserve the sanctity of Eastern traditions (as he imagined them) and reproach Japanese artists who failed to do so. In a 1933 review, Edward Alden Jewell argued the same, concluding that Kuniyoshi had survived cross-cultural exchange and the dangers of mixing artistic influences:

> Modern Japanese artists have to deal with some pretty tough problems. Turning to Occidental forms, they are accused, often justly, of having left in the

> lurch their own marvelous racial art heritage. There have been some pathetic instances of . . . borrowing. . . . And if one cares to pursue the biblical analogy, one is bound to confess that in this case a mess of pottage can become metamorphosed into something peculiarly desirable and abiding. Kuniyoshi has proved that and is handsomely, from year to year, entrenching his position.[37]

Jewell is complimentary, yet his comments are shot through with anxiety about the deficiencies in the hybrid, an amalgam that presumes uncompromising belief in the stable purity of its entities, namely, the Occidental and the Oriental personalities.[38] Kuniyoshi, who was treated as an enemy alien during the World War II years, recognized the heightening of such sentiments and tried to reason them out of a fearful American consciousness as the nation entered that international conflict. In a 1940 lecture at the Museum of Modern Art titled "What Is an American Art?" he asserted, "American art today is the product of a conglomeration of customs and traditions of many peoples . . . a culmination not only of native but [also of] foreign forces. . . . If these artists [Degas and Van Gogh] did not find alien influence a menace, why should we?"[39] On the one hand, Kuniyoshi's title suggests that many styles might happily co-exist under the heading "American art," and retain their individual characteristics; on the other, his definition makes national art the product of a melting-pot process.

In the 1920s and 1930s there was a general fascination with the ways—both imagined and manifest—that modernism was foreign.[40] As Samantha Baskind has written, artists able to claim the white, Anglo-Saxon Protestant (and normalized) identity position were expected to dig deep into their souls to uncover their modernist aesthetics; in contrast, the raced artist merely had to hold on to her or his non-WASP heritage.[41] The ethnocultural and racial identities of Johnson, Kuniyoshi, and Weber made each of these artists foreign to the WASP archetype; they were exotic moderns to the curious. This was the case even for the Protestant-raised, North Carolina–born Johnson, who could never occupy the American nativist ideal; he stood outside of it, as distant as were the immigrants Kuniyoshi and Weber. In essays appearing in issues of *The Nation* in 1926, two African American intellectuals, George S. Schuyler (1895–1977) and Langston Hughes (1902–1967), debated which collectivity blacks belonged to: the West or Africa, both symbolic "nations" singularly conceived in terms of their racial majorities.[42] Schuyler, in "The Negro-Art Hokum," argued that "the Aframerican" was "merely a lampblacked Anglo-Saxon."[43] In his reply, "The Negro Artist and the Racial Mountain," the poet Hughes forwarded a particularist conception of "Africa-America"—discrete and defined by atavistic ties to the African continent—and wrote admiringly of its "eternal tom-tom beating."[44] Since its publication in the 1920s, Hughes's essay has been widely praised: cultural critic George Hutchinson has deemed it a "classic expression for black artistic autonomy" and "an example of the power and suppleness of the American ideology of democratic individuality."[45] In contrast, Schuyler's "The Negro-Art Hokum" has been roundly criticized for its nationalism: for Paul Allen Anderson, Schuyler's "antiracialist assault . . . suffered through its dependence on counterassertions about a culturally non-differentiated 'Americanism.'"[46] These assessments of Hughes's and Schuyler's positions aside, what seems especially important is the heightened language used to situate conceptions of the United States and definitions of its people that depended on conjoined racial and class binaries: "American" is linked to the white, upper-class designation of "Anglo-Saxon," while "African" is unrelated to either of these terms. Even for cultural pluralist Schuyler, "American" was a designation that did not include nonwhites and so was in need of a descriptive modifier, that is, "Aframerican." The addition of an ethnoracial adjective when discussion turned to the perceived nonwhite subject is an indication that the black American citizen was perceived not as native but, in some ways, as foreign as the immigrant.

Commentators constructed special cultural, ethnoracial, and national interstices in which Johnson, Kuniyoshi, and Weber might operate, ones that they assumed ought to have been impervious to any other influences, including that of the School of Paris.[47] But Kuniyoshi and Weber traveled to Paris to study, and Johnson aspired to do so as well. Cézanne's work, in particular, influenced each of them. Certainly, Weber's detractors blamed Cézanne (1839–1906) for Weber's abstract paintings of the teens; moreover, in that decade, Weber wrote the appreciative essay "Cézanne's Water Colors" for the Montross Gallery's publication that accompanied an exhibition of the French artist's work.[48] As I will demonstrate in chapter 5, Johnson's Southern landscapes evidence his familiarity with Cézanne's paintings of Mont-Saint-Victoire; contemporary sources observe this fact as well.[49] Lastly, Kuniyoshi wrote of his circle's interest in "Cézanne and modern painting" in his 1940 autobiographical essay "East to West."[50] Such statements, I believe, say as much about Cézanne's growing reputation in the United States in the early twentieth century as they do about these three Americans' taste. Indeed, in 1931 Thomas Craven, a grudging admirer of the French painter's technique, and one who judged its affect too mechanical, admitted, "Since his death twenty-five years ago, Cézanne, the most despised artist of his time, has become the most famous painter of the nineteenth century."[51] Cézanne's figurally abstract nudes, still lifes, portraits, and landscapes, once derided as willfully clumsy, registered with Johnson, Kuniyoshi, Weber, and others during the interwar era. American artistic interventions during these years were not radical ones, and precisely for this reason they struck a chord in critics generally bored with "the polite oblivion of the academic" and with naturalistic paintings that were technically solid but weighted down by "the lifeless arrangements of pots and pans, birch trees and boats at rest in harbors."[52] Curiously, lifelessness was an oft-cited fault of abstract and geometric modernism, which was deemed too distant from "real" human experience. The desire for painting that audiences judged emotional and personal fed the market for art by cultural others: among them nonwhites, non-Westerners, the country folk, the poor, the working classes of the United States, and children (as innocents) were situated as the chief members of the primitive collective.[53] To wit, critic Forbes Watson (1880–1960) identified two Weber styles on display at the artist's 1930 retrospective at the Museum of Modern Art, and he was clear about his preference:

> His exhibition has two distinct sides: the international, theoretical side and the purely racial side. . . . Perhaps a trifle too consciously aesthetic to vivify the whole tragedy he is capable of feeling Mr. Weber does, in his best Jewish pictures, rise completely above mental self-consciousness or suggestabilty to the heights of a poetical and biblical tragedy.[54]

Racial art was both specific and universal, grotesque and poetic, old and yet new to its admirers.[55]

PRIMITIVE

It is still accepted that "objects are primitive or modern, but certainly not both."[56] Like the foreign and the essentialized, the primitive emerges from fields of contrast, mapped upon class, race, gender, geography, and time.[57] Locating the primitive in the twentieth century was a circumscribing act: the praiseworthy other, placed on a pedestal, was immobilized; merely fixing the other was an opportunity to separate the "us" from the "them," to make claims about the superiority of the former at the expense of the latter.[58] Writing of the longstanding American fascination with the Native American, Robert K. Martin asserts that "the idea of the Indian is a representation of the other, which can be used positively or negatively. The Indian illustrates that which we are not, thus confirming our superiority for some, our inferiority for others."[59] In the same vein, Janet Wolff has argued that early twentieth-century notions of Jewish art in England—considered primitive and identified with alien modernism and foreigners—were important to "the project of producing an English identity."[60]

What did race bring to primitivist discourse of the nineteenth and early twentieth centuries? In Europe's major cities, the racial often referred to distant nonwhite peoples in the perceived wilds of the Americas, Africa, Australia, Asia, and the Pacific Islands. Such others, represented in the commercial culture by postcards and other visual products of ethnographic curiosity, were displayed at international fairs and expositions. But the various nationals of Europe's modern states—the French, the English, and so on—and European religious, linguistic, and ethnic groups such as Jews, Slavs, and Romanies—also were ordered into unified racial groupings. In the United States the situation was different: there was special interest in the lives and cultures of Native Americans.[61] In a transvaluation of Native American art, Max Weber said in 1941, "True modern art is more a rejuvenation than an innovation. . . . The real surrealists are right here: the American Indians."[62] In the United States, modernists' admiration of indigenous art as a precursor to their own efforts was a related but separate matter from the taste for dime-store novels and other popular literatures, Indian characterizations in vaudeville, cigar store Indians, and commercial art. The exhibition of Native Americans at U.S. fairs and road shows, along with the collection and exhibition of the cultural production of Native American artists—ancient and contemporary woven baskets and blankets, murals and ground paintings, sculpted earth mounds, Kachina dolls, and arrowheads—intensified at the end of the nineteenth century with the assumption that, following genocide, imperialism, and warfare, Indians comprised a "disappearing race."[63] The market for Indian craft followed a demand for replicas of the Native American past; these were new, manufactured objects that worked like fossils, as the archaeological evidence of history. Hence, whatever comparisons can be drawn between the anthropological fascination with the primitive and the Western consumption of its artifacts, Native American artists as known, named, and identified makers of textiles, sculptures, and paintings purchased and admired by the public—did not enter most racial art discourses of the interwar period because they were anonymous and relegated to the "past."[64] Although similarly primitivized, Johnson, Kuniyoshi, and Weber—along with others who were present and discussed in the cultural press because they were artistically and commercially active in a fine-arts economy—were assigned to a distinctively contemporary project to make twentieth-century visual culture, new art for a new century.

In a manner inconceivable today, the primitive was part of everyday language in the first half of the twentieth century.[65] A Cole Porter song for his 1929 musical "Fifty Million Frenchman" included these lyrics: "Find me a primitive man / Built to a primitive plan. / I don't mean the kind that belongs to a club / But the kind that has a club that belongs to him."[66] Notably, the primitive in this example was not firmly tied to the nonwhite body; indeed, audiences would have been jarred, if not outraged, to hear Porter's white heroine admit desire for a nonwhite man. More palatable was the singer's disturbing (however comically expressed) preference for the rough, violent, and self-sustaining survivalist who, following primitivism's symbolic reordering of social hierarchies, was the better of Babbitt, Sinclair Lewis's fictional hero. And although many African Americans chafed under the assumption that they were primitives, others, particularly those familiar with the modern attraction to the word, utilized its rubric.[67] From the nineteenth century, black vaudevillians presented primitivist revues. In the twentieth, African American painter Cloyd Boykin (1877–?) named his Greenwich Village art school the Primitive Art Center. His contemporary, the widely traveled William H. Johnson (1901–1970), explained that his catholic tastes and expressionist approach were modified by his embrace of primitivism. In 1935 Johnson told an interviewer, "I myself feel like a primitive man, like one who is at the same time both a primitive and a cultured painter."[68] Elsewhere, referencing his "family of primitiveness," Johnson could issue such claims and not face questions from either critics or audiences, for nonwhites and their cultural expression were seen as "authentically" primitive. In contrast, non-blacks working primitively were questioned and their production scrutinized for affectations.

Weber's Jewish body and religious subjects were assigned to the "primitive" category following a centuries-old Western stereotype of the coarse, unsophisticated, and dull-witted Jew, a characterization that diminished in the twentieth century even as racist portrayals of Jewish avarice and craftiness survived and flourished. Primitivism, which was unproblematically assigned to black Africans, orientalized Asians, and indigenous Australians and Americans—and those visibly descended from them—right up until the twentieth century's end, was contingently attributed to Jews. Indeed, art historian Hal Foster has argued that in Europe and the United States, "Jews were often regarded not as too primitive but as too civilized—that is, as cosmopolitan and so deracinated, decadent, degenerate, and thus, paradoxically, as primitive once again in another sense."[69] Nonetheless, Weber's identification with the primitive archetype was explicit: his praises of it are clear in his 1926 poetry collection *Primitives*, which followed the equally indexical *Cubist Poems* of 1913. In turn, observers situated Weber so close to modernism's primitives as to make him one as well. For instance, Alfred H. Barr Jr. (1902–1981) surmised, "He came to know most intimately Henri Rousseau *le douanier*. His naïve vision and ingenious spirit impressed Weber deeply. More thoroughly than Matisse, Weber studied Persian and Indian miniatures. More earnestly than Picasso, he absorbed not merely the form but something of the spirit of negro sculpture."[70] In contrast to Picasso and Matisse, Weber, in Barr's view, was both more studious and less cynical than his French counterparts. In the catalogue essay for Weber's one-artist exhibition at the Museum of Modern Art in 1930, Barr made African ritual sculpture's influence on Weber a corporeal transformation when he likened the Russian-Jewish "spirit" to the black African artist's.[71] Importantly, Weber himself maintained a lifelong identification with the conceptualized primitive, telling the *Portland Oregonian* in 1952 that he almost felt like a "primitive Indian."[72]

The stereotypes applied to Kuniyoshi were also constructed along a temporal continuum, another site for primitivist conceptualization. Because Asian cultures and civilizations were valued for being among the world's oldest, American critics located Kuniyoshi's modernism in Asia's venerable past. For example, the artist's 1921 painting *Wild Horses* (fig. 1.6) generated many admiring comments for its perceived relationship to historical Asian art, considered more sophisticated for its very antiquity and more organic than the twentieth-century industrial landscape. In this painting, said the *New York Times*, "We catch the deeper note of an art that has known for many centuries that motion is life. . . . With his Western training, Mr. Kuniyoshi has not forgotten the instruction 'to carry the mind at the point of the pen.'"[73] Henry McBride, Kuniyoshi's most vocal supporter in the press, favorably compared the artist's paintings to "old Chinese damask."[74] Linking Kuniyoshi's painting to the well-made textile, McBride looked to credit the artist for tapping into ancient, ethnic resources, sources that the critic valued. In contrast, C. J. Bulliet (1883–1952), in a 1927 review, "On Trying to Smile in Front of Kuniyoshi's Babies," combined binary characterizations to dismiss the artist and those who would embrace the "primitive":

> Kuniyoshi has taken the two children—the one from the modern Primitive Rousseau, and the other from the ancient Primitives—put a dash of his own psychology to them and produced what indignant observers last Friday were pleased to view as monstrosities. Whether his "Babies" would constitute a poster suitable for a "bitter babies" campaign is a question that probably never entered Kuniyoshi's head—a question that certainly would not disturb, in the least, the artistic instinct of the young Japanese.[75]

Bulliet makes everything about Kuniyoshi strange, discrete, and distanced from the everyday. Even his reference to artistic practice seems meant to undermine Kuniyoshi's learned skills, for Bulliet describes his impetus as unshakably instinctual and tied to his youth and nationality.

ESSENTIAL

Essentialism is a reified quality or set of qualities that is subsequently assigned to be the defining aspect of individuals grouped together. Essentialist definitions contain what we put in them: they are containers of ideas, both informed and unfounded.[76] They produce a reliable and expected outcome, and although the pathway of the essentialized identity is neither direct nor indexical, it forecloses interruption.[77] By "essentializing" I do not mean "generalizing." Instead, I am identifying a pattern of tying production to what philosophers would term a possible (and not necessarily real or actualized) property and world. As is the case with definitions of the foreign and the primitive, essentialism depends on binaries to advance its meanings. A 1932 article announcing Diego Rivera's exhibition at the Museum of Modern Art makes this plain. "Ugly or Beautiful, New York Sees the Art of Diego Rivera" starts off:

> Whether the art of Diego Rivera is representational and ugly and repulsive to the Anglo-Saxon aesthetic instincts of the United States, or whether it (being typically Mexican) contains, as Dr. Elie Faure of France believes, the germ of all future great artistic expression for the American continent, it is compulsively on view at the Museum of Modern Art in New York. The American art world can judge for itself.[78]

The unnamed writer ostensibly offers his readers choices, but the rigidity of the presented categories is, of course, undisguised: Mexican as opposed to Anglo-Saxon, U.S. instincts that contrast with the representational, ugly, and repulsive.

Modernism's essentialism was more expansive than that of previous artistic movements, and as a phenomenon of modernity, it bled into the fabric of everyday life in countless places. Modernism was grounded in essentialist logic, whose first precept is that the bloc group's characteristic—whether of the majority or the minority—is the individual's writ large.[79] For example, in an undated clipping from the interwar era one American critic informs readers: "Jewish Artists take part in many exhibitions," a claim that reinforces and instantiates Jewish difference while it simultaneously tries to refute a broad-reaching anti-Semitism and the historical dominance of Christian majorities over religious minorities in the West. Indeed, the appositive nomenclature of Negro, Oriental, and Jew that trailed Johnson, Kuniyoshi, Weber, and other nonwhite American artists is the evidence of determination from without, as theorized by both Franz Fanon and Jean-Paul Sartre.[80] Observers identifying the Negro, the Oriental, and the Jew subsequently defined racialized and ethnicized collectivities, for the individual stood among and embodied the minority collective.

Many twentieth-century immigrants to the United States—European Jews among them—eventually became acculturated and assimilated into American society as the outcome of shifts in the legal code, the political landscape, demographic realities, and cultural mores.[81] But the voiced opinions about Jewish particularity were nonetheless persistent through the 1930s and 1940s. Certainly, the dominant "technology of racial exclusion," as sociologist Roderick A. Ferguson has termed it, was evident in sociologist Robert Park's 1914 estimation:

> The fact that the Japanese bears in his features a distinctive racial hallmark, that he wears, so to speak, a uniform, classifies him. He cannot become a mere individual, indistinguishable in the cosmopolitan mass of the populations, as is true, for example, of the Irish and, to a lesser extent, of some of the other immigrant races. The Japanese like the Negro is condemned to remain among us an abstract symbol, and a symbol not merely of his own race, but of the Orient and of the vague, ill-defined menace we sometime refer to as the "yellow peril."[82]

Labeling and defining a bicultural subject was even more arduous. Assessing Japanese American Isamu Noguchi's drawing exhibition at the John Becker Gallery in New York in 1932, Henry McBride struggled to address the duality of the artist's Japanese and white American parentage:

> His drawings are not profound. . . . They have no deep emotion and they lack the stern sense of plan that is expected in great Eastern art, but they have a flowing rhythm and a bold attack that is undoubtedly alluring. Being essentially Eastern, he may eventually arrive at profundity through this virtuosity of his. We must give him the benefit of that surmise. But if he were Western, on the contrary we should never surmount so much cleverness to arrive at sincerity.[83]

Rhetoric about the essential character of U.S. ethnic and racial minorities, more than the analogous perceptions formed about the nation's WASP majority, comprised a legitimized focus of modernist discourse.[84] From the nineteenth century on, some American commentators exhorted U.S. artists to paint national themes in a uniquely national style, a mode that would once and for all replace European approaches. These directives were attempts to slow the international circulation of images and the inevitability of artistic exchanges and influences; they also failed to grasp America's multicultural origins. In the early twentieth century, investigating into the national past to uncover the origins of modernity was a special labor of American WASPs thought to have lost touch with their honest and most potent roots. Conversely, most believed that excavation was unnecessary for minority Americans: they only had to be themselves to achieve the modern, to hold on to their conceptualized and particularist differences.[85]

Johnson, Kuniyoshi, and Weber alternately embraced the terms of this essentialist discourse and struggled against them, for one consequence of adopting a single identity is that it creates expectations of rejecting all others. In February 1930 Johnson responded to a critic's charge that African American artists had failed to express the race's "peculiar rhythm and directness of feeling" by arguing, "We Americans of both races know and live the same life."[86] Yet a month prior, Johnson had written in his unsuccessful application for a Guggenheim Fellowship, "As a Negro artist, I am trying to depict in line and color, creations of that one thing my race possesses—Music, devoting most of my painting to composition of Negro spirituals, folk and work songs."[87] Johnson recognized the desires of the marketplace and sought to satisfy them. Similarly, Weber at times embraced racial particularity, for he occasionally attributed his own poetic and musical interests to his Jewish heritage, furthering a singular notion of Jews, however multiethnic and multinational, as "a separate homogeneous race."[88] In the popular imagination, the Russian Jew, no less than the black, was colorful, mystical, and musical. At midcentury, less than a decade after the Nazi holocaust and at the dawn of Israel's founding, Jews remained marked with racial difference. Critic Margaret Breuning, praising Weber's palette, attributed his skills not to study and experimentation but instead to his Oriental birth: "Born in Russia, he inherited the Russian delight in color and, just as Russia seems in many respects 'an Oriental nation, looking to the West,' so he seems to possess a native affiliation with the arts of the East, particularly of China and Japan." If Breuning, writing during the Cold War, tentatively deemed Russia an Oriental space, interwar commentators were steadfast in such dichotomous assignations.[89]

Johnson, Kuniyoshi, and Weber found ways to manipulate their outsider status. Hence, although Kuniyoshi's work had little in common with that of his Japanese contemporaries (a fact that commentators in Japan and some in the United States noted), the artist buttressed his critics' Orientalism with his own. In his artist's statement for the Six Living American Artists exhibition of 1939, Kuniyoshi asserted, "I have wished to express the thought of the East, my race, using the tradition of expressing the inner thoughts through the full realization of my experience."[90] If Kuniyoshi, like Los Angeles–born, Japanese American sculptor Isamu Noguchi (1904–1988), thought it was possible to transcend the constructed worlds of East and the West, then puzzled responses in the United States and Japan ought to have indicated that his work contained inconsistent or insufficient essences of either.[91] Even as Kuniyoshi's tireless advocate Henry McBride proclaimed that the artist belonged to "the American School," the critic, in most instances, made Kuniyoshi's heritage his strongest selling point. That Kuniyoshi remained "true to the stock he sprang from," as McBride once put it, was a sentiment expressed in support of the authentic, the traditional, and the predictable identity, concepts so evidently under siege in early twentieth-century America.[92]

Critics regarded Kuniyoshi's forms of the teens and twenties—bloated, decoratively colored, and occupying impossible pictorial spaces—as caricatures of the white American body, gesture, and landscape, and advanced arguments of Occidental and Oriental purities to explain them.[93] According to this logic, the presumed makeup of each world was, in the Hegelian sense, the polar opposite of its other. Hence, some American viewers, while sensing that Kuniyoshi's approach was humorous, admitted that they failed to get the joke because they believed it untranslatable. Even if at times Kuniyoshi pushed away from exotic views of Asia, his comments only reinforced the Orientalizing framing of his work. In 1937 the artist complained to *Esquire* journalist Harry Salpeter that his art had wrongly been "classified on a racial basis, as that of a Japanese or

Japanese-American. I can't be very much Oriental. I have spent most of my life here. I have been educated here and I have suffered here. I am as much of an individual as anyone—except that I have Oriental blood in my veins."[94] Here, Kuniyoshi argued for his individuality, a quality that stands in as American. Pointedly, the artist rejected hyphenated American status: "Japanese American" deictically brought him closer to Asia than he wanted to be and further from the designation he desired—that of American. Kuniyoshi put forth his years of acculturation—through education and his untold suffering—to mitigate the metaphor of blood, an essence often summoned for its singular and singularizing power. Kuniyoshi's rhetoric followed his own reflexive moves amid modernity's binaries and within his own interiority. No matter how expressed visual signs of difference are rendered, no matter the context of their representation, they advance essentialist ideas, reifying and systemizing them for consumption. Like Johnson and Weber, Kuniyoshi claimed a racial interstice he had inherited and shored up its structure so that those who followed him might do so as well.

THREE

MAKING RACE IN AMERICAN RELIGIOUS PAINTING

IN 1923 NEW YORK CRITIC HENRY MCBRIDE, MAX WEBER'S FRIEND AND advocate in the press, wrote:

> Weber always was Biblical in his seriousness, but heretofore he appeared to assume the Christian note and addressed himself to Christians. This was understandable as was his custom of using the American language in his poetry, to express himself to Americans, but the something that has happened to him since his last appearance as an artist and that has made him Jewish also made him doubly important. It is an immense thing to have a background and speak for a race. Weber may not have intended it consciously, and it may simply be the result of added years, but the result is an eloquence and an authority that cannot be denied.[1]

McBride's assertion that in Weber's art there were different Christian and Jewish motifs and visual languages presents a startling and telling polarity, even if the critic does not fully define the terms of opposition.[2] In McBride's assessment, there is also a clear line of division—which would be drawn and redrawn by Weber's observers throughout the artist's career and posthumously—meant to periodize and site his artistic production in discrete programs: School of Paris cubism as opposed to expressive and documentary realism. The oeuvre of Weber's contemporary, Marsden Hartley, also generated a similar assessment, namely that the artist was once modern and then, abruptly, was not.[3] Contemporary admiration for either artist's production did not wane; instead, their early paintings were placed in contrapuntal opposition to their late ones: critics perceived no relationship between Weber's *Chinese Restaurant* (1915) and Hartley's *Portrait of a German Officer* (1917) and their post–World War I genre works of Hasidic Jews and Acadian fishermen, respectively. The disjunction, no doubt, stemmed from widespread agreement that modernist artists interpreted the world bizarrely while those committed to realism honestly depicted it. The take on Weber, which was different from the response to Hartley's genre portraits of swarthy, suntanned men firmly located in a white working class from which the artist did not emerge,[4] was that Weber's Jewish subjects were natural, inevitable, and indeed welcome themes from the native best equipped to document them. To use McBride's term, Weber had the "background" and therefore the right to speak, to represent, and to present what was perceptibly "his" community to the American majority. Doing so was (and still is seen as) the very duty of the minority artist, that is, to be the native informant and accept a role never imagined for her or his peers belonging to the dominant groups. Representing one's minority culture is the way to be additively and most effectively modern, by adding difference to the central, anchoring aspects of American identity, namely, whiteness and Christianity.

Weber and Johnson visualized religious particularity for American audiences interested in their exoticism—for Weber, Hasidic Jews in ecstatic song and Talmudic study, and for Johnson, black performance of Protestant "Negro" spirituals. Although Kuniyoshi twice painted Judeo-Christian motifs in realist still lifes—a traditional Lenten snack in *Pretzels* (1927) and a loaf of challah in *Rolls on a Chair* (1930)—religion seems not to have been an important aspect of this artist's life or art. In this way, the careers of Weber and Johnson provide a striking contrast to Kuniyoshi's. Over five decades, Weber created more than two dozen works that explicitly referenced Jewish religious life and culture.[5] Johnson represented the spirituals in nine known oil paintings during the years 1927–1931. As important as the artists' religious backgrounds (the focal point for contemporary critics and present-day art historians alike) is their interest in and study of religious practice; these also must be considered if we are to analyze the very making of their paintings. While painting his spiritual series, Johnson looked for inspiration to the lyrics published in compilations of these songs.[6] Weber's 1934 painting *The Talmudists* followed his observation of scholarly debates at a synagogue on New York's Lower East Side.[7] Still, references to his religiosity accompanied assessments of his work, although it was clear that, like Johnson, he was ambivalent about the essentializing of his identity.

Reaction to these projects included praise of the paintings' emotional and poetic affect. Weber's *Invocation* (1919), on view at the Montross Gallery in New York in 1923, was routinely cited as a picture of "essentially Jewish types," one that asserted "strong emotional power."[8] Reviewing the Montross show, McBride grounded the images in the artist's memory and cultural atavism, proposing that

> the new quality is not based upon the lugubriousness of Weber's themes, nor the long beards of the Jews who wail upon the housetops after the manner of the prophets, but rather it comes to me in an abstract way and from the colour chiefly. It is the richest, most distinguished, most eloquent use of colour I have seen this winter. In a way I scarcely know how to define, it seems to have come straight from the Old Testament to Weber. It is somber and with something in each tone that seems to crystallize a human experience.[9]

Johnson's *Swing Low, Sweet Chariot* (1928; fig. 1.3) was similarly cast as a recovery; it was described by the *Washington Post*'s Ada Rainey as being "typical of the hidden music and feeling of the race."[10] The words "emotion," "feeling," and "spirit" resonate in interwar discussion of Johnson's and Weber's paintings, and these characteristics, assigned to Orientalized Judaism and primitivized black Protestantism, were central in critics' analytics.

To their admirers, Johnson's and Weber's religious art was latently authentic because it presented sincere qualities absent from or perhaps overcome by secular modernism. Art historian Mary Ann Calo has rightly characterized this expectation of African American artists:

> Mainstream critics looking for racial qualities in the work of African-American artists were especially pleased when they discovered evidence of an emotional sensibility rooted in the black folk culture and religion. They were in fact looking for the visual equivalents of the Negro spiritual. . . . For many white Americans, the so-called "sorrow songs" were the most familiar, and therefore most representative, form of black expression.[11]

Matthew Baigell has noted and criticized similar tendencies among early twentieth-century critics addressing Jewish artists' production. Citing Jewish cultural writer Paul Rosenfeld's 1921 assessment that Weber's career demonstrated "the assimilative power of the Jew" as opposed to "the mystical metaphysical Jew," Baigell has judged Rosenfeld's comments as "stereotypical" and proclaimed that "to assume that Jews (or Weber) are mystical and metaphysical is nonsense."[12] In addition to asserting that birthright gave these artists license to interpret ethnoracial subject matter, the critics praised them for trading in figurative abstraction for a figural aesthetic reflective of their "true" identities. In his 1923 review of Weber's one-artist exhibition at Montross Gallery—the first after the artist's self-imposed, year-long hiatus—McBride concluded, "In retirement, Weber's art has become Jewish. In another publication I already so qualified it hesitatingly, not because of any uncertainty of my feeling in regard to the work—that was clear and profound—but because of an apprehension that the term might be misunderstood."[13] Such commentary ultimately influenced art history surveys, among them Jerome Melquist's *The Emergence of American Art* (1942), where it is written about Weber: "Unwanted by the galleries, compelled to teach for a living, and yet refusing to terminate his experiments, he gradually discovered that in his greatest inheritance from the past he could admit his own identity and be free."[14]

The perception that Johnson and Weber had recovered something once misplaced or lost seems central to their paintings' accredited success as authentic creations. As philosopher Kwame Anthony Appiah has explained, "Authenticity speaks of the real self buried in there, the self one has to dig out and express."[15] In search of this quality, commentators wrote of "hidden" culture in Johnson's *Swing Low, Sweet Chariot* and forgave its technical shortcomings. Comparing the painting to other works he saw in the Harmon Foundation's Exhibition of Painting and Sculpture by Negro Artists of 1929, reviewer Robert Bordner wrote, "Imperfect technique, faulty by many rules, it stood out as a stirring painting expressing powerfully something of the experience of the race. . . . Many of the paintings are of better workmanship, show a firmer grasp of artistic technique, but they lack the vitality of the artist's emotion."[16] In *Swing Low, Sweet Chariot*, Bordner found both a collective experience that had an indescribable racial characteristic and the individual artist's indomitable personality. Most importantly, Bordner charted a short distance between the artist and the painting he made. Johnson, whose student works, without legible, black figuration, were not and are still not well-known, was identified with his painted subjects, which satisfied a desire for a black visual idiom—homogenous, monological, stable—peremptorily fashioned in the observer's mind. If critics failed to look for Jewishness in Weber's early paintings because there was no index—titular or visual—to it, they mapped with relief a collective Jewish heritage and the artist's individual history onto his paintings of yeshivas and rabbis. In Weber's case, the critics believed that authenticity in his religious paintings had finally emerged from the pall of cubism. The critics failed to consider that the self is made, just as pictures are.

Johnson's and Weber's Judeo-Christian representations existed in an expanding field of American Christian visual culture in the early twentieth century. As visual cultural historians David Morgan and Sally M. Promey have demonstrated, both Catholics and Protestants made devotional objects—from holy cards of pious saints and illuminated bibles to inexpensive reproductions of Warner Sallman's realist oil painting *Head of Christ* (1940)—critical to their religious practices and to the decoration of their homes and churches.[17] At the other end of the representational spectrum, the spiritually inspired, abstract paintings of Roman Catholic artist Augustus Vincent Tack (1870–1949) were avidly collected by Duncan Phillips from the midteens onward. As with the Phillips Collection in Washington, D.C., American museums displaying modern art supported religious painting and made a place for it. Two prominent social realist paintings that located Christian values at the heart of the

American national character are exemplary. The fledgling Whitney Museum of American Art purchased John Steuart Curry's *Baptism in Kansas* (1928) in 1930. In the same year the Art Institute of Chicago first exhibited and then acquired Grant Wood's *American Gothic* (1930). Right up until the time of his death in France, African American artist Henry Ossawa Tanner interpreted Biblical parables in Symbolist paintings that entered French and U.S. collections. Lesser-known white American regionalists, such as New York–trained artists John McGrady (1911–1968), Coulton Waugh (1896–1973), and Ruth Starr Rose (1887–1965) traveled to the South in the 1930s to study worshipping black Baptists, subjects they rendered in a magical realist style. Still, in the same era, the visual satire of European Americans Ben Shahn (1898–1969), George Bellows, and many of their contemporaries sharply criticized the Christian temperance movement and itinerant, evangelical preachers as well.

How did Johnson and Weber, in an increasingly secular American art market, make images that convincingly communicated that their religious subjects were true to life? Who were these audiences? Lastly, what were the limits to audiences' consumption of religious art? I will address these questions to each artist's projects separately, for they produced different numbers of objects in different media as part of their creative agendas. The artists' expressionist styles were, of course, particular to their individual aesthetics and abilities, and yet they shared a vision that expressionism—a broadly exaggerated and abstract handling of figures and ground—was the best strategy for presenting ethnoracial religiosity as a particularity, one at once familiar and strange to the American majority. Decorative, direct expressionism made their imagery readable to overlapping, cross-cultural, and interracial groups: the Christian majority of the United States—an elite, predominantly white American artistic establishment—and other patrons of racial art.

ROMANTIC FORMS AND THEMES IN JOHNSON'S SPIRITUAL PAINTINGS

Johnson's surviving paintings and the available reproductions of his unlocated paintings allow us to characterize the dramatic swing from his academic and naturalistic approach of the early and mid-twenties to the moody expressionism

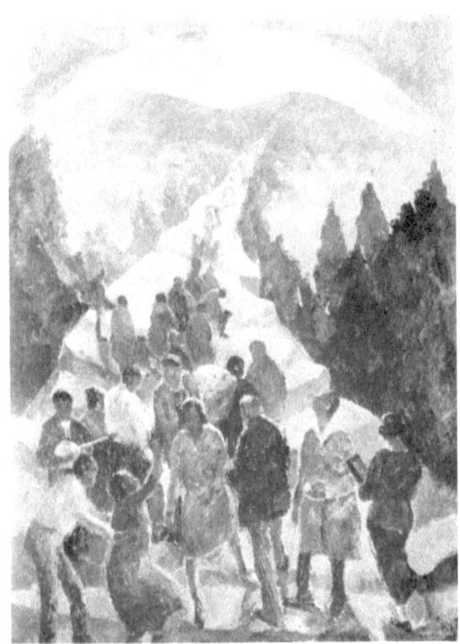

3.1 Malvin Gray Johnson, *Climbing Up the Mountain*, 1929. Oil on canvas, dimensions unknown. Painting no longer extant. Formerly in the collection of Wilson J. Lamb, Newark, New Jersey

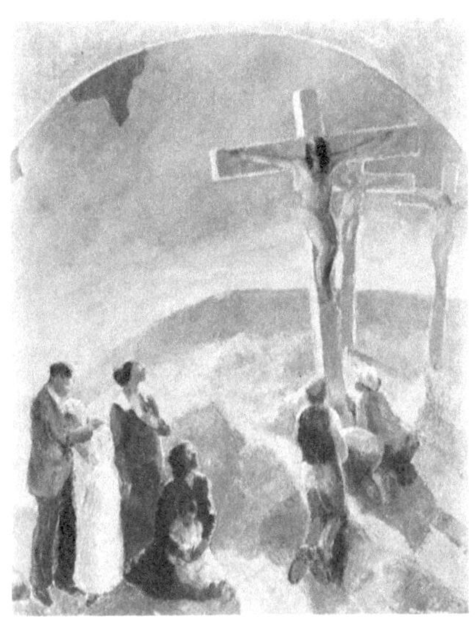

3.2 Malvin Gray Johnson, *(Wasn't That a) Mighty Day*, 1929. Oil on canvas, dimensions unknown. Painting no longer extant. Formerly in the collection of Wilson J. Lamb, Newark New Jersey

marshaled to interpret spirituals in the late twenties and early thirties. From 1927 through 1931, Johnson interpreted nine of these songs in oil. The unlocated paintings are *Deep River* (1927); *Lord, I Want to Be a Christian* (1928); *I Know the Lord Laid His Hands on Me* (1929); *Climbing Up the Mountain* (1929; fig. 3.1); *Down by the Riverside* (1930); *Great Getting Up in the Morning* (1930); and *(Wasn't That a) Mighty Day* (1929; fig. 3.2). Only *Swing Low, Sweet Chariot* (1928) and *Roll Jordan, Roll* (1930) are known to have survived.[18] Among these works, there are subtle variations in style. *Swing Low, Sweet Chariot* (fig. 1.3) provoked a critical comparison to Albert Pinkham Ryder's art, and Johnson may have been one of the many who admired that turn-of-the-century painter's expressive romanticism.[19] Through 1931 Johnson remained committed to the romantic symbolism of the spiritual as a subject even as he developed a sparer language to visualize them. *Roll Jordan, Roll* (fig. 3.3, plate 5) evidences Johnson's desire to manipulate tonal relationships and his increased facility

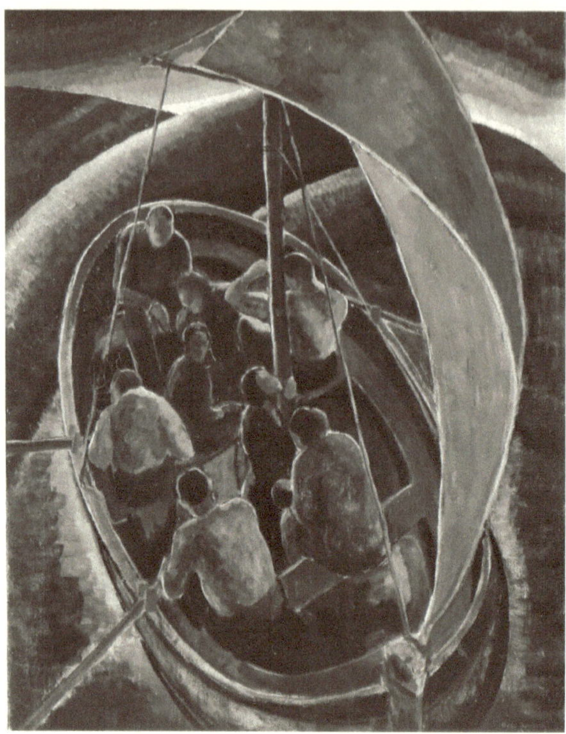

3.3 Malvin Gray Johnson, *Roll Jordan, Roll*, 1930 (plate 5). Courtesy Steve Turner Gallery, Los Angeles, California

in doing so. While relatively blunt value and color contrasts define forms in *Swing Low, Sweet Chariot*, those in *Roll Jordan, Roll* emerge from a closely keyed color scheme and more delicate transitions between light and dark areas. Although both paintings are heavily symbolic, *Roll Jordan, Roll* is less narrative in purpose and, arguably, less delineative than *Swing Low, Sweet Chariot*. The former resembles a modernist genre picture that nonetheless shares the evoked somberness of *Swing Low, Sweet Chariot*.

In his spiritual interpretations, Johnson tested the boundaries, gauging how far out on the limb of figural abstraction he could go while also providing imagery that would be enthusiastically received by audiences who wanted legibly black representation and racial symbolism. He started conservatively, for the very structure of the early spiritual paintings demonstrates that he meant to make them contemporary altarpieces. With their golden, arc-shaped framing sections, *Swing Low, Sweet Chariot*; *Mighty Day*; and *Down by the Riverside* proclaim their debt to precedents in Judeo-Christian religious art. The lunette schema invests each of these works with the sanctity of the altarpiece and the stained glass window. The gold chrome, the scintillation of rich purple hues, and the luminosity of the oil medium—insistent effects of precious artifacts—infuse the paintings with ecclesiastical authority; structurally, they look as if they were commissioned by a liberal Protestant church.[20] Their specific images of celestial spectacles effectively add to their hallowed aura. In *Swing Low, Sweet Chariot* and *Down by the Riverside*, angels and chariots traverse the heavens, a sight that commands the gazes and gestures of pious mortals. In *Mighty Day*, what look to be land masses (perhaps the fragmented sections of earthly continents) are mapped on the sky, while worshippers bow before the crucified Christ. Divine, supernatural, and oneiric, the imagery in these skies is a meaningful index to mortals as well: in order to be awe-inspiring, these miracles must be seen by the pictured, human witnesses and, subsequently, by viewers before the made paintings. In sum, religious experience is thrice-stated in each canvas: in the narrative representation; in the sacral, altarlike presentation; and in the spiritual title.

In contrast, the later work *Roll Jordan, Roll*, with its skewed cubist and compressed spaces, is a step away from the conventions of academic naturalism and its storytelling. A medium-sized easel painting in the traditional rectangular format, it makes no obvious claim on Christian iconographical form. It is a figurally abstract rendering of nine African Americans in a sailboat on high seas. The huddled passengers of this painting are simply figured, bluntly shaped masses painted with immediacy and occasionally distinguished by bright color accents against tonal schemes. The curvilinear hull of the heaving boat is made with flat strokes of tonal color as well: it is this flatness, along with the composition's interlocking forms and the frontality of its imagery, that announce Johnson's maturing modernist style. Between 1927 and 1931 Johnson discovered that the cultural currency of the spirituals could be used to communicate mood, history, ideas, and racial symbolism.

WEBER'S TALMUDIC SCHOLARS AND HASIDIC JEWS

Art historians and critics have called the 1919 oil painting *Sabbath* Weber's first Jewish painting, if for no other reason than that Weber himself did.[21] In so doing, Weber either forgot his 1913 painting, *Still Life Judaica*, or purposefully banished it to its eponymous genre category. *Still Life Judaica* pictures ritual items from the festal "set table" in the kind of compressed space often evidenced in Cézanne's still lifes and Weber's synthetic cubist works. Yet why wouldn't *Still Life Judaica* be Jewish? And what of other paintings with human figures that preceded *Sabbath*—from the genre portrait *A Cup of Tea* (1910) and the allegory *The Geranium* (1911) to the landscape *Maine* (1914) and the urbanscape *Rush Hour, New York* (1915)? What made them "not Jewish?" Figures in these works could have been Jews or painted after Jewish models, and both forest and city scenes without human forms may have been spaces where Jewish people lived.[22] It is the titles of works such as *Sabbath*, which denote Jewish ceremony, and their representations of typed bodies of observant Jews that make us realize that Weber's unmarked imagery has been located in categories that overwhelm those of race and ethnicity, namely, "American art" and "modernism."

For his part, Weber claimed that formal concerns always drove his production, saying in 1938, "I shall never make my art subsidiary to subject matter."[23] Much earlier, in a 1919 essay, he described the ideal artistic product: "Art is neither national nor racial. It is neither Bolshevik nor autocratic. Art is the universal tongue of mankind."[24] As we have seen, discussion of Weber's art did not escape such binary terms. In 1930 Weber's first biographer, Holger Cahill (1887–1960), wrote that he found "Hebraic quality" fused with ancient non-Western art in *The Worshipper*, a 1918 oil painting, and *Prayer*, a 1918 woodcut.[25] It is easy to follow Cahill's reasoning, for, in title, *The Worshipper* and *Prayer* announce the religious act, one represented by a religious painter. But what struck Cahill as a "Hebraic quality" in either? Like *Prayer*, *The Worshipper* presents a single standing meditative figure; yet in both the bodies are abstractly rendered. In *The Worshipper* the female worshipper crosses her hands across her chest in a convincing gesture of piety, no less so because her fingers are long and stiff-looking. Weber went for the same effect when incising the woodblock for *Prayer*: its wasp-waisted nude male body has attenuated features—the head, the nose, the fingers of the clasped hands—that are heightened by the composition's vertical orientation. Both of these austere figures are related to the aggressively crude wood and bronze sculptures Weber executed in 1915, in which he demonstrated his study of non-Western and precolonial sculptural traditions, as well as of the School of Paris artists inspired by them, namely, Cézanne, Matisse, Picasso, Braque, and Modigliani. The 1915 sculptures, with their activated surfaces, distorted figures, and simplified forms, clearly referenced these artistic sources—contemporary and premodernist—and the same could be said of *Prayer* and *The Worshipper.* Weber's move to primitivism was driven by his search to find unmarked, universal motifs, ones different from his early academic nudes, such as *La Parisienne* (1907), and post–World War I neoclassical nudes, such as those in *Tranquility* (1928). Cahill, too, admired "the art of the ancients" and "the primitive" (including, as has been noted earlier, folk art), and he recognized Weber's broad, stylized incorporation of these vocabularies into his work. After praising *The Worshipper* and *Prayer,* Cahill summed up:

> At the sources, the expressions of all races are akin. At the level of the primitive, art still knows a universal language. In the highest expressions of a world art, of which such work as Weber's is a prophecy, this universal language may be recovered. In Weber's matured expression, many elements have been fused and tempered in the fire of the great tradition of Europe and America to make a powerfully expressive art.[26]

Cahill, rapturously descriptive of Weber's means and ends, leaves the "Hebraic quality" of the artist's work ambiguous. Yet, we might surmise, that for this critic, it meant something like antiquity—old, extinct, and represented by its artifacts—a quality that, as Henry McBride's review of Weber's Montross Gallery exhibition of 1923 indicates, many believed was embodied in or translated through the artist himself.

Three other precedents to *Sabbath* in Weber's oeuvre also trouble our acceptance of the category "Jewish paintings": a 1907 Fauvist sketch, *Adam and Eve*; a 1916 oil painting of the same title; and a 1908 oil painting, *My Christ.* Both paintings depict their Biblical subjects as nudes, another indication of Weber's search for universal symbols and the unifying ties that bind Christianity and Judaism in Western art's stable visual conventions. These subjects certainly spoke to human fallibility and martyred suffering, phenomena and events that weighed on the minds of viewers, whether believers, agnostics, or atheists. They also may have emerged from Weber's awareness of anti-Semitic pogroms in Russia (and, later, in the Soviet Union) and his desire to denounce sectarian violence.[27] Yet no commentators have discussed the semantic and philosophical ramifications of Weber's taking up of these Judeo-Christian icons. Rather than narrow Weber's range of interests to his Jewish experience in Bialystok and to the Orthodox Jews he observed in Manhattan, I would expand it, for *Adam and Eve* is a composition of confounding signs and puzzled expressions, typical of the artist's willingness to reconsider conventional iconographies and pursue cross-cultural meanings. Like Weber's 1920 woodcut *Mother Love,* a well-balanced image of a woman and an infant with its title phrase in Yiddish script below it, *Adam and Eve* and *My Christ* have been dismissed and ignored.[28] Nonetheless, they seem especially important indications of Weber's search for universal icons.[29] The 1916 *Adam and Eve*'s monumental protagonists are crammed into the nearly square format of the canvas and share the distorted physiognomies of other Weber genre subjects, including those understood to be observant Jews. Like the figures of *Hasidic Dance* (1940), rabbis and Talmudic scholars, the heads and limbs of Adam and Eve are disproportionately large, imbuing the figures with raw power.[30] The similarities among forms indicate that Weber purposefully developed an expressionist template, heroic and potent, for symbolic personages, human and holy, ancient and contemporary.[31] Although Lloyd Goodrich said as much in his essay for the 1949 Weber retrospective exhibition at the Whitney Museum, neither he nor earlier writers seem to have genuinely understood the implications of this notion. Goodrich, taking in the breadth of Weber's oeuvre to date, did not relate the artist's cubist abstraction of the teens to his expressionist exaggeration in the proposed Jewish pictures.[32] In a mounted defense of Weber's "intensification of Jewish character in certain subjects," Goodrich wrote, "To a Gentile Weber's attitude may seem to have an element of caricature, but he himself disclaims this vehemently, and actually his attitude here is no different than that towards other subjects."[33]

Expressionism suited Weber's project of representing observant Jews of European descent and some of their practices both in latent and unmistakable terms. Whether *Sabbath* was Weber's first "Jewish painting" or not, this painting, and *Invocation* as well, are significant realizations of religiously marked Jews inserted into an American catalogue of images that included anti-Semitic stereotype—the enduring caricature, as described by art historian Robin Reisenfeld, the racist portrayal of "heavy eyes, attenuated nose, elongated face, big ears, and beard."[34] Weber's single figures, such as those of *Prayer* and his rabbi genre portraits, to be discussed in chapter 4, are designed to assert iconic force. *Sabbath* and *Invocation*, on the other hand, as compositions of figural groups, depend heavily on formal relationships that suggest social interactions. The linked forms of *Sabbath*, for instance, are compressed in the picture, making their bodies seem as if they have been flattened under glass. Differentiated as two females and two males, all four bodies are figured with the elongated faces with slitted eyes that are common to Modigliani portraits and indebted to the Dan and Fang masks that influenced that Jewish painter and other European primitivists. Such stylization emerged early on in Weber's post-Paris oeuvre, and long before he or any observer deemed his pictures Jewish. Weber built nude studies, genre portraits, and religious figures on the armature of these wooden-looking heads, subtly varying and aggressively accessorizing them for the intended context. Once stripped down, Weber's heads are generic within his oeuvre even if they are put to service as the foundation for a Jewish type recognized in the visual terms of expressionism. We also know that Weber revised Jewish images to work for "secular" ends: Daryl R. Rubinstein has reported that the artist's 1936 social realist print, *Pensioned*, was made from an earlier woodcut "originally executed with a Rabbi or religious theme in mind."[35]

American opinion about expressionism shifted during Weber's lifetime. Once dismissed and reviled as the offensive and unskilled approach of cynical artists, expressionism was later considered an entitlement afforded to creative, poetic producers. In the 1920s, Weber's detractors described him as a poet, a designation they meant to be uncomplimentary, for unlike admirers of his literary and visual production, they found his verse too oblique to enjoy.[36] The societal change in attitude over time is thrown into relief in writer Dorothy Adlow's 1957 comment that Weber was "an expressionist with discipline."[37] Her remark reflects her view that expressionism, however undisciplined, had become a recognizable branch of modernism. As early as 1939, expressionism was described in positive terms in Martha Candler Cheyney's survey of American art:

The use of the word *expressionism* has been urged variously as a broad term for all modern art, whether psychological, abstract, or nonrepresentative; for that goes beyond *impressionism* and the conception of *realism* and *naturalism* of art's recent pasts.

Expressionism is conceived as capable of giving plastic reality to the artist's intuitive perceptions of things—intuitive perception being understood as belonging to a deeper and more profound range of experience than intellectual perception. The formal abstract structure of a painting or a sculpture conforms with the principles of a basic order that underlies all natural forms, and it is universal in operation, whereas the meaning and the feeling have to do with a subjective reality underlying all consciousness. [Emphasis in the original.][38]

When produced by minority American artists readily conceived of as primitive, original poets, expressionist imagery came as no surprise to some audiences. For Museum of Modern Art curator James Johnson Sweeney, writing in 1944, Weber's expressionism was "inborn."[39] Critic Forbes Watson also cast the artist's expressionism as an "inevitable" outcome of his development, his "more thorough and searching study of what was once the healthy movement of modern art." In a 1941 profile of Weber, Watson surmised:

This is the art of a man who lives deeply in the spirit. It is pure, speculative, and racial—not national and colloquial. I say this although I am devoted to colloquial art. Besides, the homely can be universal.

. . . . . .

It was when the Hebraic quality came into Weber's work that his destiny as a great modern religious painter began to show fulfillment. By religious painter I do not mean a painter of religious subjects. I mean a painter who looks upon life from a deeply religious point of view.[40]

Watson raised Weber's expressionism above satirical or primitivist depictions, to the level of ancient religiosity and sincere racial art. If expressionism that included figural representation, however abstract, had emerged by the 1940s as a preferable alternative to nonobjectivity, it was in part because it had been promoted by minority American artists such as Johnson, Weber, and Kuniyoshi.

By the mid-1950s, expressionism was "realism in varying degree combined with abstraction," according to Ralph M. Pearson, author of a 1954 survey of U.S. art.[41] Realism was tied to "inner and outer truths or facts,"[42] and it was also tied to authenticity and sincerity, and, by extension, so was expressionism. Expressionism, then, was tempered and, in some cases, expected as the raw, atavistic production of the racialized artist. That is, with so much rhetoric generated around the inner worlds and minds of minority American artists, expressionism was a predictable outcome.

MODERNIST EMOTION AND RACIAL ART

Just as Johnson received praise for the emotion of his paintings, so did Weber, and not just for works considered Jewish. Rallying to Weber's defense decades after critics first denigrated the artist's figurally abstract mode, Holger Cahill situated emotion squarely in the trajectory of Western modernism:

> Weber does not use arrangements of forms and spaces to make exact statements about things. He uses them in such a way as to evoke the whole situation of seeing and the emotion aroused by it. . . . Many people interpret works of art as scientific statements about things, and they refer to their memory of things similar to those they see represented. If the objects as represented in the picture agree with this memory the picture is judged to be a good one, true to nature, and even beautiful if the painter and the beholder are in agreement as to what constitutes "seeing beautifully." This is not the way to look at pictures, certainly not at the pictures of Max Weber. His pictures, and those of any other artists worthy of the name, are intended to be looked at as objects in which the search of the beholder comes to rest, and not as symbols which refer to other objects.[43]

Yet when Weber and Johnson gave titles to their works, they initiated referential and intertextual readings of their images. Both artists realized that images generate associations in their audiences' minds, and perhaps reasoned that figural distortion, exaggeration, and abstraction could be mitigated by the cognitive appeal of their religious themes. Weber explained his intentions with respect to *Invocation*, a composition of tightly interlocking geometric forms, in these terms: "Sculpturesque, dynamic form was sought for in this picture, but the chief aim was to express a deep religious archaic spirit in fitting attitudes and gestures."[44] Johnson had a similar ambition in painting *Swing Low, Sweet Chariot*, which he stated in a publicity release: "I have tried to show the escape of emotions which the plantation slaves felt after being held down all day by the grind of labor and the consciousness of being bound. Set free from their task by the end of the day and the darkness, they have gone from their cabin to the river's edge and are calling upon their God for the freedom for which they long."[45] Johnson and Weber employed received images—the "Old South" and "the village Jew"—in such a way as to suggest not only their familiarity with such vehicles but also their awareness that they were recycling them. Far from smashing stereotypes, both artists depended on their long-standing reliability.

Johnson and Weber expanded stereotypes of blacks and Jews, respectively, and gave them new lives and relevance. From the turn of the nineteenth century, some persons within their American ethnoracial groups were putting forth (not unproblematically) new identity paradigms, that is, "the New Negro" and a new Jewish American—subject positions that were variably pluralist, assimilationist, and nationalist. As German Jews in New York looked to "Americanize" their immigrant coreligionists from Eastern and Central Europe, African American elites in Chicago and New York similarly instructed Southern migrants on the required manners of their new environs.[46] Working against the program of assimilation, Johnson's and Weber's religious paintings effectively intensified essentialized identities, fixing them in a niche of uniqueness and simultaneously drawing attention to them as cultures that were paradoxically strong and yet threatened with extinction by modernity. Both artists aspired to the role of visual historian endeavoring to document religious customs—some from the historical past and others believed to be disappearing or seriously threatened by radical transformations in society. While Johnson, in his own words, hoped to capture the look of the antebellum American plantation and communicate something about the emotional lives of enslaved blacks, the spiritual of his own era was performed by free black citizens in their churches and cultural spaces and in integrated concert halls internationally. Similarly, Talmudic recitation and Orthodox and Hasidic Jewish rituals, although viewed as traditions that remain unchanged from the days of antiquity, were (and are) dynamic cultural practices. I quoted above Weber's hope of expressing "deep archaic spirit" in *Invocation*; his comments with regard to *The Talmudists* (1934) likewise reference the past, eternity, and age-old customs:

> I was prompted to paint this picture after a pilgrimage to one of the oldest synagogues of the East Side in New York. I find a living spiritual beauty emanates from, and hovers over and about, a group of Jewish patriarchal types when they congregate in search of wisdom in the teaching of the great Talmudists of the past. Their discussion of the Talmud is at times impassioned, inspired, ecstatic, at other moments serene and contemplative. . . . To witness a group of such elders bent down and intent upon nothing but the eternal quest and interpretation of the ethical and spiritual significance and religious content of the great Jewish legacy—the Torah—is for me an experience never to be forgotten.[47]

Matthew Baigell considers this Weber memory—articulated in 1935—a nostalgic one, and yet his biographical analysis of the artist's identity generates other readings of his intention. In response to Weber's explanation of *The Talmudists*, Baigell, subtending and negating the artist's self-representation and the popular cultural representation of minority artists as insiders to their communities, concludes:

> In 1934, when the painting was completed, this was less a living tradition for Weber than a trip, perhaps a guilt trip, down memory lane. No doubt, he still remembered many prayers and blessings, perhaps even said them from time to time, but he was in truth an outsider reveling in remembered customs, immortalizing in his art and giving witness to a kind of life he respected and revered but had never lived as an adult. Weber also ignored the Orthodox insistence on feminine modesty in his many paintings of nudes at this time. What we can tentatively conclude, then, is this: for whatever reasons, Weber could not or did not want to become an assimilated American, nor did he find a sustaining home within the world of modern art. Rather, he chose to become a hyphenated American and expressed that kind of existence through his art. His approach was elegiac, nostalgic, and retrospective rather than concerned with the flow of contemporary events. In this regard, he is an early example of

> what today is quite common—artists whose works are inspired by their multiple identities, be they racial, religious, and gender oriented.[48]

Baigell marks and divides the historical periods of Weber's life: he separates the artist's adolescent and adult experiences in New York from his often referenced childhood in Bialystok. (This split parallels that of the two other artists in this study: Johnson, the Southern-born, adolescent migrant to New York, and Kuniyoshi, the Japan-born, adolescent immigrant to the United States.) Baigell also notes the evident contradiction between Weber's attitude toward Orthodox ways and his artistic practices. Indeed, each artist's work is informed by her or his life; each life, whether artistic or not, is formed by social identifications, individual assertions of identity, and never-ending negotiations around both. Weber's artistic life was a public, professionalized identity that must have influenced his choice of subject matter. Whether his hyphenated American status was a personal and private choice or not, he contended with its ramifications in his professional life. Just as with Johnson's spiritual paintings, stable popular notions of what Weber's ethnocultural group "looked like" and what they "did" in their particular environments animated his religious imagery.[49]

This is to say, minority American artists and their audiences collaboratively made the convention of the picturesque "other." In the present, observers (scholarly and popular) know Weber and Johnson for their genre paintings, *Chinese Restaurant* and *Negro Soldier (Rattlesnake*; fig. 3.4), respectively, because such paintings are now privileged in our inescapably dominant narrative of early American modernism—the teleological march of antinaturalistic forms toward triumphant Abstract Expressionism.[50] Yet during Johnson's and Weber's careers, their admirers focused upon the religious content in their pictures, which, however figurally distorted, exaggerated, and summarized, presented a recognizable stereotype. If Weber's genre painting included American Jews who were not purposefully marked by Hasidic or Orthodox accoutrements or their location in ethnocultural and religious environments, such figures were part of the United States in a way that those identified by this artist as Jewish were not.[51] The genre types that Weber labeled as "Jews" engage in the unchanging same. How could Weber or his fellow Americans (Jewish or non-Jewish) see them as anything but "primitive ancestors" of non-Westerners?[52] They

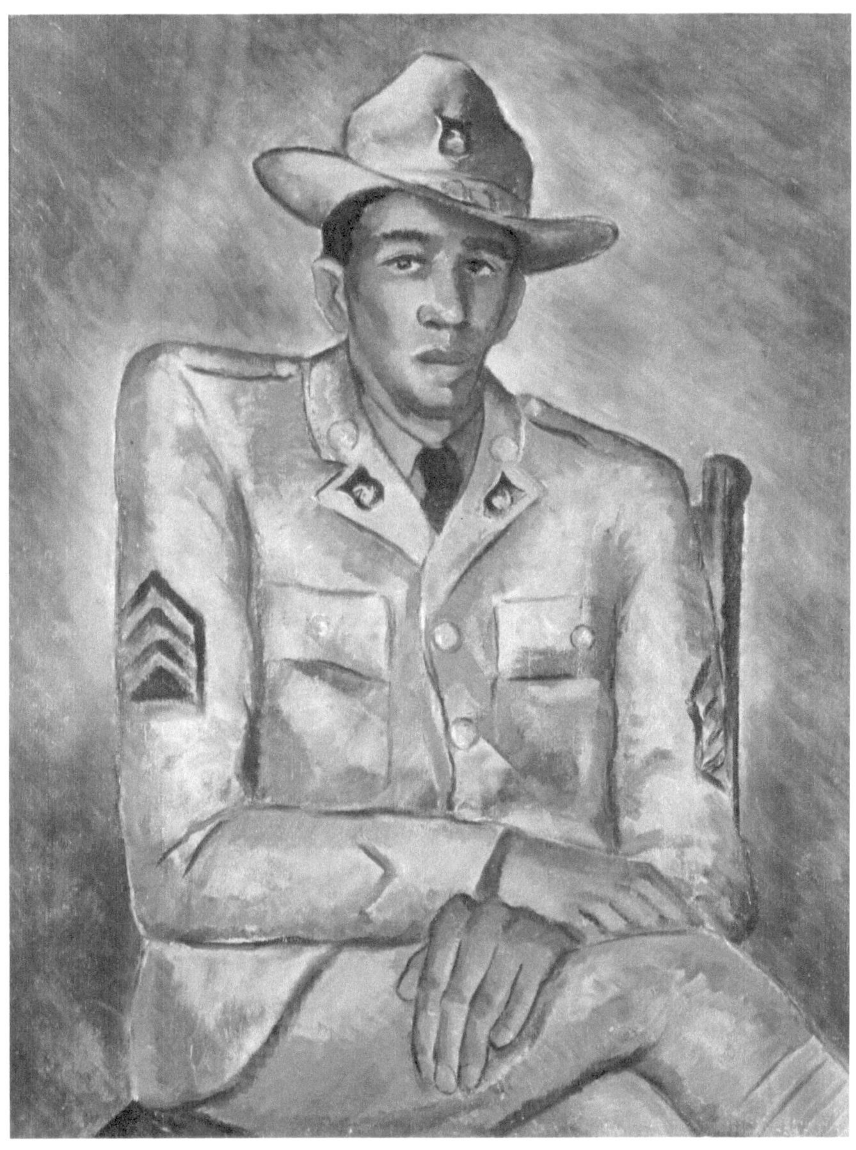

3.4 Malvin Gray Johnson, *Negro Soldier (Rattlesnake)*, 1934. Oil on canvas, 38 x 30 in. Art & Artifacts Division, Schomburg Center for Research in Black Culture, New York Public Library; Astor, Lenox and Tilden Foundations, New York

look heavenward in *Invocation*, scrutinize ancient texts in *The Talmudists* and *Students of the Torah* (circa 1939–40), and celebrate rites in *Hasidic Dance* and *Adoration of the Moon* (1944). Such pictures, which take account of institutional anti-Semitic segregation as well as self-selecting community building, shore up stereotypes of Jewish immigrants and Jewish Americans as isolates resolutely locked into Old Country folkways and entirely restricted New World ghettoes.[53] Interwar era critic Edouard Roditi (1910–1992) simultaneously problematized and reductively simplified the paradoxes within Weber's romantic renderings and his subjects' identity positions:

> His elegiac reconstructions of a vanishing Jewish world, for instance, are as humorous as the tales of Sholem Aleichem, in spite of an undercurrent of anxiety and nostalgia. His humour is more metropolitan than that of Chagall: it springs from New York's Lower East Side, not from Issachar Ryback's ideal shtetl or Chagall's Vitebsk. Weber's helpless and melancholy female nudes, with their heavy Semitic features, are no odalisques from some exotic Orient, like those of Matisse or Piscin [sic], but fugitives from Lower East Side sweat-shops, in fact girls from under-privileged Jewish homes. Weber's elderly bearded men too, so urban in their habits and so complex in their reasoning as they stand arguing at streetcorners, seem to illustrate an almost incredibly and slightly guilty prosperity between a pogrom from which they have escaped and a future that they have not yet learned to trust whole-heartedly. The society in which Weber's Eastern European Jews live is a transitional get-rich-quick world that includes its none-too-chaste Susannahs at whom the tired businessman occasionally leers.[54]

Weber, often compared to the Russian-French Marc Chagall (1887–1985) and once called "our Chagall" by American cultural critic Lewis Mumford (1895–1990), here is contrasted to his contemporary.[55] According to Roditi, a Jewish writer born in Paris to American parents, Weber reconstructed the quaint customs of Russian Jewry in order to memorialize them and then subsequently developed realist pictures of modern life with more depth than decorative Orientalism. This writer lays atop his conceptualization of the "New York Jew," described in Biblical metaphor and doubtlessly informed by Jacob Riis's photographs from some decades prior, his conclusion that Weber was representing a particular gritty experience of urban American capitalism and the psychology of the Jewish Diaspora. Even outside of the U.S. context, this trend was evident: reviewers commenting on British artist Jacob Epstein's (1880–1959) Old Testament illustrations exhibited at London's Redfern Gallery in 1932 were especially interested because the maker was Jewish: "Where his work differs from that of other Bible illustrators is in its strong racial flavor. To our thinking the best of his drawings are those that touch the supernatural."[56] Like this unnamed critic, Roditi and others (in both the majority and minority ethnoracial groups) firmly established that the minority artist authentically represents her or his collective, an idea that is still operational today. The notion, in short, is "it takes one to paint one." On both sides of the Atlantic, the taste for this kind of racial art bloomed in the twentieth century.

Certainly, American minority artists, citing unsympathetic, hostile, and racist characterizations, made strong claims that only they could accurately picture their respective groups. (The minority American artist's nonobjective work poses the greatest challenge for viewers who desperately search and sometimes find indices to racial and cultural reference points.) But what do we do when these artists' images of their groups are clearly exaggerated, grotesque, or caricatured?[57] Writing about Weber's *Invocation* in 1946, the German-born Jewish art historian Franz Landsberger (1883–1964) argues,

> In scenes of contemporary Jewish life, Expressionism offered new possibilities. Max Weber, one of the first exponents of Expressionism in America . . . painted three Jews gathered around a table, dreaming, arguing, and one of them lifting his hands and his eyes heavenwards. This is intentionally drawn beyond the limits, because the feelings of the Jews are likewise far removed from nature. These three figures have stepped beyond their material existence and are mystically bound to God.[58]

Empathetic interpretations are the scales that cover our eyes, blinding us to the complicated relationship between any artist and her or his subject. In eliding the hierarchy of artist and subject, writers of art history and artists themselves also ignore the fact of representation; that is, they forget that art *is* a representation and not the thing itself. All artists choose subjects, devise compositional strategies, and try to effect them. To state the obvious, Johnson, Kuniyoshi, and Weber were not the consistent subjects of their paintings; whatever the parallels between them and their working-class and historical protagonists, their depicted subjects could not adequately stand in for them, and their populist scenes could not illustrate their lives.[59] Yet commentators, sometimes emboldened by the artists' pronouncements, consistently folded the maker into the work. Collapsing these two entities was especially insidious in the case of minority artists, which robbed these makers of agency—both creative and intellectual. Critics outlined the form of racial art by locating its characteristics, suggesting adaptations in form and content, and noting absences of feeling and rhythms.

AFRICAN AMERICAN SPIRITUALS: BLACK FOLK TRADITION, LOST AND FOUND

Johnson's spiritual paintings made their debut during a period of sustained interest in African American religious traditions, and especially in sacred music. The renowned Fisk Jubilee Singers, a black college choir founded in the nineteenth century, and soloists Roland Hayes and Paul Robeson, entertained audiences in the United States and abroad with their performances of African American spirituals. For Alain Locke, writing in *The New Negro* in 1925, these songs were "the most characteristic product of the race genius as yet in America"; they constituted "America's folk song" and "a classic folk expression."[60] The white playwright Marc Connelly incorporated spirituals in *Green Pastures*, his 1930 Pulitzer Prize–winning adaptation of Old Testament literature; the African American Eva Jessye Choir performed spirituals in the Broadway production of *Four Saints in Three Acts* (1934), a Virgil Thompson, Gertrude Stein, and Florine Stettheimer collaboration; and the white choreographer Helen Tamiris interpreted spirituals in her modern dance compositions starting around 1929.[61] The spiritual, quite evidently, had moved decidedly beyond black Protestant churches and social spaces to the secular and integrationist society, where it inspired new cultural production in different media.

Johnson appreciated spirituals and recognized their currency in the arena of popular culture. Significantly, he attended a Robeson recital in New York in April 1927, and the program likely included spirituals.[62] In 1934, during his summer sojourn to Virginia, he painted *Come, Sinner*, which in title references the nineteenth-century Baptist hymn penned by William Witter and Horatio Palmer, a standard in black Protestant churches. The artist said of this unlocated canvas that it was "an impression that I gained after attending one of their revival services in a little church."[63] Yet in the scant literature on Johnson's project of interpreting the religious songs, there is little effort to problematize or historicize his choice of subject.[64] Instead, present-day scholars, like Johnson's contemporaneous critics, presume that religion was a "natural" subject for a black artist, especially considering the centrality of Protestantism in African American lives and the popular perceptions of blacks as America's most pious Christians. Nevertheless, even in Johnson's era, American intellectuals disagreed about the origins of the spirituals and the purity assigned to them. White southern scholar George Pullen Jackson offered improbable arguments that African American spirituals were simply artful mimicry of Anglo-Protestant religious music, a conclusion that resonated with period accusations that too many African American artists were slavish imitators.[65] The very definition of the spiritual was far from stable in the early twentieth century. The writer Zora Neale Hurston (1891–1960), an anthropology student of Franz Boas at Columbia University, maintained that what was being performed in concert halls was, in fact, not the African American spiritual but, instead, a "neospiritual," that is, a too-sophisticated version of the willfully dynamic and improvisatory musical form originated by ecstatic church worshippers.[66] At its core, Hurston's charge raised questions about concert hall performances: had the church spiritual—archetypically raw, vernacular, and improvisational—been mellowed and made less "black" for predominantly white concertgoers, American and foreign?

Johnson was probably aware of these contentious discussions, which certainly complicated any project devoted to interpreting and privileging the spiritual; the arguments threatened the spiritual's status as a stable symbol of blackness whether in music or in art. Moreover, as an individual born in the late nineteenth century, Johnson likely knew that many middle-class black Americans of his generation and socially ambitious members of the preceding one were ambivalent about the preservation and performance of spirituals, "mellows," "himes," "ballets," and other black musical traditions bound to the history and cultures of black enslavement in the United States.[67] Divergent constituencies of black leftists and cultural nationalists agreed in their shared skepticism of the preservation and performance of spirituals.[68]

Nonetheless, for many progressive blacks and their nonblack allies during the early twentieth century, "the black folk"—a pure, racial group unified by means of their rituals and Southern location and relatively untainted by history and time—was a discursive formation, one in which cultural pride and political power could reside.[69] Observers from W. E. B. Du Bois (1868–1963) and Alain C. Locke (1885–1954) to Langston Hughes and Zora Neale Hurston spoke confidently of black folk, and numerous "Negrophiliac" whites in the ranks of the press and patronage did as well.[70] For all, the black folk constituted one half of a binary relationship, in which they stood for simplicity, purity, and homogeneity, and stood against complexity, heterogeneity, and uncertainty. Considering this taxonomy, it is not surprising that a debate over spirituals, neospirituals, and pseudospirituals erupted.

Given their currency, spirituals may have seemed like a marketable subject for a struggling artist like Johnson, who was desperate to succeed. Johnson's patron and friend, John Wilson Lamb (1879–1950?), an African American vocalist and choral director, may have commissioned some of these paintings, for he was the first owner of *Swing Low, Sweet Chariot*; *Roll Jordan, Roll*; and *Climbing Up the Mountain*.[71] If Lamb did not actually commission these paintings, his purchase of them likely encouraged Johnson to continue working in this vein.[72] Certainly Johnson was not the only artist inspired by African American spirituals in the Depression era. Several artists interpreted "Swing Low, Sweet Chariot" in particular: there are eponymous paintings by Frederick Coulton Waugh (1896–1973) in 1935, John McGrady (1911–1968) in 1937, William H. Johnson (1901–1970) in 1939, and Dan Lutz (1906–1978) in 1940; and a lithograph by Ruth Star Rose dating to 1939. Malvin Gray Johnson's *Swing Low, Sweet Chariot*, reproduced on the cover of the *Art Digest* in 1929, may or may not have spurred these artists' efforts. McGrady was also celebrated for his painting of the same title.[73] As a white American, however, McGrady was questioned about his motivations for taking up this subject. In contrast, African American artists, such as William H. Johnson and Malvin Gray Johnson, faced no such scrutiny, and their practices were believed to be unmediated.

What were Malvin Gray Johnson's own religious convictions? Rather than assume a fervent religiosity as a consequence of Johnson's blackness, we might consider the conspicuous absence of statements about religion and his spiritual outlook in his history. Although he proudly noted his NAD study, high school degree, and membership in the Elks fraternal organization, Johnson never noted a religious affiliation on Harmon Foundation forms that asked for it. His sister, Maggie Gilmer, writing a biographical essay about the artist in 1956, stated, "Malvin had a very Christian mother who sent him to Sunday School and Church every Sunday."[74] In light of the prevalence and strength of Southern black Protestantism—documented by historians, sociologists, anthropologists, musicologists, and visual artists—it is likely that Johnson was brought up in a Protestant denomination. Yet nothing in Johnson's statements indicates his indivisible identification with that religious subject matter. What may be said is that he interpreted the spirituals' lyrics, which he read to develop ideas for his paintings.[75] After success with *Swing Low, Sweet Chariot*, Johnson submitted three paintings of spirituals to the 1930 Harmon exhibition: *Mighty Day* (1929), *I Know the Lord Laid His Hands on Me*, and *Climbing Up the Mountain*. In these three paintings, Johnson presented the spiritual as a black idiom. All three paintings are unlocated; nonetheless, reproductions of the first two indicate that they are of contemporary subjects. That is, neither *Mighty Day* nor *Climbing Up the Mountain* would appeal to audiences who enjoyed the sentimental, antebellum imagery evident in *Swing Low, Sweet Chariot*. Unlike *Swing Low, Sweet Chariot*, these three subsequent spiritual paintings received no accolades, and although *Climbing Up the Mountain*, a highly dramatized representation of black spirituality, generated several inquiries, it found no buyer. In light of his earlier success with spiritual paintings, Johnson must have wondered what juries, critics, and patrons wanted.

One answer emerged in a critic's review of the January 1930 Harmon exhibition. "Negro Painters Imitate Whites" was the banner headline; William Auerbach-Levy (1889–1964), a well-known illustrator, was the review's author. Auerbach-Levy faulted the Harmon exhibitors for not making their art "racial," asserting:

> There is lacking the particular patterns of design and color which one would expect and which one finds in other forms of Negro art such as music, acting

and poetry. . . . It is hoped that once these Negro artists learn the technical foundation that the white schools can give them they will let loose and express naturally and without self-consciousness the peculiar rhythm and directness of feeling which is a distinctive feature of their race.[76]

The course was clearly laid out here: black artists should learn the same skills as their nonblack counterparts, yet they ought not deploy those skills for the same purpose.[77] Certain forms are owned and sometimes misguidedly borrowed and inappropriately used. With his reference to "rhythm" and "feeling," Auerbach-Levy suggests that racial art is a product of intuition rather than intellect. The parallel created between the forms of cultural production of blacks is significant, too. For, like the performing arts, African American painting and sculpture, according to Auerbach-Levy, were opportunities for their makers to visualize familiar idioms of blackness. Although observers did not precisely describe the characteristics of racial art produced by blacks, Jews, and Asians, they reiteratively provided parameters that set the measure of the mode in content and style. Representing themes associated with blackness—musical performance, Africa, humorous dialect, and so on—was to fulfill only one condition; the manner of interpreting these subjects was equally critical. It is worth noting that in his review Auerbach-Levy praised Hale Woodruff's *Banjo Player* for its colorful, decorative design. Though expectations for black modernism dovetailed with expectations for modernism, the margins for deviation in racial art were significantly narrower.

Inspired by the numerous antinaturalistic strategies of modernism and the challenge to produce "racial art," Johnson recognized the desires of the marketplace. In a Guggenheim Fellowship application of January 1930, he explained his interest: "Devoting most of my painting to composition of Negro spirituals, folk and work songs."[78] Submitting three spiritual paintings—*Mighty Day, I Know the Lord Laid His Hands on Me, Climbing Up the Mountain*—for Guggenheim consideration, Johnson expressed a firm conviction (in the application's words and supporting images) that music comprised African Americans' most inviolable asset. Yet, as we will see, Johnson would simultaneously contradict such articulate sentiments. For now, the pressing question is where his visual production stood and how it ranked among what Du Bois termed the "gift of black folk."[79] Was Johnson exploring the possibility of synesthesia or mediation between musical and artistic traditions? Sometime between December 1929 and January 1930, Johnson submitted this application statement to the Guggenheim Foundation:

> I desire to go to Paris and study the works of the Old Masters in the Louvre, especially those who were so great in composition. After a stay there for [a] short while, I would like to proceed to Africa where I might make a thorough study of African folk music in its original setting, and thereby try to convey to my canvases the rhythm and tone I derive from music heard in the various African tribes. I feel this will also aid me in comparing our own Negro spirituals as far as line and color are concerned. This I know will strengthen my imagination for the art for which I am striving.[80]

Whether or not Johnson's application was directly informed by Auerbach-Levy's review, his ambition spoke directly to the racial art agenda. Yet his statements simultaneously intersect with and diverge from racial art's program. Among the pregnant terms Johnson summoned were "study," "composition," "folk," "original," "rhythm and tone," and "striving." Both canonical Western art and African music were areas of knowledge that the artist sought to further investigate as intellectual pursuits. Perhaps his plan was to learn from each as he found useful to his own development. From the paintings of the Old Masters he expected to expand his knowledge of "composition," the design sensibility that he wanted to improve in his own work and the quality that Auerbach-Levy found mostly lacking in the 1930 Harmon Foundation exhibition. In African music, specifically "folk" and "original" forms, Johnson identified expressions of "rhythm and tone" and anticipated that he would heuristically discern its shared qualities with African American spirituals and the potential for interpreting them in "line and color," visual elements mentioned by Auerbach-Levy. Certainly "striving" underscored Johnson's understanding that art making was labor—intellectual and creative—and his language resonated with the desires of early twentieth-century African Americans, that is, the "New Negroes," to elevate themselves in social, cultural, and economic terms.

Overall, music was foregrounded in Johnson's Guggenheim application in concrete and conceptual ways. First, while he claimed music as black cultural property, his differentiation of African and African American categories is striking. Second, his very case for comparison and contrast undermined the claims that racial art could be atavistically released from stirred, ancestral memory. Third, as many modernists—from Europeans Paul Klee and Wassily Kandinsky to New Yorkers Arthur Dove and Stuart Davis—did in the early twentieth century, Johnson cited affinities between music and art.[81] For the rest of his brief career, he occasionally returned to musical themes, in *Harmony* (not dated), *Blues* (1933), and *Platform Dance* (1934); all evidence the artist's progressively expressionist style. Yet music did not collapse seamlessly into visual expression. Instead, the spiritual—a conservative musical genre in contrast to blues and jazz—like Old Master art, the romantic narrative of antebellum slavery, and the urban culture of Harlem, was one of many sources available to Johnson.

Johnson was clearly ambivalent toward the project of racial art. In February 1930 he was quoted in a reply article to Auerbach-Levy's review titled "Art Not Racial, Negroes Tell Critic." Addressing the critic's charge that black painters imitated their white counterparts, Johnson maintained:

> No doubt this is true. Not so much from the standpoint that they imitate white artists of this or any other country, in as much as they are trying to do what artists of all races do—follow the principles of fine arts technically. We are taught to use lines, forms, and colors, never being told to look at these things from a racial viewpoint. That distinguished etcher admits most of these things himself, but says, "While few of the Negro artists used subjects of Negro life, the approach is no different than that of the white painter." How can it be? We Americans of both races know and live the same life, except that the Negro encounters racial restrictions.[82]

Johnson's reference to art training carried special irony. The critic Auerbach-Levy was a long-time instructor at the School of the NAD, where Johnson had studied. Although Johnson was not his student, the two may have known each other. In presenting art school as an ideal, color-blind space, Johnson noted that racial art was not part of the curriculum he and Auerbach-Levy knew. Johnson's comments deftly refuted the possibility of racial expression and couched his lofty principles in an eloquently phrased acknowledgement of racism and discrimination. Neither entirely universalist nor assimilationist, his comments signaled his desire to be part of an encompassing artistic tradition and fraternity.[83]

FOUR

TYPE/FACE/MASK

RACIAL PORTRAITURE

DURING THESE ARTISTS' CAREERS, PORTRAITURE REMAINED AN ARTIST'S most profitable genre, operating in the way it had for centuries: the commissioned representations of middle- and upper-middle-class sitters decorated homes, offices, and public venues, announcing the subjects' social status and power to viewers who stood before them. While some portraits of American ethnoracial minorities functioned in this way, many more were valued as picturesque illustrations of anonymous, "interesting" types; these were deemed racial art. Just as race was considered to be a stable, biological fact of difference, racial art was the visual evidence of immutable racial talents. Neither naturalism nor complete abstraction seemed to provide adequate means for racial art. Instead, it was expressionism's bright hues, exaggeration, and distortion that resonated with audiences' internalized ideas about ineffable racial essences. Expressionism was perhaps the only way that the portraiture of U.S. American minorities—ethnic, national, racial, sexual, or religious—could be accepted into

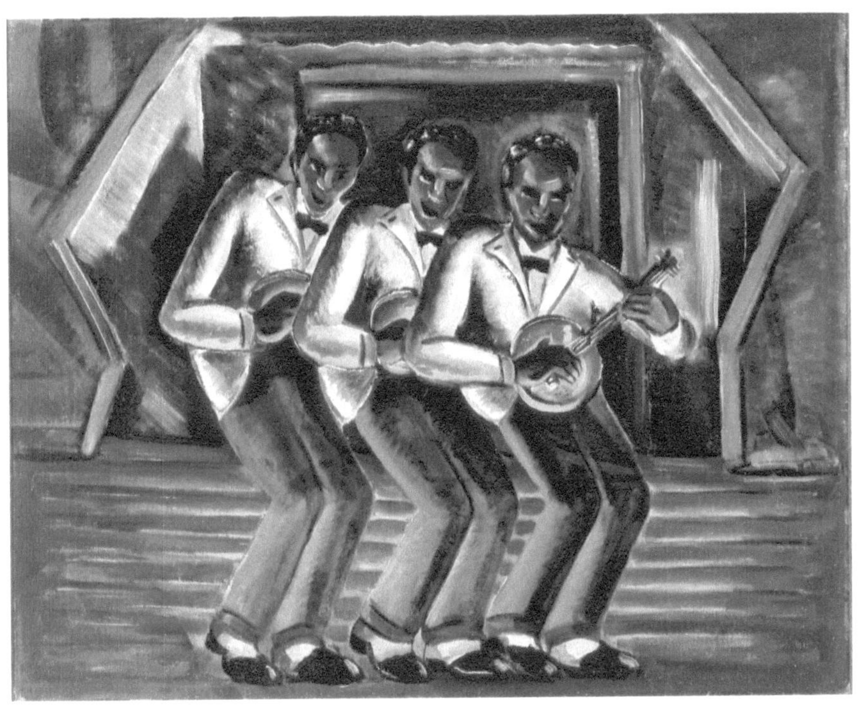

4.1 Malvin Gray Johnson, *Harmony*, not dated. Oil on canvas, 24 x 30 in. Fisk University Galleries, Nashville, Tennessee

modernist discourse, that is, as new subjects realized in a self-consciously new manner. That Johnson, Kuniyoshi, and Weber devised similarly expressionist strategies does not signal their lack of imagination or ambition. To the contrary, their parallel approaches are the products of struggle—among makers and their audiences—over figurative representation and its limits.

While they were American minorities who faced discrimination and bigotry, Johnson, Kuniyoshi, and Weber did not make portraits that consistently idealized or elevated their subjects; nor did they consistently individualize them in the manner we would expect. That these painters were engaged in the centuries-old project of depicting types complicates our consumption of their images because they do not cleanly rupture limited, binary thinking around identity. Weber's oil painting *Adoration of the Moon* (1944), Johnson's oil paint-

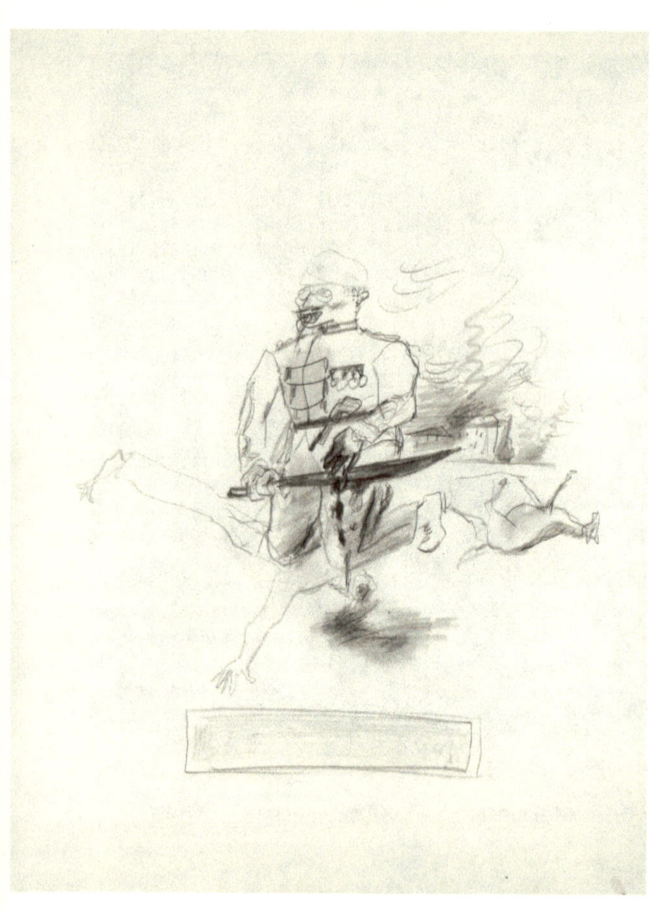

4.2 Yasuo Kuniyoshi, *Execution Scene*, 1943. Graphite on sketchbook paper, 17 x 12 3/4 in. Morgan Anderson Consulting, New York

ing *Harmony* (undated; fig. 4.1), and Kuniyoshi's graphite drawing *Execution Scene* (1943; fig. 4.2) were inextricably linked to the racist iconography these artists doubtlessly hoped to undermine and dislodge. How could it be otherwise? Ideals cannot function without the resonating presence of their opposites. Johnson, Kuniyoshi, and Weber presented enigmatic genre types and painted in ways that do not insistently oppose racist exaggerations. The subjects of these pictures are stereotypes, handled in expressionist terms: caricatured black vaudevillians in the saturated palette of *Harmony*, cartoonish Hasidic bodies described by a wavering line in *Adoration of the Moon*, a marauding Japanese officer schematically drawn in *Execution Scene*. With these inflected forms, the artists draw our attention to portraiture's impossible claims to be faithful to its subjects, to be specific and revelatory.[1] Still, observers invested these likenesses of the other with truth and authenticity, for portraits produced by Johnson, Kuniyoshi, and Weber were read first and foremost through these artists' minority American bodies.

TYPE

A discussion of portraiture need not start with the body but may begin with a conceptualization such as body type. In eighteenth- and nineteenth-century European thought, "the 'American' type is 'red, choleric, erect,' the Asiatic is 'yellow, melancholy, rigid,' and the African is 'black, phlegmatic, lax'"—characterizations informed by the classification of humors in ancient Greek philosophy.[2] Nineteenth- and twentieth-century Americans—white and nonwhite—were aware of these archetypes and stereotypes, and traded and produced them as well.[3] Like many polygenetic hypotheses formed in scientific communities, artistic concepts about types fueled racism, elitism, and other particularizing and exclusionary epistemologies.[4] In the twentieth century, the idealized representation of types who had long faced discrimination—blacks, Asians, Jews, Native Americans, the poor—numbered among cultural relativists' remedying responses to scientific racism and stereotyping in popular media. Yet types were inextricably bound to, if not embedded in, racism's iconographical logic. The minority genre portrait, outnumbered by those of the majority, carried the weight of a documentary: it was presented as objective information about a minority group's difference and particularity to be set against the conceptualization of the majority.[5]

Types have always been critical to figural representation because they facilitate quick and uncomplicated readings of bodies.[6] In "Picturing the City," Robert W. Snyder and Rebecca Zurier identify numerous types in popular illustrations of the early twentieth century: the black, the Chinese, the Irish, the Italian, and the Jew were among the most salient.[7] These types were effectively stereotypes, and, like all stereotypes, they define difference through the presentation of arbitrarily chosen characteristics—some physical, some cultural—and they make claims that such features are standard, naturally occurring, and unvarying.[8] Certainly, racist stereotypes and caricatures inspired progressive artists to redraw the minority body that had been denigrated by malign, aggressive racialization across the breadth of visual culture.[9] In the early twentieth century, mean-spirited racial types were challenged by what I call reform portraits, including the lyrically drawn *Morning Prayer* (1909; fig. 4.3) by Jacob Epstein and the bravura painting *Paddy Flannigan* (1908) by George Bellows (plate 6). Rather than attempt to neutralize their subjects, Epstein and Bellows strategically mark their young male subjects as pious Jew and Irish urchin, respectively. I suspect that Bellows and Epstein knew that audiences could only appreciate the figurative representation of these lower-class, urban heroes if they incorporated some aspect of a long-held and long-recognized stereotype—here, Epstein's yarmulke- and tefillin-wearing young man and Flannigan's bared toothy grin, reddened nose, and lank brown hair. What is self-evident is that the visual stereotype is augmented by descriptive and indexical titles in both cases, as if Epstein and Bellows doubted that images alone could advance what they wanted to communicate about these youths' identities.

Two portraits of the early Depression years demonstrate the stark con-

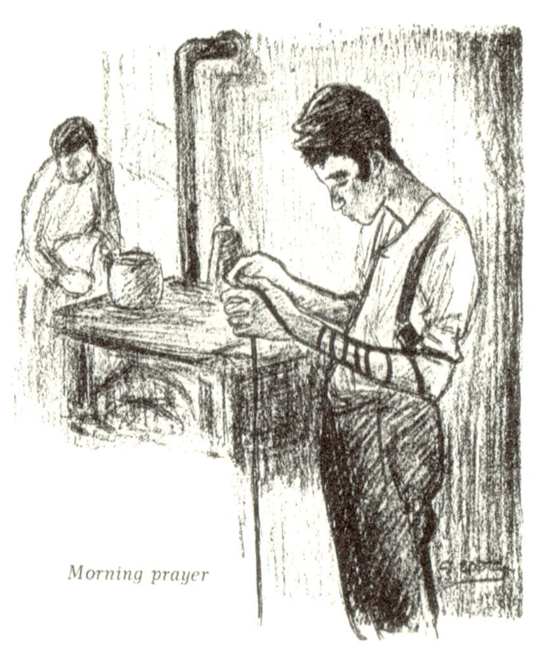

4.3 Jacob Epstein, *Morning Prayer*, 1909. Drawing, dimensions unknown. Collection unknown. Reproduced from Hutchins Hapgood, *The Spirit of the Ghetto* (New York: Funk and Wagnalls, 1902), 19

trast between a type and a stereotype: John Sloan's *Artist's Model* (not dated) and Edward Kemble's watercolor *Black Man with Pipe* (1929). In the former, an oil painting probably dating to the 1930s, Sloan offers a torso-length portrait of a black woman with large earrings and dressed in a flashy red turban and shoulder-baring dress. A realist painter of the Ashcan School, Sloan was interested in the decorative potential of his subject's body, for his palette here—much brighter and more intense than usual—contrasts with his use of local, true-to-life hues in other genre scenes and portraits. He also designs the model's form sculpturally: the variably colored, crosshatched lines make this figure both wooden and iridescent. Sloan, who was a white American, clearly articulated his interest in black sitters as types, stating, "Among the racial strains we have in this country, the Negro furnishes the most beautiful individuals. . . . more artists might find them a rich field for color-sculptural study."[10] In contrast, the illustrator Kemble (1861–1933) offers generalized information about his subject. His drawing's focal points are the man's purplish skin, his dark, similarly colored pipe, and the reddened whites of his eyes. A well-regarded caricaturist whose drawings expressed his cultural biases, Kemble offers few individual details about his subject and seems to rely on his audience's visual memory of black folk stereotypes. Tellingly, Kemble, the illustrator for Mark Twain's *Huckleberry Finn: Tom Sawyer's Comrade* (1891), bragged that he was considered "a delineator of the South, the Negro being my specialty" long before he visited the region.[11]

In the twenties, black types were the focus of well-meaning debates and forums about art. In 1926 the black monthly *Crisis* posed the question "The Negro: How Shall He Be Portrayed?" to a number of black and white cultural commentators and published their responses in seven consecutive issues. All respondents expressed the belief that black culture was rich; the outlook ranged from Anglo-American paternalism to resigned acceptance of it and the pitfalls of cultural speciation.[12] To wit, white photographer Julia Peterkin asserted that "the Irishman or Jew who know that his people have racially so lived and wrought and achieved … is not remotely disturbed by … portrayals of Mr. McManus and Mr. Gross." Peterkin stated that she wrote about "Negroes because they represent human nature obscured by so little veneer."[13] Several white respondents—Sherwood Anderson, Vachel Lindsay, and Peterkin—

advised African Americans not to worry about the predominance of racial stereotypes. Nonetheless, the poet Countee Cullen wrote that white writers were not "under the same obligations" as their black peers."[14] Cullen and other black artists felt hamstrung by the task of presenting the best of African American experiences in order to counteract negative stereotypes.[15] African American novelist and *Crisis* literary editor Jessie Fauset and historian Benjamin Brawley, in advocating for the recognition of "the complexity of Negro life," sounded the call for creative freedom and for art that was not principally designed to compensate for centuries of racist depictions. Yet even as progressive black artists and their likeminded allies sought to create a catalogue of New Negro imagery, they effectively used and maintained a recognizable "old Negro." In order for audiences to recognize and appreciate the strides and achievements of early twentieth-century African Americans, the bodies of "Zip Coon" and "Uncle Tom" were required for contrast.

As a type, Johnson's *Meditation* (1931; fig. 4.4) is a form radically different from his prior representations. Its centralized female sitter is a solid volume,

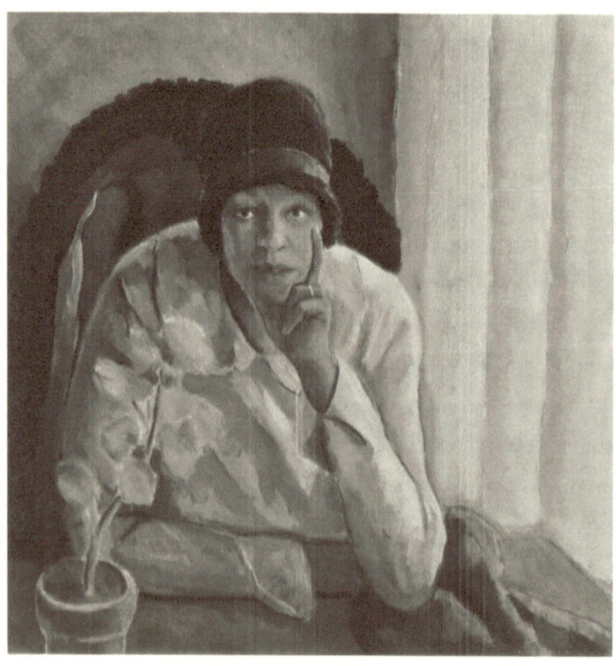

4.4 Malvin Gray Johnson, *Meditation*, 1931. Oil on canvas, 29 x 25 in. Strawberri Lucas, East Orange, New Jersey

4.5 Malvin Gray Johnson, *Sailor*, 1933. Oil on canvas, 30 x 23 in. Fisk University Galleries, Nashville, Tennessee

4.6 Malvin Gray Johnson, *Postman*, 1934. Oil on canvas, 37 x 30 in. Art & Artifacts Division, Schomburg Center for Research in Black Culture, New York Public Library; Astor, Lenox and Tilden Foundations, New York

and the artist has clearly abandoned the sincere, linear realism of his *Study of a Head,* an ink drawing of 1920.[16] The variably painted surface and higher chromatic values of *Meditation* also distinguish it from the spiritual interpretations Johnson had begun painting in 1928. In those dark, impasto works, Johnson rendered pious black Protestants as generalized, small-scale forms defined mostly by symbolic gesture. In contrast, the head and torso of the woman in *Meditation* fill up the picture space, and both figure and ground are energized by Johnson's varied brushwork: he alternates between quick flourishes and deliberate scrubbing motions, and likely used a palette knife as well to build up paint on some passages and scrape it off of others. After *Meditation,* Johnson similarly activated the canvases on which his subsequent genre subjects are represented: *Domestic* and *Sailor* (fig. 4.5), both 1933, and the often-exhibited *Negro Soldier* (fig. 3.4) and *Postman* (fig. 4.6), both 1934. He had devised an expressionist style using high-keyed colors and angles to emphasize the body's angles and to flatten the space the body occupied. The degree of figural exaggeration, distortion, and summarization indicates that he was not solely or consistently interested in

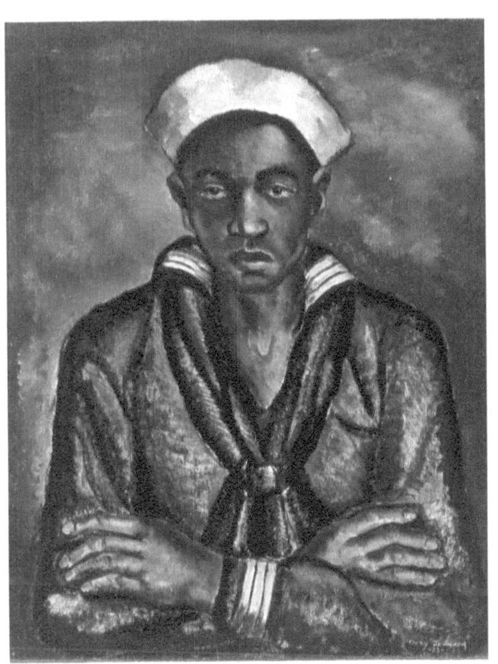

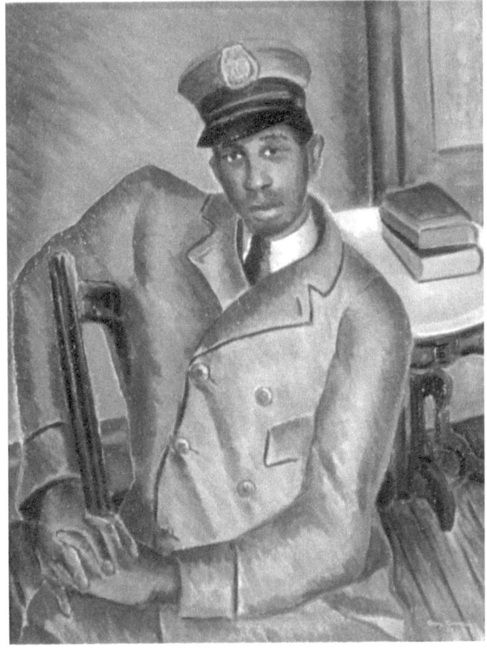

picturing the individuality of his sitters. Instead, the portraits offered key opportunities for him to experiment with figural abstraction as he associated Depression-era black bodies with labor. These paintings straddle modernist abstraction and the unwieldy category of social realism, which is generally excluded from formal analysis.[17]

Histories of social realism absorb Weber's Jewish types and yet still have not addressed the politics of such images with respect to essentialism and anti-Semitism. Weber's genre pictures do not depict Jews handling money or menacing Christians, two of the most insuperable and noxious anti-Semitic representations. Instead, Jews are shown studying, praying, or charismatically worshipping, as in *The Talmudists* (1934): these activities were less threatening to a society that would demonize Jews. Still, to today's viewers, Weber's Jewish genre portraits, much like his paintings of Talmudic debate and Hasidic ritual, strain to avoid the label of racist caricature. They seem to reify, rather than strenuously reject or challenge, Jewish stereotypes both physical and cultural. Weber built up these forms using expressionist means, which always veer toward energetically grotesque exaggeration even as they "celebrate" the pictorial subject. Like the exaggerated physiognomies in Johnson's and Kuniyoshi's paintings, those in Weber's paintings trouble scholars and other viewers in search of affirming realizations of a modern subject. All three artists' raced portraits engage the historical typing of races, nationalities, and ethnicities and bespeak the modernist's butting up against their binding limits.

Type images were quite common in the interwar years. In 1921 Austria-born artist Lionel Reiss (1891–1988) started his travels through Europe and the Middle East "to follow the trail of the wandering Jew" and ultimately published a book of 178 images in different media titled *My Models Were Jews: A Painter's Pilgrimage to Many Lands*.[18] Over his lifetime, German artist Winold Reiss (1886–1953) drew hundreds of realist portraits of Black Forest and Swedish peasants, Native Americans, African Americans, and Mexicans. In 1930 the Field Museum of Natural History in Chicago commissioned white American sculptor Malvina C. Hoffman (1885–1966) to produce more than 100 bronze sculptures to be displayed in its Hall of the Races of Man. "Antwerp to See Foujioka's California Types" was the *Art Digest* headline announcing Japan-born painter Noboru Foujioka's exhibition of genre paintings in Belgium in 1932.[19] In each case, these artists spoke of the nobility of their subjects, whose bodies they said they studied firsthand in order to better document them.

Before hypothesizing about Weber's ends, let us examine the artist's aesthetic means, because, as we will see, some observers said that his style conveyed the inviolable truth of racial authenticity. What convinced Weber's audiences that his pictures were Jewish? Characterizing the symbolic weight that Jews, Judaism, and cultural Jewishness have historically borne, historian Max Silverman has written, "'Jew' is one of the most malleable signifiers . . . the site on which unruly desire and ambivalence can, supposedly, be transformed into a coherent and univocal discourse."[20] While, unlike African Americans and Asian Americans, Jewish Americans were accepted citizens of the republic from the time of its founding in the eighteenth century, they were not considered Caucasian, the pseudoscientific racial category designed to map the "logic" of European superiority.[21] In U.S. debates over immigration policy in the nineteenth century, nativists made Jews people of color in order to place them outside of the founding myth and nationalist narrative of a white, American leadership stock that was superior to their fellow inhabitants.[22] Primitivizing and Orientalizing Jewish archetypes dominated the pictorial field as depictions of "not-whites" whose non-Anglo-Saxon, non-Christian otherness was conveyed with broad hand gestures and their deictic location in yeshivas and synagogues.[23] Weber historians have made much of the artist's emphatic pictures of identified Jews, considering them visual documents of shtetl traditions and their continuation in the United States. But, if there are forceful representations of minority difference in some of Weber's images, it should not, by default, mean the presence of majority sameness elsewhere in his oeuvre. What, in addition to descriptive titles such as "The Talmudists" and "Rabbi," made some images Jewish and others not? Rather than consider particularity and difference as definitive qualities, we might consider them desired ones, the outcome of a willingness to see qualities of alterity, succinctly described by art historian Richard Brilliant as "the perceived distinction that separates one class of person, or any particular individual from 'others.'" [24] Seeing Jewish subjects, like seeing any racially inflected subjects that embody difference, then, is work that is both conceptual and perceptual, necessitating what Matthew Frye Jacobson has called "a double task of first 'recognizing' (that is, *assigning*) resemblance and then, second, reifying that resemblance by 'likening' the two disparate objects of perception."[25]

Weber approached his subjects with a sociological interest in their lifestyles as part of a disappearing past—a Hasidic community in Manhattan to which he did not belong (and that had not disappeared)—and with knowledge of the iconicity of the Jew in Western art. While Weber's observations of New York's poor and immigrant Jewish communities provided information for his works, the outcome was not a visual catalogue of Jewish groups in New York. Nonetheless, Weber's images were read as documentary imagery and were deemed successful because they coincided with his audience's preconceived notions. Viewers added the already-read body—cultural and collective—of the Jew to Weber's primitivized visages. Despite these pictures' modernist aura, art historians and critics who admired them presented them as emblems of Weber's retreat from modernism and return to the fold of his heritage.

But Weber never left modernism behind. He artistically managed the School of Paris modes he had studied and advanced in his own work, and he never completely abandoned any single approach in favor of another.[26] In late 1919 Weber wrote of his frustration with cubism and his ambition to "humanize geometry."[27] The Jewish genre portraits fall short of this goal. In them, geometricization and distortion of the human form are still wedded to stereotype—itself a distortion—and parallel historical and cultural flux and complex shifts of identity along national, ethnic, and racial lines. Weber's genre portraits, which are thoroughly mediated by School of Paris primitivism, frustrate ethnographic readings and hopes of discovering an artist's uncomplicated nostalgia for the "Old World." Instead, the portraits suggest that Weber, like the Polish émigré writer Isaac Bashevis Singer, was "at war with the Jewish culture he memorialized."[28] They also make clear that, whatever the aspects of Weber's identity, they were not completely coincident identifications with Old World stereotypes.

Three Weber genre paintings, each titled *Rabbi*, include stock attributes assigned to the male spiritual leader's body; similar dress, expression, gesture, and facial characteristics type the starkly posed subjects, cutting off the intrusion of other signs.[29] Indeed, Weber's choice of the half-body portrait format suggests that no important information can be conveyed through a figure's stance or height. Considered together, the works demonstrate Weber's virtuosity and his nod to the archetype. The 1918 oil *Rabbi*, angular and blocky, appears materially close to *Prayer*, Weber's woodcut of the same year, and to small-scale figural sculptures he had made three years earlier. Like the modernist print and the totemic forms of 1915, the 1918 painting coarsely interprets the human form: the rabbi's head looks chiseled and planar. As a result, the painting is endowed with modernist simplicity, roughness, and exotic character, qualities opposed to those of finished and refined naturalism. Another Weber oil, *Rabbi* of 1934, limits the geometric rendering of its subject in order to emphasize the possibility of motion: the attenuated form is built up through liquid brushstrokes and, as a result, appears less static than its predecessor. Furthermore, the exaggerations about this figure—the defining black outlines and the compressed space in which it exists—propel the pictured subject forward and manipulate it. Even more energized is the 1940 *Rabbi*, in which oil pigments nearly obfuscate the subject's expression and color the man's face in the same objectifying manner as the wall behind him. This countenance seems to dissolve rather than emerge, and the left hand is similarly abstract: it looks less like a refined human feature and makes the book in the picture look even more concrete and realized. With quick brushwork and summarizations, Weber mindfully created a theatrical presence: the bright palette and aggressive facture is like heavy stage makeup and, coupled with the gesturing right hand, this rabbi—or actor in the role of rabbi—is in high relief, as if made to be seen from a theater's back rows and balcony. Weber's interpretations transform a stock figure into hyperbole.

Exaggeration can frustrate instrumental readings of identity by underscoring the fact that a representation is not the thing itself. In Mark Gertler's 1913 painting *The Rabbi and His Grandchild* (fig. 4.7, plate 7), the British artist (1891–1939) inscribes his signature and the date of production on the adult protagonist's coat.[30] But the picture's focal point is this man's right hand, made long enough that it can be imagined as a modest serving tray. This hand is both strong—its heel is constructed as if it had shaped the bottom of the man's beard—and delicate, for it balances the granddaughter's chin on its middle finger. In addition, the gesturing hand perpetuates the exhorting rabbi stereotype. Its incorporation into a scheme of rounded shapes animates the portrait much as the piped color describing the girl's lips does. While I do not mean to uncritically compare "Jewish artist to Jewish artist" across decades, I am putting

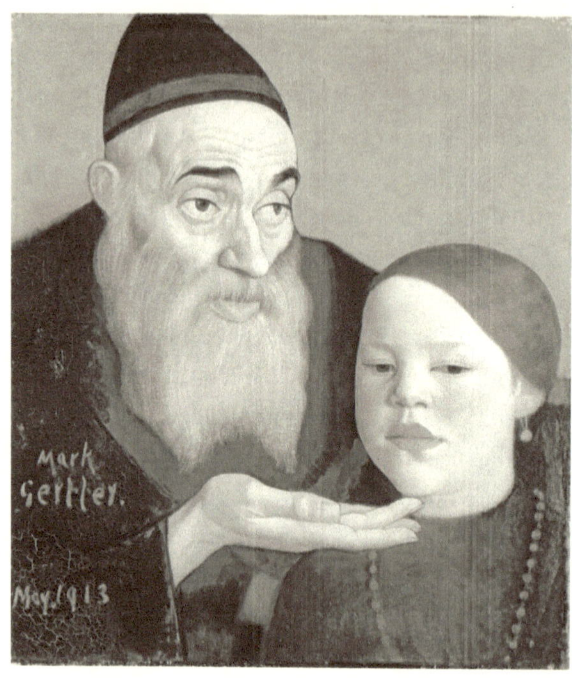

4.7 Mark Gertler, *The Rabbi and His Grandchild*, 1913 (plate 7). © Southampton City Art Gallery, Hampshire, UK/ The Bridgeman Art Library

the crisp realism of *The Rabbi and His Grandchild* in play with the primitivism of Weber's rabbi portraits as two modernist approaches to a particularizing motif. Significantly, Gertler represents not just the single figure but stretches to communicate the tenderness of a cross-generational relationship: such confluence allows *The Rabbi and His Grandchild* to escape iconicity in a way that Weber's rabbis cannot. Weber's group genre portrait, *A Family Reunion* (1944), is intertextual, like *The Rabbi and His Grandchild,* because it is analogous to a body of satiric Jewish American literature. Weber's painting spoofs the Orthodox Jewish family: in a spare interior, three men and a woman engage with each other, but their cartoonish expressions and melodramatic gestures suggest a futile negotiation. While Weber caricatured bodies in *Refugees* (1939) and *The Wayfarers* (circa 1940) that he said were Jewish, they are unmarked by any signs of Orthodox or Hasidic Jewishness, and their gnarled limbs convey brute strength and heroic, unending labors.

Weber's and Gertler's rabbinic genre portraiture is tied to a history of representation of known rabbis, such as the 1686 mezzotint of Rabbi Isaac Aboab

(1631–1707) by an unknown artist and British painter Isaac Luttichuys's 1671 oil on canvas portrait of a man believed to be Rabbi Jacob Sasportas (1610–1698). Another oil, one of London Rabbi Hakham Zevi Ashkenazi (1660–1718) anonymously rendered around 1715, even inspired copyists to reproduce it in other media. Of this phenomenon, Richard I. Cohen has explained, "A personality cult evolved around certain rabbinic figures and inspired individuals to incorporate into their own lives an idealized and glorified image of the rabbi's life and legend."[31] As would Weber, artists in Europe and the United States who were making rabbi portraits before the nineteenth century generally portrayed their subjects alone, presented only their heads and torsos, and directed viewer attention to their faces as the evidence of high character. An anonymous miniature oil on ivory (circa 1770) that portrays a clean-shaven Reverend Gershom Mendes Seixas (1745–1816), a Philadelphia cantor, is exemplary. Richard Brilliant, writing about colonial and federal-era likenesses of Jewish Americans, including the Seixas portrait, has concluded, "Non-Jewish portraits . . . reveal profound formal and iconographic correspondences with their Jewish counterparts. . . . All of them, Jew and gentile alike, appear to be members of a certain economic class, at least in terms of that class's confirmatory self-imagery."[32] Three nineteenth-century engraved portraits fashionably present Sephardic rabbis: Italy's *Abraham De Cologna* (circa 1806), England's *Raphael Meldola* (1806), and Holland's *David Leon* (1824) are attired in somber clerical dress not unlike their Christian counterparts' and sport conventional hairstyles and wigs.[33] While Jewish citizens in Europe from the thirteenth century to the nineteenth century had been identified by specific mandatory dress, Alfred Rubens, the author of *A History of Jewish Costume* and *A Jewish Iconography*, has contended that the nineteenth century brought change in several nations: "In those countries like Holland, America, and England where Jews dressed like Christians the fact that they did so is in itself significant and indicates the extent to which they had become integrated."[34] Furthermore, these rabbi portraits made by anonymous artists working in colonial America and early modern Europe reveal that the sitters were not strictly interpreting the Second Commandment, which might prohibit image making, "Thou shalt not make unto thee a graven image, nor any manner of likeness of anything that is in heaven above, or that is in the earth beneath."[35]

In the twentieth century, the market for commemorative portraits of famous and respected rabbis followed the growth of increasingly visible Jewish communities and paralleled other markets for images of racial types, such as Native Americans in feathers and buckskin, Chinese men wearing their long hair in queues, and other "picturesque" subjects of difference in painting, sculpture, graphic art, and photography.[36] A painting without the body of the rabbi, George Oberteuffer's *The House of the Rabbi* (1932), was a naturalistic street scene that notably won a National Academy of Design prize in the year of its making.[37] Many of Weber's peers, including Hyman Bloom (1913–2009), William Meyerowitz (1887–1981), and Reuben Rubin (1893-1974), earned praise for their genre portraits of rabbis, which were reproduced as representative work in the 1947 survey *100 American Jewish Artists*.[38] The rabbi even appeared where viewers—past and present—likely did not and do not expect it. The 1929 photo *Rabbi Matthew*, named for a leader of the Beth B'nai Abraham Synagogue in Harlem, was one of several images of Moorish Jews made by African American James Van Der Zee (1886–1983). Like Weber's and Gertler's rabbi genre portraits, *Rabbi Matthew* is emphatically Jewish: standing before his brownstone synagogue, Wentworth Arthur Matthew is dressed in a tallit shawl and he touches an open book, likely a sacred text, placed on a tall table before him. Van Der Zee's black-and-white composition highlights the symbols the Beth B'nai Abraham Synagogue proffered to the world: the building's exterior boasts a banner bearing the congregation's name in English and Hebrew, and U.S. and Zionist flags. Another Jewish American, Rabbi Alexander David Goode of York, Pennsylvania, was posthumously depicted on a U.S. three-cent stamp issued in 1948. Commissioned by his employer, the U.S. Postal Service, the Orthodox Jewish American artist Louis Schwimmer (1897–1995) first made a naturalistic pen-and-ink drawing of Goode and his fellow chaplains who went down with the World War II army transport ship the US *Dorchester* after it was torpedoed on February 3, 1943. In Schwimmer's drawing and a lithograph reproduction of it that he made in the 1980s, Reverends George Lansing Fox of the Methodist Church and Clark V. Poling of the Dutch Reformed Church, and Father John Patrick Washington, a Roman Catholic, are presented as they were in life—clean-shaven white men—and all but Goode are fair-haired. Each is dressed in a military uniform and surrounded by descriptive text: "These

Immortal Chaplains . . . Catholic, Protestant, Jewish," "Interfaith in Action," "Died to Save Men of All Faiths." The Post Office adapted Schwimmer's linear drawing style and head-and-shoulders rendering of the men, but the stamp omitted the text stating the ministers' religious affiliations and the line about their sacrifice.[39] Critically, the released stamp bore the words "These Immmortal Chaplains . . . Interfaith in Action" and an image made by an unknown artist that obfuscates Goode's chaplain insignia—Hebrew tablets and the Star of David—while making his colleagues' Christian crosses quite visible. Heroicism and martyrdom are highlighted for the Christian subjects, and yet the same qualities exhibited by a Jew are not.

Without question, Weber's rabbi genre portraits were markedly different from Gertler's painting, Van Der Zee's photo, and the renderings of the "Immortal Chaplains." Yet the genre portraits had to have been informed by the abstraction and exaggeration of Weber's own work, including the futurist New York landscapes and Fauvist still lifes of the teens and the chunky, Cezanne-inspired nudes and roughly rendered landscapes he painted throughout his career. Weber's negotiation of such motifs and styles, I suspect, made observers who preferred naturalism uneasy, and the rabbi genre portraits relieved their anxieties and doubts. Yet Sheila B. Braufman has noted that many writers seemed "unable to give a tangible definition of what [the writers themselves] were trying to communicate" about the Hasidic subjects.[40] What Braufman takes as confusion is essentialist rationalization. For example, Alfred H. Barr Jr. assigned originality to the period of the Hasidic genre portraits' debut, circa 1918: it was then, argues Barr, that Weber "seems to have first discovered a style which is unmistakably 'Weber.' . . . The extraordinary intimacy and depth of feeling of the year 1918 is transformed in the following years into a more objective and monumental style in which figure composition and still life rival each other to the accompaniment of an occasional landscape."[41]

Similarly, the outspoken New York gallerist Samuel M. Kootz, who wrote about Weber in *Modern American Painters*, located the artist's individuality in "religious" genre portraiture. Kootz was a supporter of modernist efforts and in this 1930 publication included Weber in the list of eleven artists he considered "important American painters of today." Kootz reproduced Weber's *Chinese Restaurant*, the Cézannesque *Table with Still Life* (1929), and three neoclassical figure studies with women: *Oriental Scene* (1918), the genre portrait *Woman* (1918), and *Alone* (1929), which featured a pensive, gargantuan seminude. Kootz was specific when dismissing Weber's landscapes that "follow nature in the same realistic, factual presentation that characterized Courbet's work" and still lifes that "relied too greatly upon his color palette," and was general in his praise of the artist's "essentially Hebraic creations":

> Weber is essentially a student, carrying on others' researches and tentative discoveries. Sometimes he rises above his assimilations and by sheer racial emotionalism sweeps his painting into the realm of personal expression; his colors attain decided values and his forms become taut above reminiscence. . . .
>
> It is in his religious paintings alone that Weber becomes the fine artist, the individual. He is an expert in the mysteries of faith; his rabbis and brooding woman have the curious melancholy significance, the almost fanatical appearance that is inherent in the ecstatic worshipper. In these works we feel the imaginative stirring of his intelligence, a delicate sensitivity, a statement of faith, of exaltation, that is rare in this time. His views become more his own and his construction assumes a more original aspect, one of greater individual perception.
>
> In these assertions Weber has reached his highest plastic values. . . . He becomes the architectural romantic, emotional, colorful, drenched in feeling.
>
> In these religious paintings Weber goes beyond mere subject matter. Their spiritual essence, their devotion, portray for us something of the artist's own communion, of his Slavic and Jewish heritage.[42]

Weber asserted that he participated in all his iconography—"I paint myself all the time," he told Forbes Watson in 1941—and the Orthodox and Hasidic Jewish subject, in particular, gave Kootz and others license to look for and locate difference in all of Weber's production and to look for Weber in it.[43] One of the artist's most vocal supporters, Henry McBride, weaves together his ideas about human evolution, race, psyche, and modernism to describe the work's praiseworthy aspects: "What was wonderful in them was the fact that they echoed the racial anguish of mind without recourse to brutal facts or prosaic argument. They did it musically, symbolically, eloquently, and though so modern in texture, still bore accents that seemed to reach back to the beginning of time."[44] The unstated binary to subtle rendering was aggressive social realism, a broad field of "brutal facts" and "prosaic argument." Equally deft is the balance struck in McBride's characterization of Jewish subjects: for the critic, they are the primordial (if not archaeological), psychically revelatory, and au courant descriptions sometimes applied to Weber himself.

FACE

While Kuniyoshi's favored genre subjects—working-class women, some of whom may be sex workers—are legible and recognizable types, it is for good reason that scholars have deemed these pictures "idiosyncratic."[45] This assessment is worthy of a push. Many of the bodies, male and female alike, that Kuniyoshi represented in paintings and drawings are physiognomically strange. Because Kuniyoshi was a Japanese immigrant to the United States, it is tempting to think that his figures' strangeness is simply a product of the artist's bicultural history. Yet Kuniyoshi's bodies exceed the parameters that define race purity and stable identity, much less neat combinations and blendings of cultures, nationalities, and ethnicities. Notably, Kuniyoshi's women fit neither his era's ideals of Japanese nor European American beauty, nor are they clear hybrids. They are often placed, moreover, in bare environments and improbable settings, making cultural contextualization more challenging. In viewing them as the outcome of Kuniyoshi's deliberately confounding "racial art" strategy, I am not making race real; as a construction, it is not. Rather, I am arguing that representation is often designed, marshaled, and repeatedly deployed for the project of making race material, visible, and logical.

Kuniyoshi's figures resist the binaries of the conceptualized Orient and Occident, and instead open the discussion of the complicated spaces in between. The ambiguous look of Kuniyoshi's women of the 1930s and of subsequent decades is foreshadowed in the figures—male and female—that preceded them. In Kuniyoshi's early production, human forms promise accessibility and even intimacy, for they are posed frontally and painted near the front of the picture plane: we find them poised to meet our viewing gaze, and their colorful, volumetric, and relatively large bodies perhaps invite our touch. But

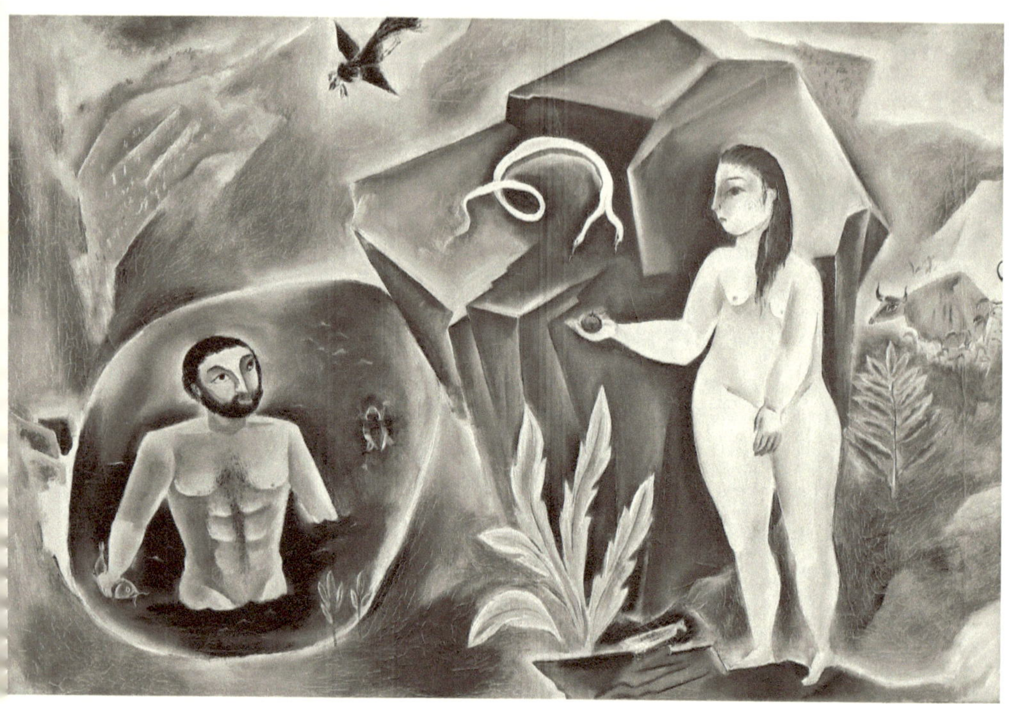

4.8 Yasuo Kuniyoshi, *Adam and Eve*, 1922. Oil on canvas, 30 x 20 in. Private collection

Kuniyoshi frustrates such contact, even as he allows some within the composition. Adam stares at Eve, who looks over his head in *Adam and Eve* (1922; fig. 4.8); two women hold hands and still ignore each other and the threat rising behind them in *Sisters Frightened by a Whale* (1923); a mother regards the son she holds aloft in *Child Frightened by Water* (1924; fig. 4.9). Each is a distracted and deformed character, as are those in *Strong Woman and Child* (1925), *Nude* (1929), and other paintings where heads are tilted and eyes are crossed. The human form, quirky with its illogical and impossible appearances, as we have seen elsewhere in Kuniyoshi's oeuvre, is made strange and independent of the audience's reality. For his part, Kuniyoshi explained his project in the terms of universalism, a problematic and yet dependable framework for the liberal humanist/artist-intellectual of his generation. In 1944 he wrote in an unpublished autobiography: "I am much more interested in painting women, because

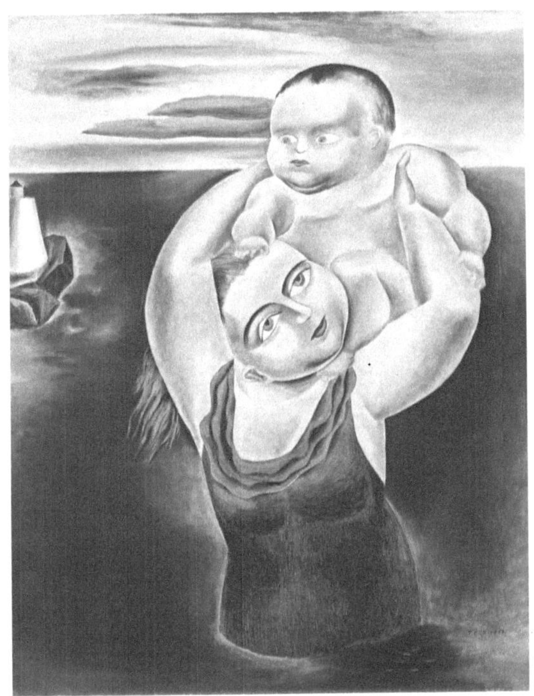

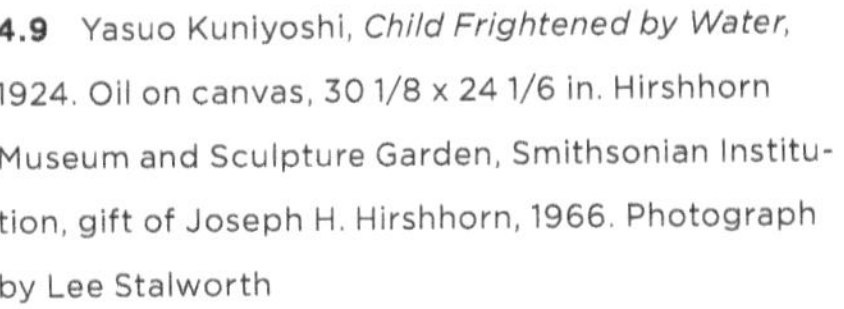

4.9 Yasuo Kuniyoshi, *Child Frightened by Water*, 1924. Oil on canvas, 30 1/8 x 24 1/6 in. Hirshhorn Museum and Sculpture Garden, Smithsonian Institution, gift of Joseph H. Hirshhorn, 1966. Photograph by Lee Stalworth

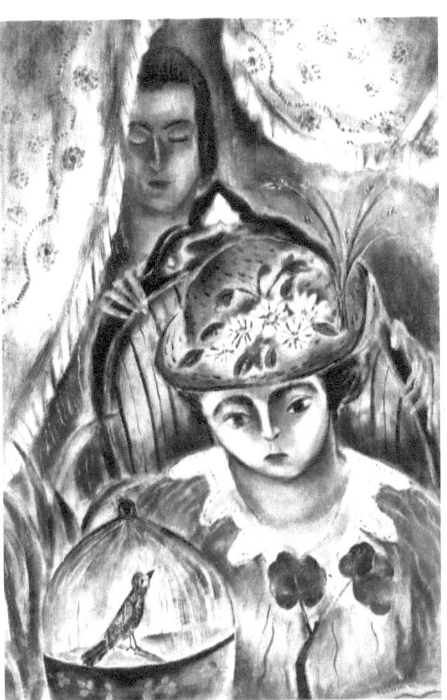

4.10 Yasuo Kuniyoshi, *Sisters*, 1920. Oil on canvas, 29 2/3 x 19 9/10 in. Collection of the National Museum of Modern Art, Tokyo

woman is more decorative, and I think for me to admire woman is natural. I paint universal women, as I dream woman should be."[46]

In examining Kuniyoshi's women, it is clear that the universal is not synonymous with the generic—the subject without markers, designed to fit into any context. Instead, Kuniyoshi's women have numerous and, occasionally, conflicting features that work against reading the universal as an apotheosis of female beauty. Analyzing an early example in the circa 1917 oil painting *Girl at Table*, art historian Tom Wolf identifies "a slight Oriental cast to her features and her dress."[47] More striking is the conical shaping of the sitter's head, which echoes the woman's pulled-back coiffure, and the angles that construct the eyebrows, the kimonolike dress sleeves, and the compressed, cubist spaces of the common

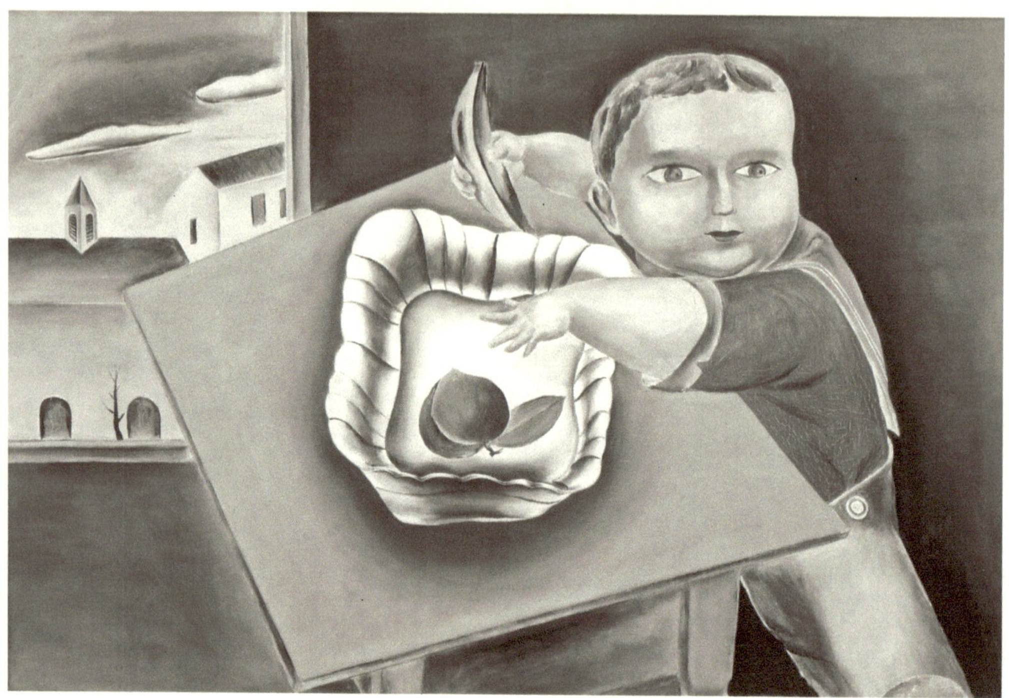

4.11 Yasuo Kuniyoshi, *Boy Stealing Fruit*, 1923. Oil on canvas, 20 x 30 in. Columbus Museum of Art, Ohio; gift of Ferdinand Howald (1931.194)

rooms she occupies. This female body, neither completely Occidental nor Oriental, is just another passage to decorate, no different from the brightly colored interior, the still-life setup, or the natural world. When compared to Kuniyoshi's protagonists in a later, Matisse-inspired oil, *Sisters* (1920; fig. 4.10), the female in *Girl at Table* looks more like the cubist motif that we have racially neutralized, normalized, and considered white. It may be that, juxtaposed to *Girl at Table*, the figures in *Sisters*, like many in Fauvist and cubist painting, can be finally read for their self-evident nonwhiteness. Subsequently we must ask: what problems do such analyses pose for the imaging of whiteness and its claims to neutrality and universality?

Kuniyoshi adopted some of the conventions that denote whiteness and rejected others.[48] In his pictures' bold details—crystalline and light-value

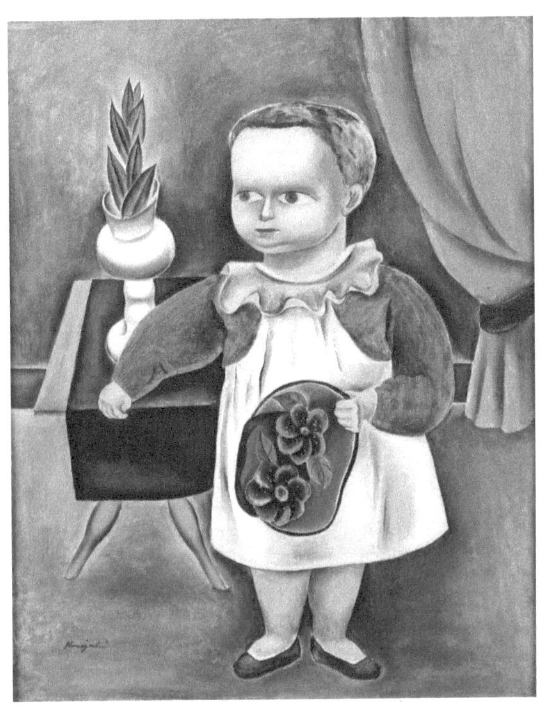

4.12 Yasuo Kuniyoshi, *Child*, 1923. Oil on canvas, 30 x 24 in. Whitney Museum of American Art, New York; gift of Mrs. Edith Gregor Halpert (55.1). Photograph by Sheldan C. Collins

irises, blond and straight hair—are Nordic accents on bloated, corpulent bodies wielding Western modernity's tools and displaying its mores. Throughout Kuniyoshi's oeuvre, both male and female figures are presented in this manner, with the latter in revealing costumes, using curling irons, or smoking cigarettes: *Between Two Worlds* (1939), *Bather with Cigarette* (1924), *After the Bath (Captain's Daughter*; 1923), and *Waiting* (1938) are typical. In these works and others, whiteness or white "American-ness" is destabilized as the artist actively queries race and racial purities. Inspired by colonial painting and American folk art styles, Kuniyoshi did not adopt their chalk whitening of bodies; color was just another visual element available for modernist abstraction. Brown shading suggests less skin tanned by sun and more burnished and varnished wooden surfaces. As a result, skin, a critical site of race and ethnicity, seems less human, natural, and biological and instead more material and synthetic in appearance. One could find *Boy Stealing Fruit* (1923; fig. 4.11) and *Child* (1923; fig. 4.12) to be lacking in gravitas and outside of serious art's limits—to be, indeed, in the realm of cartoon.[49] Alternatively, we might read whimsy and puns in the former: a jaundiced and vapid-looking boy grabs a banana in a scene replete with phallic symbols and rhyming yellows. Kuniyoshi's choice of motifs and his manipulation of them make these paintings distinct from the colonial and U.S. folk art he admired. If limning and vernacular painting number among the countless pre-twentieth-century projects that constructed whiteness and made it, ideologically, the defining norm of American character, Kuniyoshi's paintings always seem to make whiteness strange and, most importantly, visible.[50] In his work, whiteness's status as "flesh color" is undermined: the arbitrariness of race and the stark color assignments of white, black, yellow, brown, and red to racial, ethnic, and national groups are thrown into relief, and even crisis.

Although Kuniyoshi had moved away from his deliberately naïve style by 1930, he continued to problematize race by representing the female genre subject and nude for the rest of his career. Kuniyoshi scholars address race through the conceptual polarities of the Occident and the Orient, and it is usually the early works of the teens and twenties that are scrutinized for evidence of such tensions. Race is made peripheral in discussions of Kuniyoshi's later work of the thirties and forties, mostly because historians have viewed the subjects as white and hence not raced. Accounts of Kuniyoshi's production are usually periodized: Kuniyoshi was interested first in race, and subsequently in gender.[51] The bind is not unlike the one evident in the Weber literature: the early, figuratively abstract work epitomizes avant-gardism and then gives way to Jewish subjects—authentic, "astylistic," if you will, and certainly not modernist.[52] Critics found Kuniyoshi's twenties style and preoccupations disquieting. In a short exhibition catalogue essay of 1939, one unidentified writer expressed relief at seeing changes (quoting an earlier critic's description): "Having gone through the period when he was 'wildly distorting his cows into queer triangular shapes and equipping children with inflated bulbous heads,' he has successfully survived the stage of mere pleasant romanticism and is developing 'a sound classical technique that will make his contribution even more important than it now is.'"[53] We can see how the writer mounts a case against distortion and romanticism by opposing them to the classical, that is, the critically accepted technique and motifs of the nude and the woman in the interior. Working with the acceptable, the known, and the familiar, Kuniyoshi found a site of the real that could be transformed.

If Weber's rabbi portraits suggest that, in the artist's mind, the male authority figure unequivocally communicates the Jewish archetype,[54] Kuniyoshi's genre portraits of women in the 1930s likewise betray a creative decision to make a gendered body a vehicle for the racially particular. Earlier I noted that Kuniyoshi considered women decorative rather than beautiful; interestingly, he also used the term "decorative" when explaining his interest in painting cows and babies, subjects he chose for their strangeness.[55] For Kuniyoshi, the female body was a familiar entity that could be defamiliarized and made racially ambiguous, reflecting, I believe, his thinking about the complexity of identity and appearances. Kuniyoshi experimented with female forms, as he had with colonial painting and American folk art motifs, turning to them repeatedly to present the body not as a recognizable ideal but rather as a field of exploration, where, he explained, "reality and imagination" were combined.[56]

Kuniyoshi's female subjects of the 1930s and 1940s, commonly read as erotic and sexually available, generate questions about several aspects of identity, and gender is just one of them. His renderings of mothers, female performers, nudes, and sex workers hide neither their artifice nor their artificiality. Most are made up, their features darkened by mascara, eye shadow, and eyeliner. Kuniyoshi's interest in the cosmetically transformed body did not mean that he intended to make pictures of flawlessly beautiful women: in fact, his figures fall short of the glamorous and have many imperfections. Figures that do effect whiteness, as in *Girl in a Pink Slip* (1932; fig. 4.13, plate 8), are quite literal with their exaggerations of stony form and alabaster color. In contrast, the vanitas subject of *The Mirror* (1933) generates no reflection, only darkness. And two of Kuniyoshi's best known female genre paintings, *Daily News* (1935; fig. 4.14, plate 9) and *I'm Tired* (1938; fig. 4.15, plate 10), present sitters whose skin colorations resemble the objects they're paired with: in the former, a metal radiator, and, in the latter, a varnished wooden table. Although we do not know whether Kuniyoshi's depictions are mixed-race women, there is no question that he repeatedly presented a darkened whiteness, moving whiteness as category away from ideals and absolutes, and throwing the certainty of race altogether into doubt.[57]

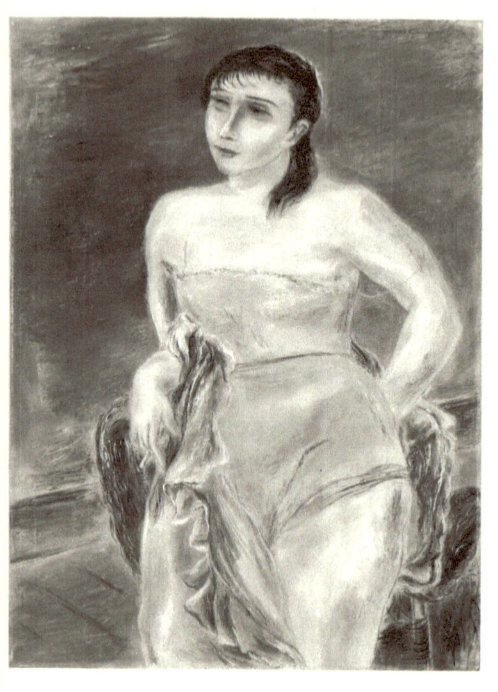

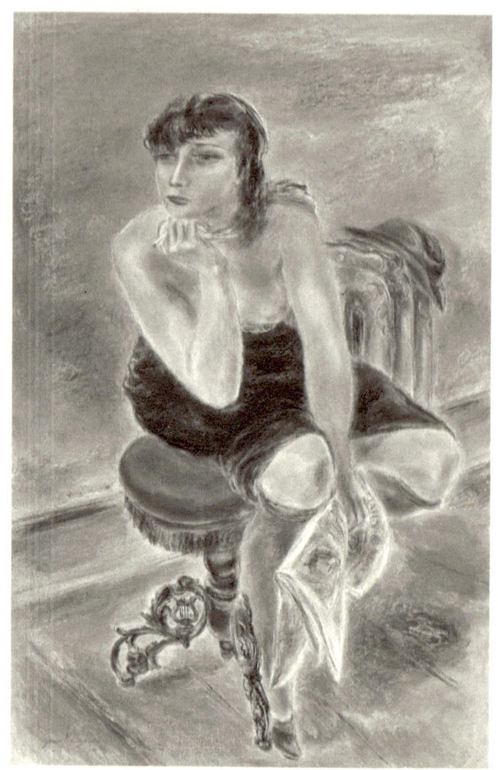

That Kuniyoshi visualized the evidence of racial mixing in the early twentieth century set him apart from many African American artists and their nonblack, antiracist counterparts who put forth a particular black physiognomy in order to privilege it. By creating a "typeface" of strong, heavy, "African" features, these artists simultaneously exalted a historically denigrated appearance and contradicted the heterogeneity of black looks (in Africa and elsewhere).[58] They were motivated by the impulse to bury stereotypes and revise the black image in art; ideologically, they subscribed to a notion of truth in representation, and yet, under examination, their production raises questions.

In 1936 African American painter Charles Alston asserted that "when you paint Negroes who look like Greeks, you're just faking."[59] Notably, Alston's desire not to "fake" approaches denied his own "European"-looking countenance—a light-skinned complexion, angular nose, and lank brown hair—in favor of a new, stock type. In self-portraits Alston took the naturalist approach to rendering himself, but in genre portraiture he rarely presented people who

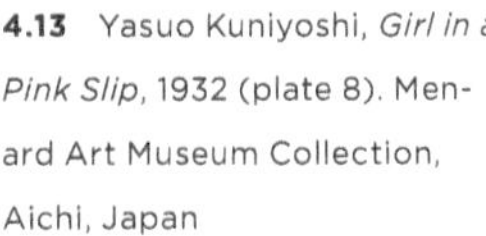
4.13 Yasuo Kuniyoshi, *Girl in a Pink Slip*, 1932 (plate 8). Menard Art Museum Collection, Aichi, Japan

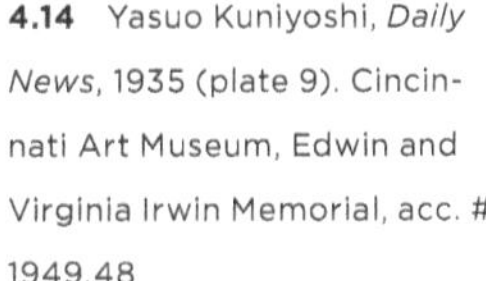
4.14 Yasuo Kuniyoshi, *Daily News*, 1935 (plate 9). Cincinnati Art Museum, Edwin and Virginia Irwin Memorial, acc. # 1949.48

4.15 Yasuo Kuniyoshi, *I'm Tired*, 1938 (plate 10). Whitney Museum of American Art, New York; purchase 39.12. Photograph by Sheldan C. Collins

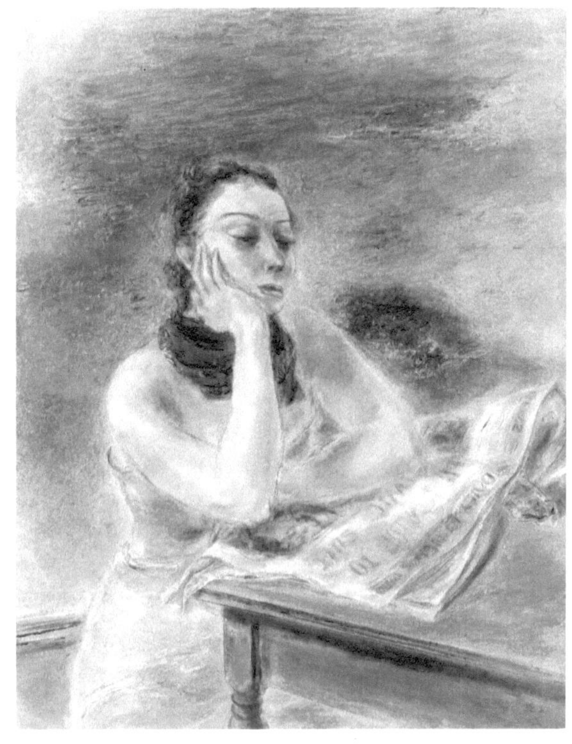

resembled him. As had Weber and Johnson, Alston created an undifferentiated type meant to stand in for the collective. In *Girl in a Red Dress* (1934; fig. 4.16) and *Farm Boy* (1941), Alston simplifies the human form: attenuated and drawn as crisp contours, faces and bodies are constructed to suggest the rigidity of dark-grained wood. Unquestionably, African ritual masks and Modigliani's portraits influenced him. Still, *Girl in a Red Dress* and *Farm Boy* function differently because they fall between the index and the symbol: their materiality points simultaneously to cultural, historical, and generic blackness, that is, numerous African sculptural traditions, while exceeding naturalistic standards of rendering and threatening to become arbitrary. Alston's goal, like Weber's in the rabbi paintings, was to make a raced image that was monolithic and indivisible. But, as is always the case with identifications, race, class, gender, sexuality, and such cannot be separated from one another.

Many of Alston's similarly light-brown-skinned, African American con-

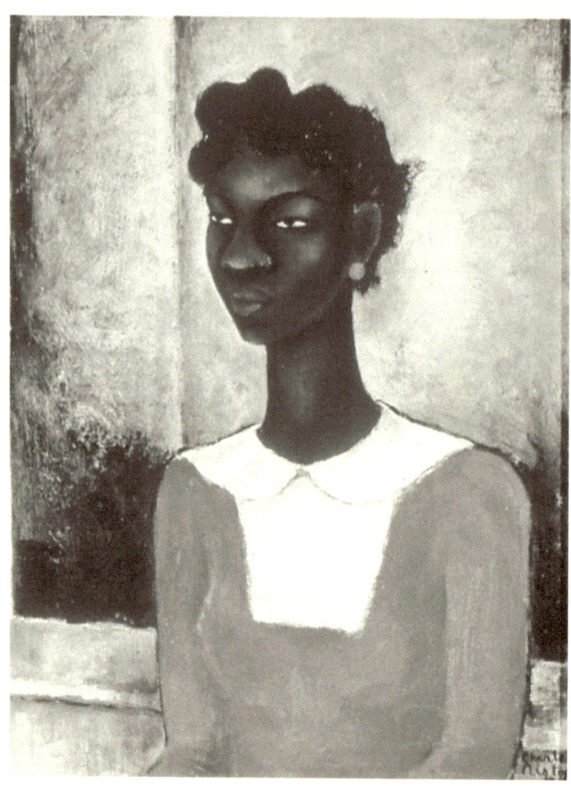

4.16 Charles Alston, *Girl in a Red Dress*, 1934. Oil on canvas, 28 x 22 in. Harmon and Harriet Kelley Foundation for the Arts, San Antonio, Texas

temporaries—among them Romare Bearden, Archibald J. Motley Jr., William H. Johnson, Sargent Claude Johnson, and James Lesesne Wells—produced mainly images of darker-skinned black subjects.[60] Still, portraits of mixed-race subjects were also being produced in the interwar period, and they frustrated notions of racial purity.[61] In the 1928 Harmon Foundation exhibition, Chicago painter Charles C. Dawson's *Quadroon Madonna* (not dated) was popular with viewers.[62] In this unlocated painting, the art-school-trained Dawson (1889–1981), deemed a "traditionalist" by Alain Locke, employed a well-known convention in a studio composition of a woman and child.[63] Dawson's sitters were socially provocative subjects, for the artist clearly intended to make a statement about the wide range of human skin tones and the conditional privilege that lighter skin color bestowed in twentieth-century America.[64] The pictured mother and son make an elegant pair with simply tailored clothes

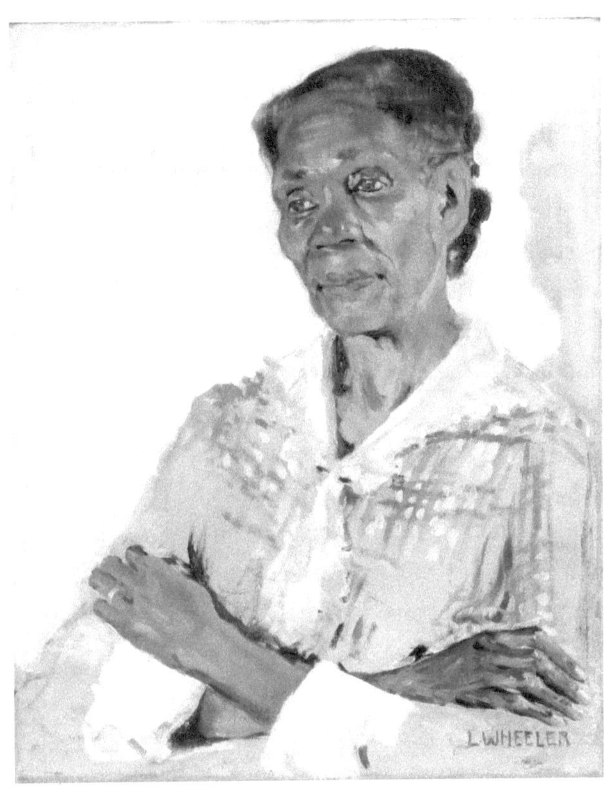

4.17 Laura Wheeler Waring, *Anna Washington Derry*, 1927. Oil on canvas, 20 x 16 in. Smithsonian American Art Museum, Washington, D.C./Art Resource, New York

marking their patrician tastes. Especially significant are their physical attributes: their hair textures are wavy, their lips thin, and their skins fair in color. The woman's bared arm is a chalk-white limb that contrasts with the darkness of the backdrop and her dress, and nearly equals the high value of her child's pristine dress and shoes. The chromatic exaggerations work in concert with bodily details that deviate from the strictest of European and European American beauty ideals of the period. The mother's nose broadens enough so as not to be perfectly aquiline; her fingers are slender and yet not perfectly tapered. Lastly, the shadow falling against the pair's foreheads is both a naturalist technique that suggests bodily volume and a realist commentary on the subjectivity of race categories. If African American communities conferred high rank on these sitters because of their lighter skin color, then the indelibility of the features considered imperfect, black, or miscegenated (which was widely perceived as a degraded, racial dilution) likely compromised or entirely blocked their entry to white circles.[65]

Similarly dedicated to depicting a range of black physiognomies was Laura Wheeler Waring (1887–1948). She wrote to the Harmon Foundation in 1928, "I have been planning to make a record of interesting characters of the American Negro in paint."[66] The following year, her twelve renderings of "American colored women of varied ages and types" were exhibited at a Paris gallery.[67] Typical Waring portraits are *Anna Washington Derry* (1927; fig. 4.17) and *Evangeline Hall* (1930). That Derry and Hall are both named in the respective picture titles affords them an identity absent from Johnson's *Meditation*.[68] Both of Waring's female subjects were friends of hers, and for this reason (if no other) she sought to portray them flatteringly.[69] Hall is presented as a corsage-wearing matron, a woman of education and good breeding whose fleshy fingers hold her place in a book. Derry has no such props, nor is her body characterized as a light-skinned elite's. Clad in a homespun dress, she is a standing figure whose crossed arms and turned-away gaze establish her confidence and her distance from the viewer. While Derry is brown-skinned and Hall is much lighter, both possess (or are depicted with) features that fall outside of essentialized inventories of racial characteristics. Derry's nose is broad, but her lips are thin, her face narrow, and her fingers long, veined, and tapering. Hall's finely textured hair and straighter nose comply with expectations for mixed-race appearances, yet her lips are fuller than Derry's. Hence, as depicted, these sitters' physiognomies combine the archetypal qualities associated with both whites and blacks. If Waring intended to starkly contrast the looks of mixed-race and full-blooded (an unlikely, if not impossible, purity) Negro types, Derry's and Hall's portraits end up complicating the issue of race, rather than neatly resolving it. Even more provocative is Waring's *Mother and Daughter* (circa 1931), a double portrait of two adult women viewed in profile. Retrospectively, Alain Locke praised this painting of a biracial mother and her lighter-skinned daughter, citing what he perceived as its lack of distortion and its documentary value. Writing in 1936, Locke deemed *Mother and Daughter* "an illuminating and thought-provoking symbol of the blending of races so taboo to art in the days of social intolerance. It is in such respects that the full documentation of race has so much to say and add to the interpretation of life, as our artists more fully grasp the unique things that can be said out of the heart of Negro life and experience."[70] *Mother and Daughter* seems to boast truth and objectivity: its realism is authenticated by the cheek-to-cheek comparison and by the image's relatively hard-edged qualities, departures from Waring's freely handled, naturalistic black portraiture. *Mother and Daughter* failed to generate comment from other reviewers and observers in 1931, when it was shown at the Harmon Foundation exhibition. Instead, the light of publicity shone upon the exhibition's portrait prizes, Lillian Dorsey's primitivist *Self-Portrait* (1930) and Edwin Harleston's *Old Servant* (1928).

Archibald J. Motley Jr. made representing women of color a quasi-scientific quest.[71] When Motley articulated his goal to represent "the full gamut, or the race as a whole,"[72] the interdependence of "positive" and "negative" (each was necessary to the definition of the other) was eminently clear. He began painting mixed-race, middle- and upper-class women around 1920, and toward mid-decade his portraits of darker-skinned, black subjects dramatized his desire to aestheticize racial heritages.[73] Late in his career, Motley explained his motives: "I find in the black woman such a marvelous range of color, all the way from very black to the typical Caucasian type."[74] He held that, while "form" was "essential," color was "more important as an expression of the numerous shades and colors which exist in great variety among Negroes."[75] By Motley's estimation, the mixed-race person, sometimes hard to distinguish from the "pure caucasian," possessed a "normal" head, "well-constructed and symmetrically balanced." He added that "the construction of the body such as elongation of the arms, a tendency toward a weak bone construction found in many of the dark purer Negroes and large fat heels are nonexistent."[76] That Motley's efforts to create a set of physiognomic traits or, more accurately, to advance an already extant set derived from nineteenth-century pseudoscience and assign them to his sitters, was received as realistic and truthful indicates widespread acceptance of the premise of pure races. In 1928 New York critic Worth Tuttle deemed Motley's attitude "desirable, not only for the fresh material it provides, but also for the emotional release it has given such an artist as Mr. Motley. Certainly, one cannot see his work and agree with George Schuyler that there is not racial art."[77]

Tuttle's praise takes the familiar tone and trajectory of "racial art" commendation, a category dismissed by Schuyler in his 1926 essay "The Negro-Art Hokum." What I would like to focus on here is Tuttle's designation of "freshness" for Motley's production. In all likelihood, the critic had seen and admired Motley's paintings in a one-artist show at the New Gallery in 1928. At that venue, Motley exhibited the portraits *Octoroon* (1922), *Portrait of My Grandmother* (1922), *Mending Socks* (1924), *Woman Peeling Apples* (1924), *Octoroon Girl* (1925), and a suite of paintings "about" Africa, a continent he had never visited and that he had represented as a place of superstition and dark mystery.[78] What Tuttle saw as artistic authenticity and truth in Motley's painting, Alain Locke deemed brash abstraction. In 1931 Locke designated Motley, Lillian Dorsey, and Malvin Gray Johnson innovative modernists for their antinaturalist modes of representation. If Tuttle located modernism in new content ("fresh material") and atavistic expression ("emotional release") in a collective racial art, Locke found modernism in figural abstraction, conceived as the artist's individual, creative interpretation.[79] For Locke, Motley's *The Snuff Dipper* (1928), Johnson's *Meditation*, and Dorsey's self-portrait were markers of the artists' "objectivity," a description meant to signal their freedom from any obligation to idealize or faithfully represent black subjects.[80]

The perception that minority artists had special expertise to represent their bloc groups likely informed the American government's decision to ask Kuniyoshi to make anti-Japan propaganda in 1942. Writing in his capacity as the U.S. Office of War Information (OWI) assistant director, Archibald MacLeish explained, "We need to describe the enemy more fully, what his intentions are, how he looks. We suggest that you might care to work on the Japanese enemy."[81] Kuniyoshi was not the only artist contacted by the OWI, yet he received unique advice on the nature of the imagery he was to make: "A poster on the recent Japanese atrocities—the water cure, for example."[82] According to art historian Alexandra Munroe, the OWI published two of Kuniyoshi drawings as posters: *Torture* and *Deliver Us from Evil* (both circa 1942–43), each of which depict victims of Japanese persecution.[83] Two more Kuniyoshi graphic examples in this vein survive: *Execution Scene* (1943) and *Rape* (circa 1943). A wavering line describes aggressors and sufferers in these sketches, in which all of the depicted faces are so plainly masklike. As a result, menacing acts seem more theatrical than real, perhaps undermining OWI objectives and expectations. More than did Kuniyoshi, Americans such as MacLeish believed that they already knew the enemy inside and out.

MASKS

I have argued that types are constructed through simultaneously reductive and exaggerating measures. That is, types are made by stripping away certain particulars and accentuating others to create a set of appearances, linked by commonalities and generalities. Masks, oftentimes, are created the same way. Certainly, in Malvin Gray Johnson's *Negro Masks* (1932; fig. 1.2) and Palmer Hayden's *Fétiche et Fleurs* (circa 1932–33), the painted mask is a skeumorph, that is, something that has been rendered in a medium different from its customary or original one.[84] In both Johnson's and Hayden's paintings, meaning emerges not only from African sources that influenced these African American makers but also from the fact of artistic "translation." The plastic medium of ritual masks in metal, ivory, and wood inspired modernist painters—black and nonblack—in Europe and in the Americas to think about pictorial space in new ways. By adapting sculptural approaches to painting, such artists were rethinking the two-dimensional format. It is especially important to stress this conceptual work when considering Johnson and other black painters, for art historians' discussions of *Negro Masks* and *Fétiche et Fleurs* typically center on reclamation of the African diaspora subject's "ancestral legacy." While heritage is a resounding factor in these paintings, the incorporation of African cultural objects in *Negro Masks* and *Fétiche et Fleurs* was an outcome not of atavism but of the creative imagination.

As a cultural practice, masking stands opposite to portraiture's claim to capture a physical likeness. Disguise, deception, and concealment are manifest in Johnson's *Negro Masks*, in *Harmony*, and in many of the masklike faces he portrayed. Pared down and squared off, the faces of Johnson's *Girl Reading* (1932; fig. 4.18) and the female sitter in *The Letter* (not dated) have the qualities of masks: eyes are mere slitted ovals, and other distinguishing features are summarily drawn. Heads are weighty-looking and appear wooden in both color and suggested texture. Such sculptural qualities are amplified in Johnson's *Sailor*, *Woman with Hat* (1931), and *Ruby* (1932). In each of these half-body-length portraits, the sitters are impassive and impenetrable subjects. Although their soulful gazes seem to meet their audience's, their painted faces and bodies are so stilled, symmetrical, and stiff that they become solemnly iconic forms, as foreboding as totems. That these subjects were not compelling, and were

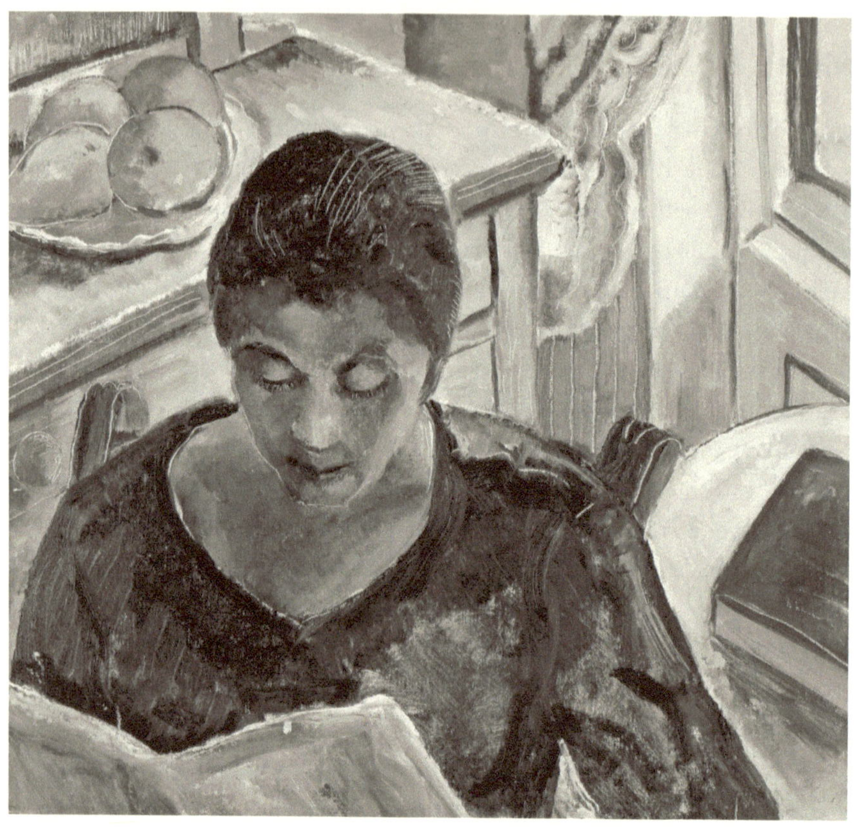

perhaps too mechanical, is suggested in one press comment: Rose Henderson wrote that Johnson's *Sailor* was a "capable but less diverting study."[85] By 1932 the artist did not seem as concerned with communicating the individuality of his sitters. He may have become overly reliant on a single device—the angularization of the body—to vary and interestingly render faces. Moreover, examining Johnson's oil portraits from 1932 through 1934 is like paging through a family album. Similarities in the gaze, the skin tones, and the strong facial features are resonant: the subject of *Portrait (Ermie,* 1934; fig. 4.19) resembles *Sailor,* which resembles *Ruby.*[86] There are, at least, two possible explanations for this. First, Johnson may not have been painting a model but instead constructing a type or a subtly altered prototype that was an informal inflection of the black portrait genre. Second, the same person or handful of related persons could have

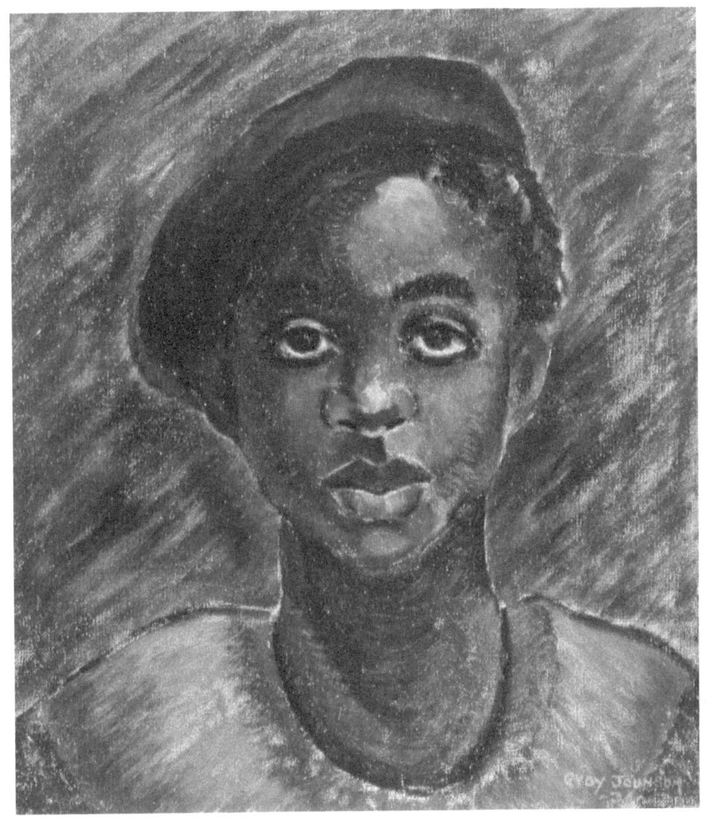

4.18 Malvin Gray Johnson, *Girl Reading*, 1932. Oil on canvas, 18 x 19 in. Hampton University Museum, Hampton, Virginia

4.19 Malvin Gray Johnson, *Portrait (Ermie)*, 1934. Oil on canvas, 16 x 14 in. Fisk University Galleries, Nashville, Tennessee

provided templates that could be gendered and costumed accordingly. Commissioning likenesses constituted a luxury for most during the Depression, and with a dwindling number of clients, many artists looking for figural subjects tapped their families and friends.[87] Johnson's familiarity and, perhaps, intimacy with his subjects promoted sympathetic rendering. His sitters bear an uncanny resemblance to the painter himself: *Sailor* and the female portraits *Woman with a Hat* and *Ermie* share the artist's sloe-eyed countenance. Indeed, the painted figures may have been kin or they may have "been" Johnson, for he likely used a mirror to make his *Self-Portrait (Myself at Work*; 1933) and could have done so to make his genre portraits. In sum, these paintings appear to be serializations of the same figure, and, simultaneously, they raise pertinent questions of autobiography in the way that portraiture as a genre always does.

As it regards African American artists' production, the presence of African mask and statuary imagery in early Depression-era painting invites discussion about the representation of ancestral reclamation as self-representation. Of the key works in this still-life genre—Hayden's *Fétiche et Fleurs*, Johnson's *Negro Masks*, Frank Joseph Dillon's *Still Life* (1933), and Wilmer A. Jennings's engraving *Still Life* (1937)—only Johnson's and Hayden's paintings were exhibited in the period and provoked comment. Most contemporaneous writers either entirely failed to address the other paintings or they briefly noted the presence of the African elements.[88] In other words, the topos of African art and its ritual sculpture did not resonate with the critics of that time to the extent that it does with today's art historians. *New York Times* critic Edward Alden Jewell, assessing Hayden's *Fétiche et Fleurs*, merely recognized the Fang statue as African and made no mention of the Kuba cloth upon which it sat.[89] Rose Henderson congratulated Hayden for composing a pleasing color design. Hers is the most extensive period description of the painting:

> Best known for his lively seascapes, Mr. Hayden shows a more sophisticated feeling for color and design in this exquisitely luscious still life. Orchids in a blue bowl suggest both the form and the inherent strangeness of the beautifully carved and polished fetish beside them. The soft, rich rose of the flowers is carried throughout the painting, in the glow of the polished table and carving, in the wall and hanging of the background. A green ashtray and a table scarf in primitive pattern add interest to the unusual and adroitly balanced composition.[90]

Henderson addressed the painting without mentioning the radical move made by Hayden, among others. The bold innovation of Dillon, Hayden, Johnson, and Jennings, as we recognize it today, was to add legible signs of Africa to the canonical Western still life, a genre grounded in symbols of nations, cultures, and academic conventions. To wit, Jennings's engraving presents a fleur-de-lis, studded wainscots, a Baule-like statue, and a Federalist-style metal urn. Beyond the juxtaposition of significant objects that confirm the artists' intention of mixing iconographies and widening the genre, the artists demonstrated their grasp of the still life tradition by making key substitutions. Where we might expect to find the skull of vanitas painting and the cheese, fruit, and meat of seventeenth-century Dutch still lifes, we find root vegetables communicating bounty and harvest in Dillon's painting and the decorative Kuba cloth in Hayden's. It is surprising that race-obsessed American critics of the interwar period, confronted with the African sculpture and mask, never linked or conflated Hayden's body with this culturally and racially inflected representation. Instead they conspicuously avoided the corporeal connection: writing several years after the painting's debut, Alain Locke, for example, straightforwardly described Hayden's painting as "an African idol on a table beside a vase of exotic wild orchids."[91] In contrast, nationalists in Germany who viewed pieces such as Max Pechstein's woodcut *Self-Portrait with Fetish and Nude Figure* (1922) denounced both the marrying of African subjects, symbols, and forms to Western art modes and the expressionists' identification with "outsider" and "primitive" cultures.[92]

American critics evaluating *Negro Masks* and *Fétiche et Fleurs* did not mull over the mask's role in performance or the metaphoric relationship between masking and representation in the visual arts. Still, a few writers acknowledged the African influences upon such images and the centrality of Africa in the modernist inflection of primitivism. For instance, Edward J. Brandford seemed thrilled to report that Malvin Gray Johnson's *Negro Masks* was "understanding and relieving" and more "intelligently interpreted" than his earlier, modernist works. In the same space, Brandford accorded "rare quality and texture" to *Fétiche et Fleurs* and an unlocated Hayden painting, *Theater Alley* (circa 1933): "One can easily distinguish the influence of an African background—gained not through his studies abroad—but rather through close contact and inspirations of that well known pioneer of primitive Negro art, Cloyd Boykin."[93]

Boykin's Greenwich Village school, the Primitive Art Center, was indeed among the many places where Johnson may have seen African art throughout the teens and the twenties.[94] An undated, untitled drawing of a mask from the Amistad Research Center (fig. 4.20) divulges more about Johnson's study of African art. Johnson copied masks, summarizing and translating the original sculpture into refined and economic forms of figural abstraction.[95] While these drawings were not preliminary studies of forms that appear in Johnson's oil paintings, they undoubtedly helped him work out composition problems. Johnson's confidence is patently evident in these differently articulated linear

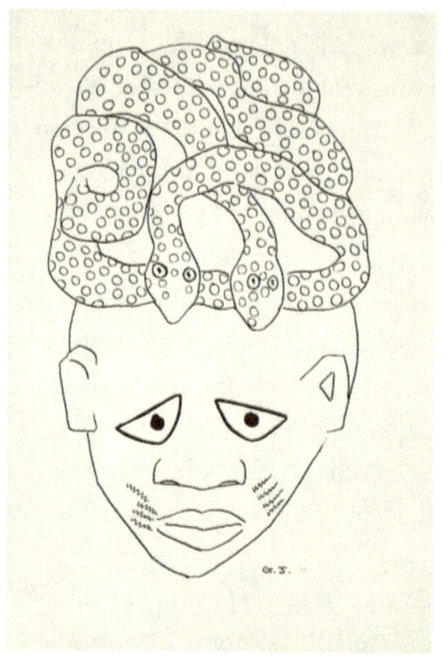

4.20 Malvin Gray Johnson, Untitled drawing (mask), not dated. Ink on paper, 16 x 10 in. Amistad Research Center, New Orleans, Louisiana

rhythms, theatrical gestures, stabilizing geometries, and bold patterns. Yet in Johnson's era few non-Africans understood the ritual and cultural status of non-Western masks that avant-garde artists found so fascinating. There is, notably, no textual evidence that demonstrates Johnson's awareness of the masks' contexts and uses. Without question, Johnson's artistic agency and creative process can be generally described as one of reclamation, borrowing, and skeuomorphic transformation. While primitivists read the process atavistically, the selection of the mask—by the era's black and nonblack artists—was a self-consciously modernist move to add it to the catalogue of Western art motifs.

Expressionist portraiture carried risks, and such handling of black figures was not kindly received in all quarters. The responses to Beauford Delaney's and William H. Johnson's publicly exhibited portraiture in 1930 are cases in point. In a small group show at the Whitney Studio Galleries in February and March, Delaney won first prize for an untitled, presently unlocated sketch (1930) of his friend, the dancer Billy Pierce, and honorable mention for his pastels.[96] Much of the same work was featured at Delaney's one-artist exhibition that April at the West 135th Street branch of the New York Public Library.

The Amsterdam News had proclaimed Delaney's success at the Whitney Studio Galleries in Greenwich Village: "Hotel Worker Wins First Prize in Art Exhibition."[97] But the headline for the *Amsterdam News*' review of Delaney's April show at the Harlem library betrayed editorial ambivalence: "Grotesque Exaggeration Dominates Art Sketches and Paintings at New Exhibit: Youthful Tennessee Artist Creates Extreme 'Negroid' Character Studies, but Shines as Painter of Portraits."[98] Delaney's genre portrait in pastel, *The Red Hat* (date unknown), is singled out for criticism because it failed to resemble anyone and fell short of meeting prevailing standards of beauty: "Repulsive in the extreme ugliness of the character portrayed, but again, perhaps that is just what the artist meant to portray. It requires, however, a vivid imagination for one to accept as an authentic likeness the grotesque figure."[99] The reviewer, identified by the initials "T. T. F.," allowed the artist creative agency, perhaps because she or he was aware of Delaney's training with a local artist in his hometown of Knoxville, Tennessee, and at prestigious Boston schools.[100] Nonetheless, T. T. F. goes on to denigrate Delaney's "exploitation of the grotesque" in his charcoal renderings:

> "Harlem Stenographer," "Harlem Athlete," and the portrait, "Harlem Chore Woman," are somehow unconvincing to the average observer. Too, one feels that the coarse features, the large nose and the thick lips depicted in each of these sketches is not the result of the artist's own observation of such types, but that rather they are the result of a very conscious effort on his part to achieve a final so-called Negroid type.[101]

T. T. F. was suspicious of Delaney's "types," judging them too unnatural and too exaggerated to be acceptable. In the mind of T. T. F., the artist did better when he painted from life: "Where he has used models . . . it is in these portraits that his true skill as an artist is at once evident. Particularly, this is true of his 'Profile of a Man,' in which one readily recognizes the musician, Morris Driggs, as the subject, and of 'An Artist Friend,' which is a likeness of Winifred J. Russell, the artist."[102] The expressionist treatment of the figure that clearly frustrated T. T. F., however, must have pleased connoisseurs of modernism such as Alain Locke, who visited this Harlem exhibition.[103] According to Delaney biographer David Leeming, in the 1930s the artist worked diligently to fulfill his sitters' demands for likenesses, rather than paint his "abstract impressions."[104] But when he was not working on commissioned subjects, Delaney relished taking liberties with form. He told a *New York Telegraph* interviewer in 1930, "I never drew a decent thing until I felt the rhythm of New York. New York has a rhythm as distinct as the beating of a human heart. And I'm trying to put it on canvas . . . I paint people. People—and in their faces I hope to discover that odd, mysterious rhythm."[105] Oddities and mysteries aside, are there any qualities in Delaney's portraits of 1930 that merit the description "grotesque"? Two of these works exist in reproductions: the charcoal drawing *A Man* (1930) and the previously mentioned Billy Pierce sketch.[106] *A Man* is a half-body-length treatment of a black subject that is posed against a neutral background. Although Delaney slightly varies his tones to suggest the fall of natural light and shadow upon the head, his grisaille treatment of his subject invests the human form with a sculptural quality. This artificiality is heightened by Delaney's deft, linear drawing style. The most exaggerated features of *A Man* are the figure's sharply arched eyebrows and the enlarged ears and nose. The long and outward-flaring ears appear summarily appended to the figure's heart-shaped head. By late-twentieth-century standards, both figures are realistic, much in the way a caricature exaggerates a bodily gesture or feature for expressive ends; both are recognizable as humans and hardly "grotesque." Nonetheless, their realistic qualities are evident, and it is easy to imagine the dismay of a viewer in 1930 who expected verisimilar imagery. Delaney's portraits announce their artificiality and made quality rather than persuade the viewer that they are pictures from life.

For some critics, figural distortion stood against the ideals of humanism, American nationalism, and "the New Negro." Their tastes reflected those of black Americans who preferred conventional approaches in art and aesthetic idealizations of black figural subjects that challenged racist visual stereotypes.[107] Theophilus Lewis, a progressive theater critic and cultural commentator for the *Amsterdam News* and the *Messenger*, skewered the prizewinning entries of William H. Johnson at the 1930 Harmon Foundation exhibition:

> This painter seems to have a flair for the grotesque and deformed in human stature and expression. . . . His self-portrait is obviously intended to be the like-

ness of the genius being consumed by its own fire. I didn't like it. One of his other portraits is a gnarled gnome and the third and last, No. 9 in the catalogue, is the figure of an aged black consumptive. This last one is the only picture of his group I liked.[108]

It is interesting that Lewis dwells on human imperfections: the psyche of the creative genius and the body deformed or contorted by age, disease, or birth defect. The two works he mentions are simply titled *Portrait* in the Harmon catalogue, so certain identification is impossible. Nevertheless, the reproduction of one of these self-portraits (circa 1929) brims with the fiery energies so disliked by Lewis; so does William H. Johnson's 1930 portrait *Minnie* (fig. 4.21). In both paintings the faces are faceted and chiseled. The artist's half-body-length treatment of the head and torso is especially weighty and forceful. The form is truncated in dramatic ways: the picture frame cuts off the right arm at the shoulder, and the left at midbicep; it also crops the artist's wildly curly hair, adding to

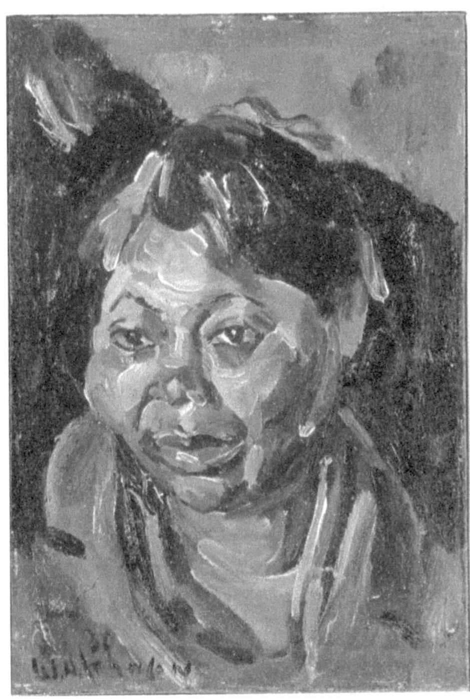

4.21 William H. Johnson, *Minnie*, 1930. Oil on canvas, 17 1/2 x 12 1/8 in. Smithsonian American Art Museum, Washington, D.C./Art Resource, New York

the edgy fragmentariness and immediacy of the painting. In fact, these qualities are what earned William H. Johnson the admiration of the Harmon jury: sculptors Meta Warrick Fuller and Karl Illava, critic George Hellmann, artist and Cooper Union instructor Victor Perard, and painter George Luks, who was Johnson's employer. In their press statement, the judges declared, "In his portrait work, Mr. Johnson has brought out characteristics of his subjects through exaggerated lines and shadings, so that his work tends toward caricature."[109] Though their assessment is consistent with Lewis's, for these judges exaggeration was a desirable quality: "We think he is one of our coming great painters. He is a real modernist. He has been spontaneous, vigorous, firm, direct; he has shown a great thing in art—it is the expression of the man himself."[110]

Art Digest similarly praised the artist with their headline "Is William H. Johnson, Negro Prize Winner, Blazing a New Trail?"[111] Unquestionably, such publicity was recognition of Johnson's break from staid portraiture. His paintings were deemed successful because they evidenced what Joanna Woodall has called the "symptomatic relationship between external appearance and an invisible, internal self," a conceit of Western artists such as Courbet and Manet from the mid-nineteenth century onward.[112] Johnson's paintings also asserted an aggressively modernist character that was different from the least experimental naturalist modes he learned at the NAD.[113] Antinaturalism alienated critics such as Lewis, who felt that much of the portraiture exhibited by the Harmon Foundation had gone too far. Lewis bitingly opined, "The principle seems to be that if the picture of a man looks like a man it isn't art. But if it looks like a head of lettuce that's been dropped in a pan of purple Tintex, then it is art."[114]

Indeed, foundation director Mary Beattie Brady voiced concern that abstraction and distortion would subvert goals for race uplift, social responsibility, favorable impressions of black artists, and idealized black images. She said retrospectively, "Portraiture [produced by African Americans] was so distorted that it was difficult to make any impact on the art-going public. While I feel very hesitant always to try to encourage artists to do something that may or may not come naturally to them, I do feel that we have a very important responsibility with our criticism to be constructive and to show dignity, leadership and positive values where we can."[115]

Both Lewis's and Brady's statements depend upon a notion of the universal that lays an impossible claim to objectivity; poststructuralist and postmodernist theorists have persuasively argued that the universal is always a subjective standard of beauty based in perfection, purity, and harmony. Lewis's and Brady's comments pit mimesis and naturalistic representation against the kinds of figural abstraction that interested Delaney, Dorsey, Malvin Gray Johnson, William H. Johnson, and many of their peers. Audiences for these black painters' portraits—a swath of diverse viewers that included conservative opponents of modernism as well as intrigued admirers of its varied forms—generally expected pictures of people to look "real" and "natural." Furthermore, as Richard Brilliant has observed, portraiture is viewed as an unmediated genre, a standard to which other genres are not held: "No one considers a collection of fruit, glasses, and bottles on a table to be a 'still life' without the intervention of an artist, and neither is an artificially constructed genre with a long history of representation that goes beyond immediate observation, realistic depiction, and schematic models of composition to convey certain meanings about the world."[116] Brilliant's assessment is especially apt in the context of the 1930s, when few viewers (for Locke was a notable exception) recognized portraits such as Dorsey's *Self-Portrait* (1930), Malvin Gray Johnson's *Postman* (1934), or William H. Johnson's *Minnie* (1930) as creative revisions of traditional picturing of the body.

Reading truth and authenticity in the work of Johnson, Kuniyoshi, and Weber was and continues to be dependent upon unmediated views of the artists themselves. Weber's biographers make much of his Bialystok birthplace: a creative and industrial center of the mid-nineteenth century, the city is cast in the literature as a quaint village where Weber absorbed timeless folk traditions and Slavic customs.[117] Although Lloyd Goodrich ridiculed critics who saw "the effect of a Hebraic heritage" in Weber's exhibition at the Museum of Modern Art in 1930, he later situated the artist's 1916 painting *Russian Ballet* in an Orientalist context. Goodrich homogenizes Russia and swings toward the other end of national and cultural stereotype, that is, Tsarist opulence: "Even more personal was 'Russian Ballet,' a subject peculiarly in harmony with Weber's love of music and dance, and his passion for color. Its vivacity and Oriental luxuriance matched its theme. Here Weber's Russian origin was again apparent."[118]

However informed by cubism and French Orphism, *Russian Ballet*, for Goodrich, was the evidence of the non-Western: its palette was the result not of Weber's study nor of artistic invention and exchange but a fact of his birth.[119] The Slavic East, in addition, was an opposing pole to the West and the United States, similarly to Hegelian conceptions of cipherlike Africa and the mysterious Orient. Notably, Alfred H. Barr Jr., after opening his 1930 monographic essay with a reference to Weber's self-conscious modernism, writes, "As a boy he brought with him to New York the memories of his childhood in Russia where both Slav and Jew had still preserved what is so lacking in America, a racial culture of authentic purity and color."[120] To shore up his claim that Weber was born to his art, Barr adds, "More than Picasso, he absorbed not merely the form but something of the spirit of Negro sculpture."[121] Picasso was said to admire "primitive art," but observers felt that artists such as Weber, Kuniyoshi, and Johnson embodied the primitive.

At times, Weber, Kuniyoshi, and Johnson inhabited the racial stereotypes that fettered them. "I am proud to belong to a race that was civilized when the French were still barbarians," Weber boasted.[122] To explain the impact of his study with Kenneth Hayes Miller at the Art Students League, Kuniyoshi once asserted that "he had been brought up seeing and feeling things in the Oriental way, that is in a two-dimensional way . . . then Miller taught him to see things in depth, one behind another."[123] Johnson both embraced and rejected the idea of a black aesthetic. In chapter 3, I quoted Johnson's January 1930 application for a Guggenheim Foundation fellowship, in which he wrote that he was "trying to depict in line and color, creations of that one thing that my race possesses—Music." One month later Johnson asserted that black American artists "are trying to do what artists of all races do—follow the principles of fine arts technically."[124] In these statements we recognize the negotiations of artists who recognize the desires of the marketplace *and* the very difficulty of separating themselves from both that market's rigid conceptions and from their own self-conceptions. Kuniyoshi's late career paintings with masked figures, among them *Revelation* (1949; fig. 4.22), speak to his interest in circus and carnival performance and, pointedly, to his multiple conceptions of self. In them masking, performing, and parody are less obviously subversive and rightly hesitant and uncertain.

Just as I have discovered a resemblance between Johnson and many of his genre subjects, I take the measure of Kuniyoshi's and Weber's stated ethnocul-

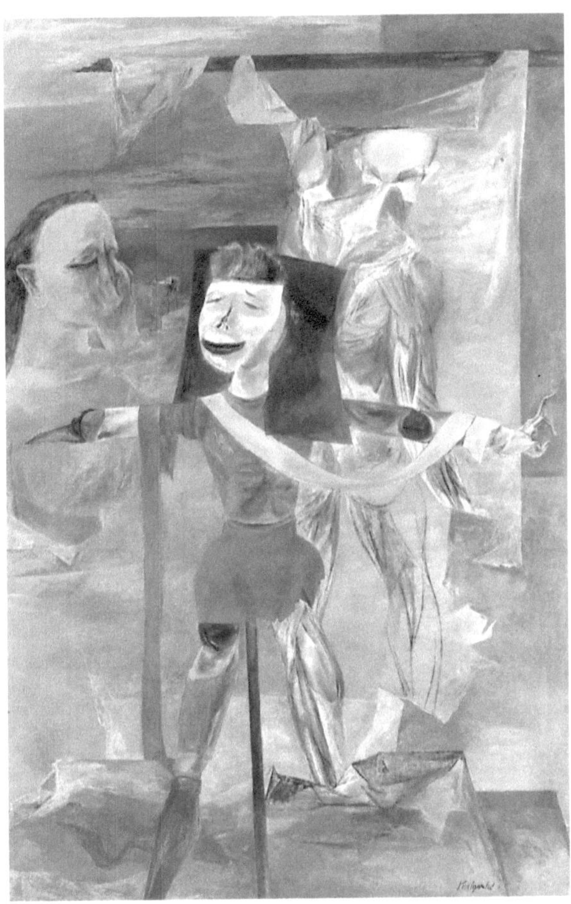

4.22 Yasuo Kuniyoshi, *Revelation*, 1949. Oil on canvas, 70 1/8 x 46 3/8 in. Roland P. Murdock Collection, Wichita Art Museum, Wichita, Kansas

tural, racial, and national identifications with their subjects in general. Their claims underscore the subjectivity of viewing, and viewing as a self-conscious experience that guides the portraitist.[125] But for all the personality and formal integrity of the painted likeness, it remains a simulacral, third-person narrative, opposing readings of the racial genre portrait that would exactly align it with the raced body.[126]

FIVE

THE RACE OF LANDSCAPE

So far, I have placed Malvin Gray Johnson, Yasuo Kuniyoshi, and Max Weber in the thick of racial art, as key producers, interlocutors, and sometime critics of a notion that emerged in the interwar decades and reverberates through present-day multiculturalism. Their production of landscapes—rural and urban—carries special significance, although this genre does not predominate in their oeuvres. The unpopulated landscape has rightly been considered an occasional turn for these artists; more often they staffed scenes of nature with symbolic human, architectural, and machine forms. Nonetheless, these artists' landscapes were seized upon as opportunities to plot identity—pinned to class, ethnicity, gender, race, and national subjectivities—on invented, imagined space. No less than their genre portraiture and religious representations, many of these artists' exterior scenes rely on long-used geographical associations: the pictures contain conventional signs and symbols that bind American regions to projected affirmative histories and affecting culturalist narratives. Hence, even as these artists wrote and spoke of discovering special characteristics of the places to which they traveled, their journeys began long before they left home. For Johnson, Kuniyoshi, and Weber, variably situated outside of centralized and privileged American identity, representing place was an opportunity to assert their belonging and commitment to the national body. The paradox is that, with their landscapes, these three artists made their cases for full citizenship, cases that often embraced and advanced an "already there" American essentialism.

"WEBER! N'OUBLIEZ PAS LA NATURE!"

Weber's best-known scene paintings are his energetic urban landscapes of the teens, paintings that are valued signposts of experimental modernism in the United States. In *Rush Hour, New York* (1915), Weber breaks down Manhattan's insistently vertical character with sharp, forceful lines, piercing rays, and multiple geometric shapes. Fragments and passages of pavement, pinnacles, and other architectural details are evident, economically delineated with directional brushstrokes and a suite of complementary hues. Weber employs cubist and Futurist techniques to proffer a vision of the city as simultaneous and ceaseless movement. His interpretation of seeing as experience extended beyond celebrations of New York as a specifically named site, for he also interpreted performance and athletic competitions in a similar manner. In both *Russian Ballet* (1916) and *Athletic Contest (Interscholastic Runners*; 1915), he deploys highlighting primary colors across the canvas in high-value vectors and dense geometric passages. Color, then, helped viewers make sense of the abstracted subject in shattered picture space. As art historians Willard Bohn and Linda Dalrymple Henderson have shown, Weber's plan in the teens was to capture the real-world energies of a conceptual space he called "the fourth dimension."[1] In his 1910 essay, "The Fourth Dimension from a Plastic Point View," Weber proposed:

> In plastic art, I believe, there is a fourth dimension which may be described as the consciousness of a great and overwhelming sense of space-magnitude in all directions at one time. . . . It is real, and can be perceived and felt. . . . It is somewhere similar to color and musical sounds. It arouses imagination and stirs

> emotion. It is the immensity of all things. It is the ideal measurement, and is therefore as great as the ideal, perceptive or imaginative facilities of the creator, architect, sculptor, or painter.[2]

Like his New York contemporaries, John Marin (1870–1953), Joseph Stella (1877–1946), and Abraham Walkowitz (1878–1965), Weber celebrated the modern, industrial age in the teens. It is noteworthy that human forms rarely appear in any of these tributes to the vital metropolis, a conspicuous absence in light of the growing and diversifying New York population.

In the pastoral landscapes of the twenties and thereafter, Weber moved away from the analytic cubism techniques that he marshaled to suggest simultaneity in his earliest work. In 1921 Weber left New York City permanently to settle in Long Island. Assessing Weber's landscapes of the 1920s, his principal biographer, Percy North, deems the moderately abstract rendering of a shimmering lakeshore an indication of the artist's readiness "to move both physically and aesthetically to the suburbs."[3] It is possible to push another of North's provocative observations: that the Cézannesque *Landscape* (circa 1925) is "a distinct contrast to Weber's figure studies from the same decade, almost as if they were created by two separate personalities." I believe that the artist sought to overlay generalized locations with a School of Paris–informed approach to create a "tough," American picturesque. *Landscape*, then, might be seen as Weber's amenable compromise to a wary public that was developing tolerance for modernist effects in traditional painting formats. After the critical uproar his art had provoked in the teens, Weber understandably searched for a viable art style and for appealing subjects.[4] One avenue was to paint neoclassicizing nudes and iconic figure groups, a de-particularizing strategy elected by many European modernists in the post–World War I era. Another was to insert the picturesque and provincial into the landscape, a format once derided as the genre without subject. Weber embraced both these tactics and sometimes incorporated monumental female forms—nude and clothed—into his idyllic landscapes.[5] He usually worked from detailed sketches, developing representation from observation and color notes to test compositional formulas.[6]

Weber's landscapes were admired in the twenties and thirties by audiences looking for moderately modern art. His *High Noon* (circa 1925) entered the Phillips Gallery in Washington, D.C., in 1926, and the collector Duncan Phillips described it as "a record of sensation and mood," adding that "all this Oriental color-orchestra powerfully affects us in its Persian splendor pervaded by melancholy."[7] While scintillating color sits on the surface of *Landscape*, it is scrubbed into the canvas of *High Noon*, making its forms—barns, fields, and fences—warm, solid, and material. Throughout the twenties and thirties, Weber's landscape painting tacked along a course toward impressionist and expressionist interpretations. In *Avenue of Trees* (1926) the eye follows broken brushstrokes across the canvas, which direct attention to multiple focal points. Weber's application of the paint medium in *Straggly Pines* (1932) and *Winter Twilight* (1938) is more emphatic: the surface of *Straggly Pines* seems abraded, and that of *Winter Twilight* bears impasto streaks of oil and palette knife–edge scratches. To most of today's observers, neither the organic subject of nature nor Weber's skilled handling makes these pictures as compelling as the cubist abstractions of the teens.[8] Yet, at the time of their debut, Weber's landscapes were considered achievements, au courant, beautiful, and modern.[9]

In 1930 Alfred H. Barr Jr. and Holger Cahill, two of Weber's most influential supporters, positioned these landscapes ahead of his radically abstract work, considering them along with his contemporaneous paintings as culminations and signs of the artist's maturity. Barr, the director of the fledgling Museum of Modern Art, wrote an essay for its Weber exhibition, and Cahill, who was affiliated with numerous organizations, including Edith Halpert's Downtown Gallery in Manhattan and the Newark Museum of Art, authored a monograph published by Halpert.[10] Barr offered, "at the risk of destruction by future historians," that Weber's oeuvre could be organized into "four divisions": "The Student Period in Paris (1905–1908)," "The Period of Experiment (1909–1917)," "Introspection (1918)," and "The Period of Maturity (since 1918)."[11] Barr's praise includes an inference that Weber, as his detractors charged, had been a School of Paris imitator, for he writes, "In 1918 he seems first to have discovered a *style* which is unmistakably 'Weber.'"[12] For Barr, Weber's subsequent painting was even better, evidencing "a more objective and monumental style." He concludes, "But it is scarcely by his still life paintings or by the drenched blue of his landscape that Weber most clearly commands our study, nor by any external or purely aesthetic quality of paint or of arrangement; it is rather by the penetrating, pathetic sentiment of his more intimate and personal compositions—by a quality of spirit."[13]

I have previously discussed the centrality of emotion and spirit in the early twentieth-century American critical lexicon, for they were terms often summoned to condemn modernism and its practitioners. The terms worked similarly in Barr's established binaries: he hoped that the MoMA retrospective exhibition demonstrated that Weber's studies, experiments, introspection, and maturation had led to an embodied modernism, an intense, colorful mode opposing cold, aloof, and soulless design. Cahill, too, looked to distinguish the artist in this way. Striking a tone of concession, he acknowledged the figural abstraction evident in Weber's 1916–20 production. Yet, Cahill qualified this statement by calling the artist's work "research" that would productively lead elsewhere, for, in Cahill's words, "even in Weber's most abstract work the personal element is felt." Cahill further explained that, while Weber's abstraction "is fundamental to all that he has since produced," he was no exception to the rule: "No artist can live for long at the level of the glacier beauty of impersonal art."[14] Like Barr, Cahill summoned effective metaphors that put artistic temperament ahead of virtuosity: "Weber's personality is felt in everything he does, yet he has never gone in for orgies of personal expression—German 'expressionism,' for instance, or the cult of the brush stroke which was so much the thing a few years ago."[15] If Barr discerned discrete and radical style shifts in Weber's practice—from abstraction to figuration, from the School of Paris to a self-discovered, unique expressionism—Cahill opined that Weber had forsaken nothing, and that he plainly knew how to strike the right balance in his work, especially in his landscapes. In them, Cahill insisted, "there is harmony between the demands of design and of nature. They show a power to handle nature's forms within the moulds of geometry, a power which springs from intimacy with the life of nature and an acquiescence in her laws. . . . Landscape of this kind is a visual poetry which might run to preciousness in the hands of a lesser man."[16] Cahill distinguishes *Avenue of Trees, High Noon*, and other pastoral landscapes from merely decorative and effete scene painting and credits Weber's powerful handling and informed awareness of art and nature for their success.

There is no doubt that Weber's descriptions of his objectives and his work informed both Barr's and Cahill's texts. The MoMA publication's exhibition checklist includes the artist's annotations of some of the displayed objects, and Weber's descriptions resonate with "poetry," "senses," and "spirit." Toward the same desired end of conveying a romantic personality to readers, Cahill liberally quoted the artist. Nature's inspiration to artists, as Weber saw it, is central to Cahill's monograph and also to the artist's story as he himself narrated it. His oft-told tale of Henri Rousseau's departing words to him in 1908—"Weber! N'oubliez pas la nature!"—resonate here and nearly everywhere in the literature by and about him. Cahill assured readers that Weber had not forgotten Rousseau's advice, adding,

> He is not trying to escape nature along the path of personal expression, nor is he trying to escape into nature along the path of imitation. He is seeking an order paralleling that of nature, and in this he is akin to Cézanne and to all artists of the past whose works have lasting significance. . . . In a very profound sense he has a message. . . . If this message could be condensed into one word it would be the word equilibrium.[17]

Cahill wrote as an advocate of modernism, simultaneously arguing for the preeminence of Cézanne and raising Weber's stock by likening him to the French artist and to a far-reaching artistic canon. Cahill's move is a bridging one, and not unlike Weber's own goal of subtly modernizing durable genres such as landscape. In measured tones, Weber and Cahill endeavored to normalize modernism, to make it less strange to puzzled audiences, to rescue it from demonization, and, ultimately, to recast it in a positive light by associating it with respected art of the past.

In the interwar era that was driven by regionalist rhetoric, Weber's generic landscapes are not bombastic jingoist celebrations of American scenes—rural or urban. If anything, Weber's work in this genre was unapologetically Arcadian: Weber painted natural paradises enjoyed by broad-featured men and women. Nude and seminude, these bodies were meant to be read as timeless and traditional indices of idealized beauty motifs. In *Pleasures of Summer*, *The Gesture* (1921), and *At the Lake* (1934), sun-bronzed, raven- and red-haired women linger near bodies of water. With their stiff and solemn poses, they provoke associations with antique Greco-Roman sculpture and with Weber studies such as

Eight Figures (1927), whose nudes, Weber explained, were "ordained more by a plastic necessity."[18] Almost certainly, Weber similarly constituted human subjects in these landscapes as plastic problems to be solved. Although their physiognomy, their nude or dishabille presentation, and their warm and rustic surroundings might suggest a Mediterranean locale, such suppositions are foreclosed. As neoclassicized forms, they seem designed to evade designations of ethnicity, race, nationality, and class. These subjects contrast with the male and female nudes in *Retirement* (1921), a painting whose title references Weber's 1922–23 self-imposed removal from the exhibition circuit. With their stylish twenties-era coiffures and wide-eyed expressions, the protagonists of *Retirement* seem to be contemporary, self-aware bodies.[19] They are, despite their proximity to one another, individuated, disengaged from each other, and anxious. The seated male figure at left, for instance, seems more undressed than naked, and rather embarrassed. Yet at least one critic, the *New York Times*' Edward Alden Jewell, deemed the work successful when it was exhibited in 1944. Weber's expressionism, Jewell wrote, was versatile, and "the exceptionally fine" *Retirement* was evidence of Weber's "moving into a realm characterized more and more by expression preponderantly his own."[20] This assessment, which noted Weber's modern manner and uniqueness, was precisely what this painter (and any artist of his era) sought.

"TO GET DOWN IN THE SOUTH AND PAINT NEGRO SUBJECTS"

In July 1934, a few months before his death, Johnson traveled from New York City to Brightwood, Virginia, a hamlet sixty miles southwest of Washington, D.C. As he put it, he had long wanted "to get down in the South and paint Negro subjects."[21] Johnson, who was born in Greensboro, North Carolina, pointedly looked outside of that crossroads city in his search for "the South." He numbered among the dozens of New York–based artists who traveled to the region in the 1930s: for African American artists and writers, in particular, the South was a symbolic crucible of a black culture that they sought to represent as paradigmatic.[22] Elsewhere, I have written about twentieth-century representations of the South that are indebted to long-held, idyllic tropes and the romanticism of the noble yeoman. Compositional strategies and chosen themes, I argued, were hardly discoveries informed by a Southern aesthetic. Instead, the art produced and sustained an enduring clapboard iconology of the South: plank floors and cabin walls, agrarian laborers and their fields, dirt roads, and small town rituals such as fairs, picnics, and livestock sales. Yet Johnson, who at the time of his death in October 1934 was negotiating to exhibit his Virginia images in New York, was disappointed by these scenes.[23] His wife, Betty Johnson, wrote after her husband's death, "The study of Negro types did not all come up to his expectation, such as he met, he may have been on the streets of New York."[24] Indeed, Johnson had already explored "Negro types" in the religious and genre paintings he had done in New York, in which he had developed the quick, expressionist manner in which he would represent Southern subjects.

If Johnson did not find exactly what he was looking for in Brightwood, he was still productive during his eight-week stay, finishing fifteen oil paintings and eighteen watercolor drawings characterized by bold, bright colors and simplified forms. The emergent expressionism in this body of work had its origins in New York: the Virginia genre scenes *Platform Dance* (fig. 5.1) and *The Ploughman* (1934) continued his experiments with geometric forms, which were manifest in the angular bodies and tilted-up perspectives of *The Elks (Marching Elks,* 1934) and *Girl Reading*. Johnson executed landscapes throughout his career, but relatively few in the period right before he traveled to Virginia. Nevertheless, landscape seemed to be a grounding practice for Johnson: he made it his first painting project in Virginia. On his second day there, he recalled that he walked "around looking for some subject matter to do in the way of landscape."[25] Among the first landscape he rendered was an oil he titled *Muddy Road*, now known as *Untitled (Red Road,* 1934; fig. 5.2).[26] More than a landscape, *Untitled (Red Road)* is a representation of social relationships meant to evoke those in a small Southern community. In it, black figures—albeit small in scale, highly abstracted, and merely one of many focal points—are pictured interacting. Two townspeople chat while leaning over a low fence; others stroll along the streets. The architecture also suggests social intimacy: modest clapboard structures—private homes, a church, and a post office—are set close to each other. Marshalling these symbols of the American picturesque, Johnson did not remove the evidence of the machine age's presence in Brightwood. A

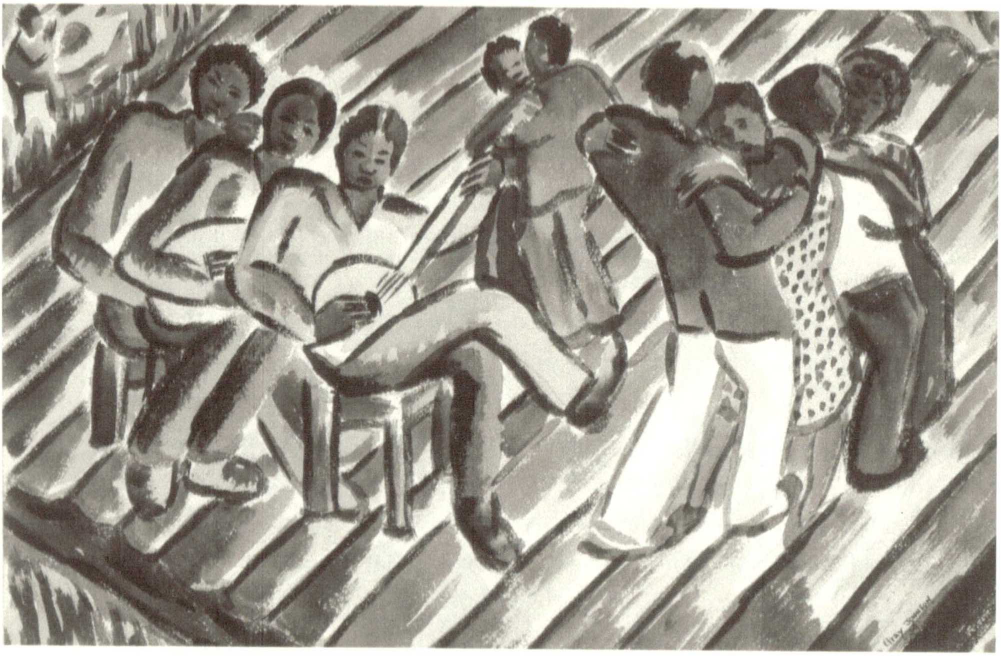

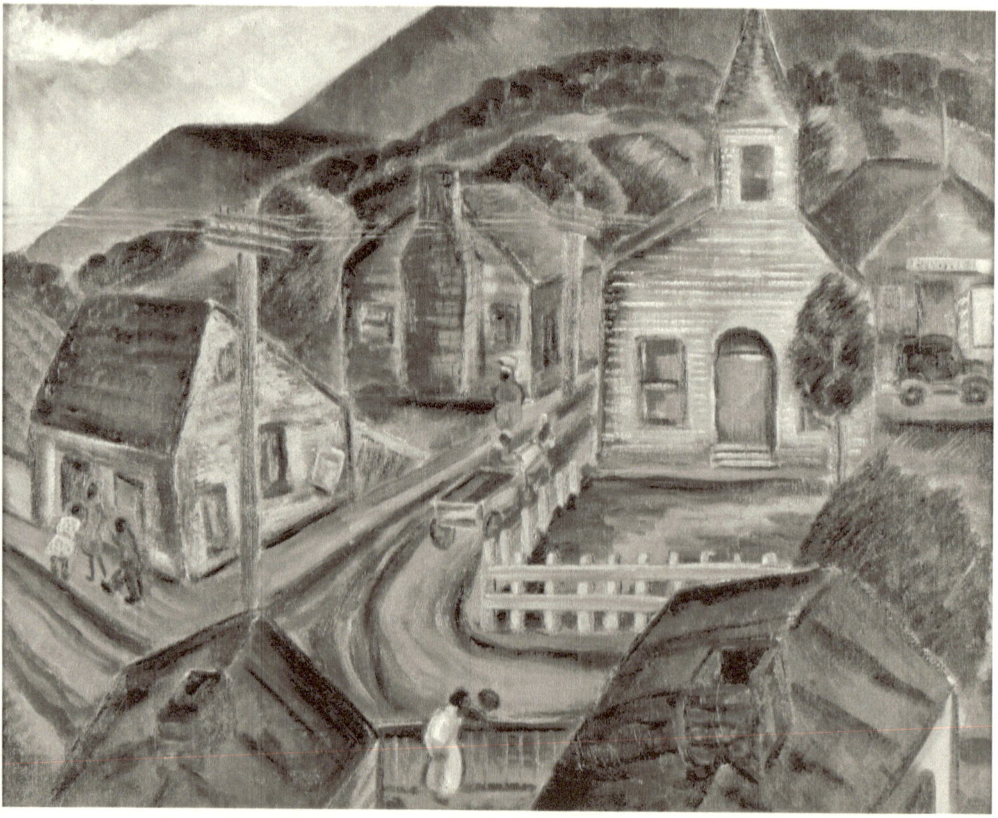

sedan, placed in the painting's rear ground, catches the eye as a solidly drawn and dark form set between the lighter-colored church and post office buildings. This car is in dialogue with the mule-drawn, open wagon at the picture's center. Similarly, the majesty of the steeply rising hills in the background is paired with another assertive vertical element: the utility poles in the middle ground. Although the church's steeple reaches higher, these poles, which bring telephone and electric service, are signs that resist readings of Brightwood as a timeless, unchanging place.

That Johnson deemed *Untitled (Red Road)* an "impression," as he did other scenes composed and painted in Virginia, indicates his modernist ambition to make accessible pictures. One oil was "a landscape impression [of] . . . the light effects of the morning—the time when this canvas was done"; another, "an impression of an after-storm effect . . . a terrific gale . . . the worst storm I have ever seen." Another was "just an impression of the combination of the beautiful blue hill, green trees and this red soil that caused me to do this composition."[27] *Fallen Trees* (1934; fig. 5.3) offers a close-up view of a storm's aftermath: dashed, angled brushstrokes are used to construct the lightning-struck trunks and boughs. Although broken, these natural forms still communicate energy because they are large, colorful, and seem to advance to the front of the picture plane. Johnson, intrigued by the dramatic climate shifts in Brightwood, depicted the foothills and forests in several paintings and watercolors. His approach was not strictly serial, but his focus on slopes and peaks—again, angular forms available for modernist exaggeration and abstraction—must have been related to his interest in Cézanne, whose work was frequently exhibited in New York, widely reproduced, and emulated by some in the United States. Hints of Cézanne's influence on Johnson's landscape compositions may be evident as early as 1933 in the waterfront scenes *Caterpillar* and *Riverboat* (both 1933); these modest oils offer verdant hills and trees as formidable presences equal-

5.1 Malvin Gray Johnson, *Platform Dance*, 1934. Watercolor on paper, 11 x 17 in. Fisk University Galleries, Nashville, Tennessee

5.2 Malvin Gray Johnson, *Untitled (Red Road)*, 1934. Oil on canvas, 24 x 30 in. Hampton University Museum, Hampton, Virginia

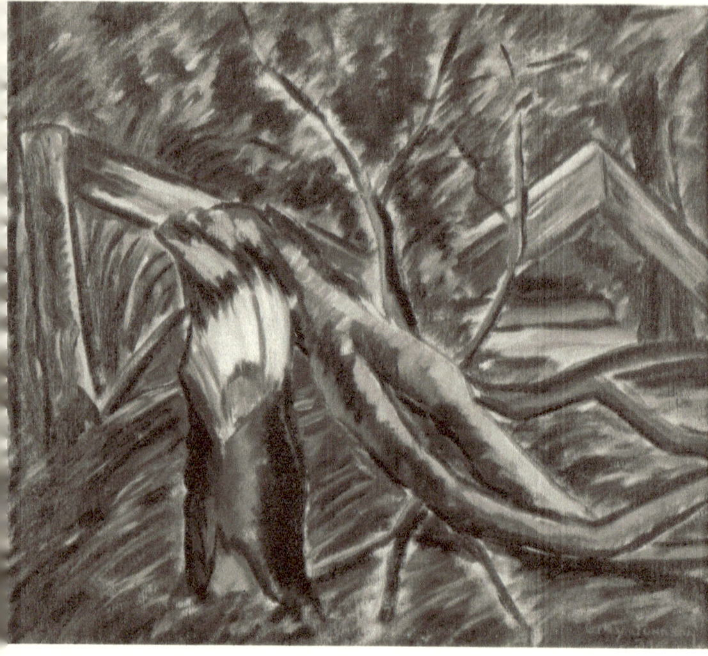

5.3 Malvin Gray Johnson, *Fallen Trees*, 1934. Oil on canvas, 16 x19 in. Hampton University Museum, Hampton, Virginia

5.4 Malvin Gray Johnson, *Southern Landscape*, 1934 (plate 11). Fisk University Galleries, Nashville, Tennessee

ing the strength of the modern machine. In Johnson's Virginia production, the artist's approach to rendering these motifs is indebted to Cézanne's paintings of Mont Sainte-Victoire. While Johnson's *Southern Landscape* (1934; fig. 5.4, plate 11) does not match the brilliant jewel-like array of color in Cézanne's best work, he clearly sought to approximate it. The painting is marked by heavily worked passages, signs that Johnson had weighed the merits of faithful representation and ultimately decided against naturalism and mimetic realism. The resulting images boast color contrasts much starker than those in nature and abstracted forms flattened and tightly compressed in the picture space.

Johnson's dissatisfaction with Brightwood's "Negro subjects" notwithstanding, he painted numerous genre portraits and figure groups that construct his sitters and their surroundings as rural Southerners: for example, the subjects in *Portrait of a Young Woman* (1934; fig. 5.5) and *Uncle Joe* (1934; fig. 5.6) are backed by a clapboard wall and an enveloping tree trunk, respectively. In these genre portraits Johnson tapped into an available inventory of Southern motifs evident in nineteenth-century U.S. paintings, including Christian Mayr's

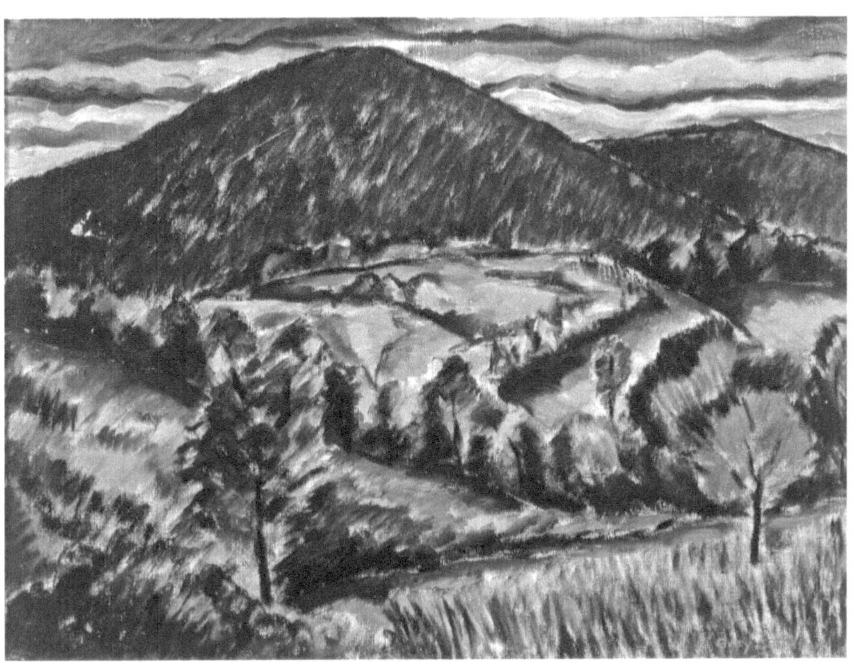

Kitchen at White Sulphur Springs (1838), Eyre Crow's *Slave Market in Richmond, Virginia* (1852–53), and Eastman Johnson's *Negro Life at the South (Old Kentucky Home*; 1859). Malvin Gray Johnson's Virginia sitters are influenced by archetypes and stereotypes, and are also related to the compositions he developed for his New York genre portraits, such as *Sailor* and *Negro Soldier*. It is notable that the four paintings *Portrait of a Young Woman*, *Uncle Joe*, *Sailor*, and *Negro Soldier* are all half-length, frontal portraits. Both the solo and group subjects of New York and Virginia bear Johnson's signature manipulations of the body: angled shoulders, steadily focused gazes, and multiplication of the human form into a patterned design. In sum, even as Johnson advanced a clapboard iconography, he relied on the format and style he had developed in New York. Planning to paint folksy "Negro subjects" and expecting to find an arcadia in rural Virginia, Johnson instead discovered that Brightwood's citizens lived in a dynamic present, as he himself did.

Mythic space is hard to construct, and Johnson found figures invaluable to his project of idyllically representing the South. Black figures, even more than folksy titles, made the Virginia pictures southern. In *Platform Dance* and *First*

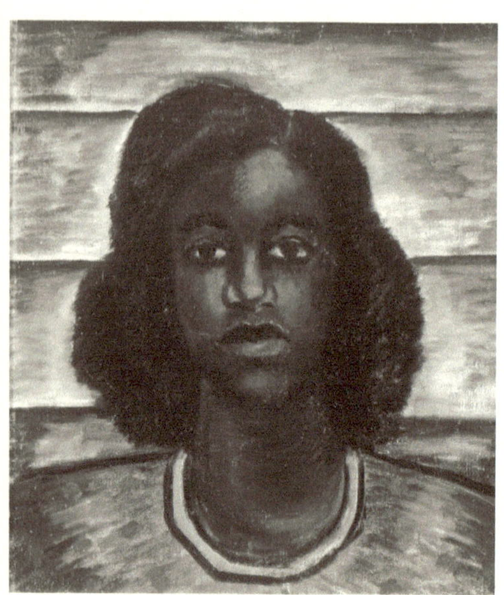

5.5 Malvin Gray Johnson, *Portrait of a Young Woman*, 1934. Oil on canvas, 12 x 16 in. Fisk University Galleries, Nashville, Tennessee

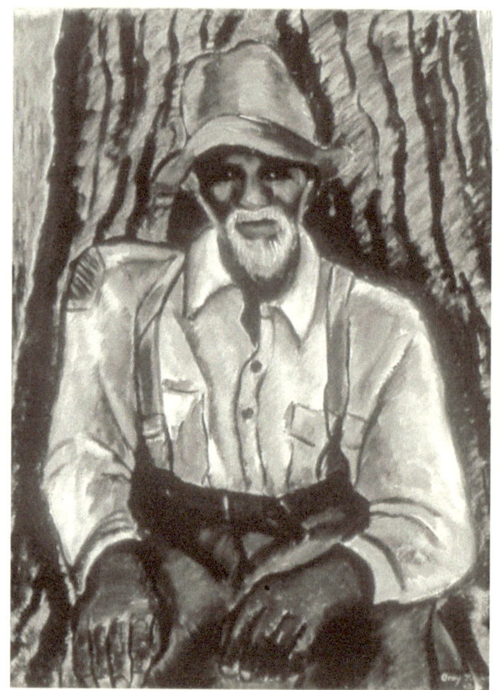

5.6 Malvin Gray Johnson, *Uncle Joe*, 1934. Oil on canvas, 30 x 24 in. Amistad Research Center, New Orleans, Louisiana

Sunday with Dinner on the Ground (fig. 5.7), the subjects are abstracted forms, summarily rendered and brightly colored. Stilled by black outline, these forms nonetheless communicate the energy of the social engagement. Aggressively cropped to accentuate the diagonal lines of the performance platform and the gesturing, angled forms, the watercolor *Platform Dance* presents paired dancers and a trio of musicians close to the front of the picture plane. Whereas *Platform Dance* is a close-up shot, *First Sunday with Dinner on the Ground* is a longer view with vignettes. Johnson struck an ethnographic tone in his explanation for painting *First Sunday with Dinner on the Ground*: "This composition was made from an impression that I gained after visiting one of the churches there on what they call 'First Sunday.' I think it's the first Sunday in September every

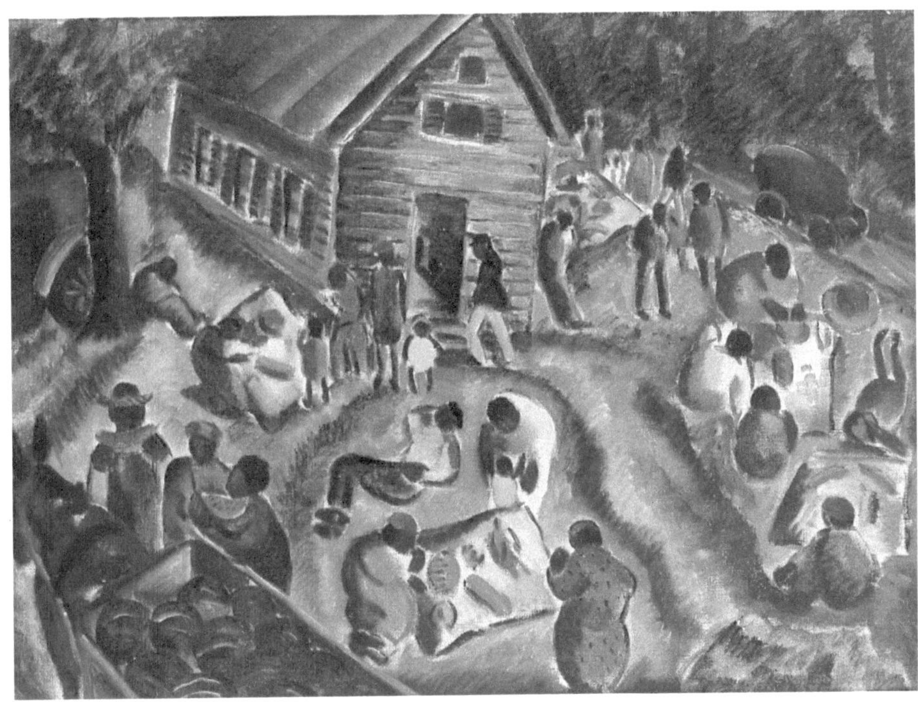

5.7 Malvin Gray Johnson, *First Sunday with Dinner on the Ground*, 1934. Oil on canvas, 17 x 23 in. Hampton University Museum, Hampton, Virginia

year that they have a celebration and they all get together for a religious service, after which they picnic on the ground. This is a very colorful affair."[28]

Scattered around a church's hilltop grounds are black parishioners in a variety of unaffected poses: a man naps; another takes shade underneath a tree; a group congregates around a picnic blanket. In the left foreground a vendor sells watermelon from a horse-drawn cart, a vehicle juxtaposed to parked and passing cars at the other end of the composition. Johnson playfully renders a woman's dress in black and red to echo the watermelon's seeds and flesh, and a patch of grass suggests the rind. This witty repetition—like the summarized figures, distorted clapboard church, and deliberately skewed perspective of the painting—underscores the artist's characterization of it as "an impression": it is a quickly gathered, though still inevitably mediated, interpretation that contributed to American regionalist iconography of the Depression era and its smaller subset of noble black yeoman types. Representations of hard-working and virtuous African Americans were favored subjects of many black and nonblack artists of the interwar period and its aftermath. Yet this imagery was overwhelmed by similarly idealizing depictions of whites. Moreover, black images were received as representative in a way that the larger set of white, regionalist types was not.[29] However broadening and successfully redeeming images of southern black folk were, they also reified a limited number of black subject positions and nearly erased many others. Black folk iconography offered a single, symbolic blackness in the interwar years, and even today maintains its hold on authenticity.

"I LIKE THOSE GHOST TOWNS, DESERTED PLACES"

Kuniyoshi's landscapes introduced him to audiences in the 1920s: his figural abstract interpretations of farmland typically startled viewers, who were confronted with distorted and compressed picture space, livestock transformed into irregular geometries, scale-exaggerated flora, and bloated human figures that glowed with unnatural energies (fig. 5.8). Some approved of Kuniyoshi's landscapes in this decade, among them an unnamed critic who praised their "richness of tones" and "powerful construction."[30] Others saw atavism rather than parody and aligned some scenes, such as *Little Joe and Cow* (1924), with a perceived Japanese interest in nature.[31] New York critic Margaret Breuning detected agreeable national flavors—American and Japanese—in his work, noting that he

> displays an unexpected interest in the American scene, which he observes with delicate perception and transcribes with amazing vitality and latent richness of color. *Little Pond* is a small landscape, which in its perception of the essential quality of the scene depicted might well be considered in the "American tradition," yet it is enriched by characteristics of design and handling which reveal the inheritance of the painter in an older and more sophisticated art than so young a country as ours can boast.[32]

Throughout his career Kuniyoshi alternately fed and rejected essentialist

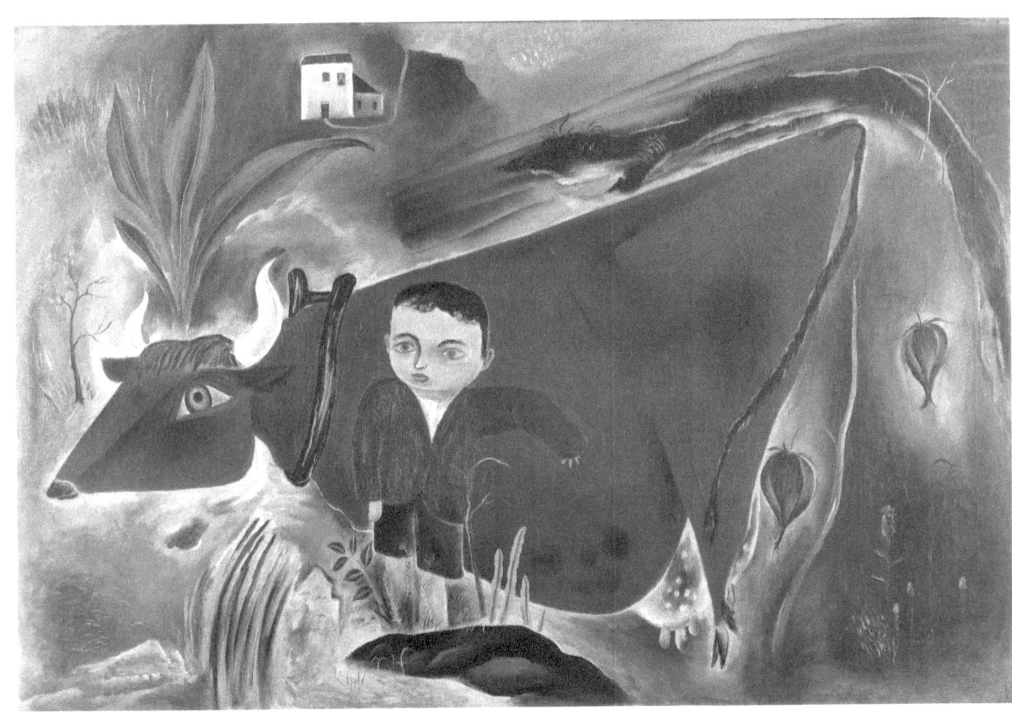

5.8 Yasuo Kuniyoshi, *Little Joe and Cow*, 1924. Oil on canvas, 28 x 42 in. Courtesy Crystal Bridges Museum of American Art, Bentonville, Arkansas

perceptions. In "East to West," his 1940 autobiographical essay for the *Magazine of Art*, he explained that in his early production

> I wasn't trying to be funny but everyone thought I was. I was painting cows and cows at that time because somehow I felt very near to the cow. Besides I thought I understood the animal. You see I was born, judging by the Japanese calendar, in a "cow year." According to legend I believe my fate to be guided, more or less, by the bovine kingdom. Also I was interested in the cow because I thought it decorative as well as ugly and so I painted cows constantly until I was exhausted.[33]

With this assertion he presented himself naively, attempting to convince his audience (and likely himself) that he—foreign-born and youthful—had merely taken a sincere interest in a farm animal as a motif, an interest singularly driven by his heritage.[34] Yet Kuniyoshi's 1920s farm scenes seem designed as parodies, as visual exaggerations that he hoped would bring scrutiny to cultural ones.[35]

Kuniyoshi's curiosity was cross-cultural and typical of modernists' interests—in the United States and internationally—in popular cultural production.[36] In the 1920s Kuniyoshi collected Japanese and colonial American and U.S. folk art, lent these objects to exhibitions of such work, and curated a contemporary exhibition that included the work of Kenneth Hayes Miller, his former teacher, as well as Henri Matisse, Joseph Stella, and the self-taught U.S. painter John Mauro. Traveling to Mexico in the 1930s, he bought and brought back common indigenous toys.[37] Contrary to suggestions—and some of the artist's statements—that he worked atavistically, Kuniyoshi instead was a student of both artistic tradition and craft conventions. Toys, weather vanes, antiques, organic material, and masks were diversifying and decorative objects in his still lifes, figure studies, and landscapes.[38] As art historian Gail Levin has shown, Japanese cultural products—from papier-mâché tigers and kites to folk tales—are central symbols of his childhood in his paintings *Japanese Toy Tiger and Odd Objects* (1932) and *Fish Kite* (1950). Yet, as Levin also points out, the evidence of American folk art in Kuniyoshi's work and the influence of its naïveté in his work of the 1920s are signs of his bond, or desired bond, with the United States.[39]

Landscape was a choice vehicle for proving and presenting such allegiances, for its scenes can be stocked with decorative and meaningful national and cultural symbols. Toward the end of his career, Kuniyoshi recollected landscape's strong appeal for him in the teens and twenties, explaining that the "severe landscape and simple New England buildings were my God. Whenever I did anything, I used to make up that type of scenery somewhere in the picture."[40] That Kuniyoshi spoke about creativity is critical: by his own admission, he "made up" compositional elements, using certain motifs that had captured his attention. An early Kuniyoshi landscape, *Thurnscoe, Maine* (1918; fig. 5.9), is executed in a cautiously modern manner: its summarized forms—a Christian church set in rolling hills—follow postimpressionist trends toward abstraction and descriptive color. *Thurnscoe, Maine* shares a Christian theme with another of Kuniyoshi's paintings, *Crucifixion* (1917). Both demonstrate that the artist was steeped in Western approaches to landscape, not surprising considering he had studied in academic settings and in artists' colonies in Woodstock, New York, and Ogunquit, Maine. In another late career recollection, creativity anchors Kuniyoshi's explanation of his work, even as he differentiated Eastern and Western ways of seeing: "As a student I was taught to see things wide. . . . But then when I was on my own I got the idea to paint things looking down on them. Like Oriental [sic], I didn't paint any sky—the ground slants up with all things on it."[41] Here, Kuniyoshi separates art school training from experimentation in terms resonant with Orientalist views, ones that threaten to obfuscate his inspirations and ideations. Yet the articulated binaries are undermined by the artist's cosmopolitan story. His connections to Asian and Western artistic modes and to the symbiotic relationship among them must be categorized as active ones.[42] He learned the aspects of different practices and the iconographies assigned to

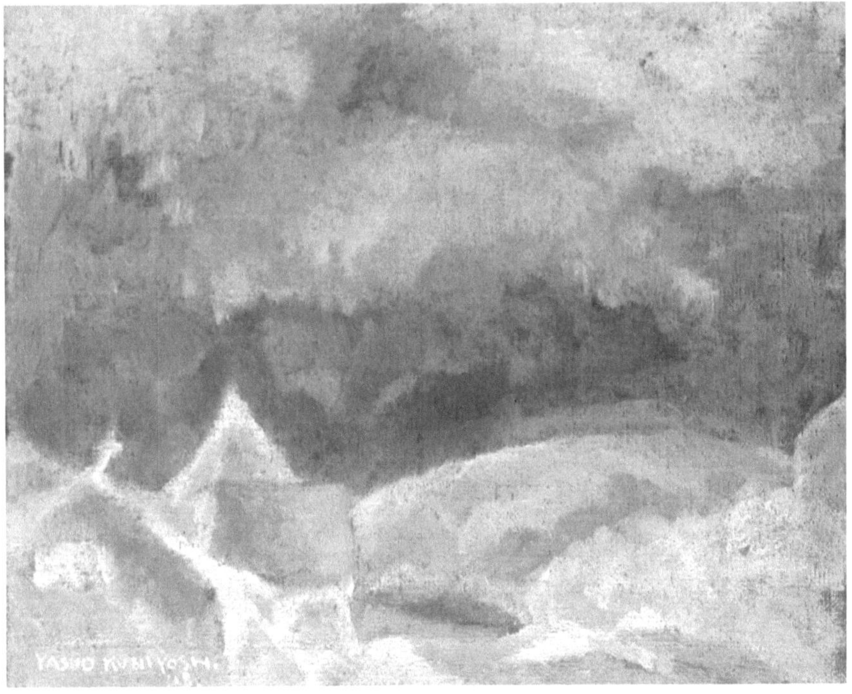

5.9 Yasuo Kuniyoshi, *Thurnscoe, Maine*, 1918. Oil on canvas, mounted on board, 8 1/4 x 10 3/10 in. Courtesy of Owen Gallery, New York, New York

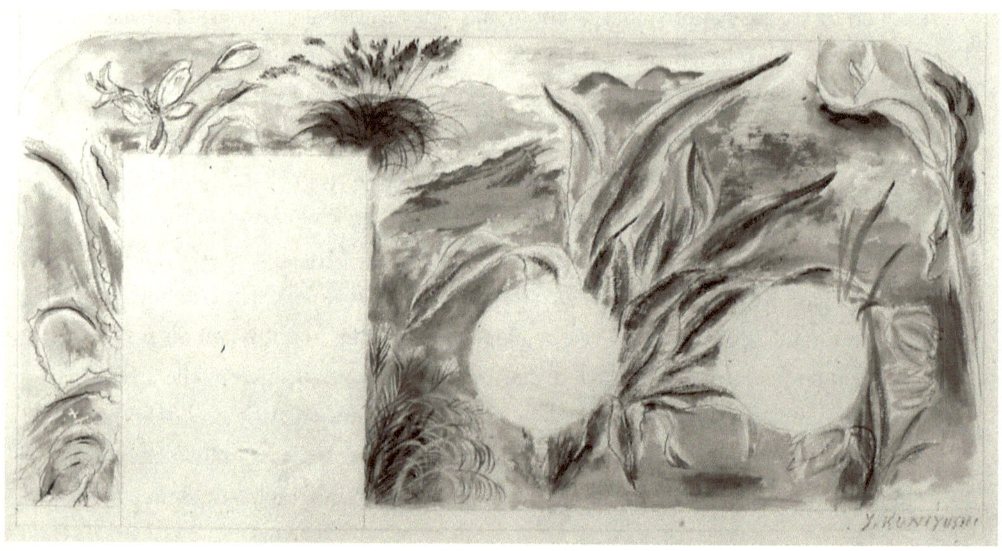

5.10 Yasuo Kuniyoshi, study for Mural for Radio City Music Hall, 1932. Gouache and watercolor on paper, 7 1/2 x 15 in. Courtesy of Owen Gallery, New York, New York

them, and his deployment of them simultaneously advanced and threatened nationalist narratives.[43] In Kuniyoshi's interviews and writings of the World War II years, he stated that he "felt foreign" in Japan during his 1931–32 visit to his birth country.[44] There, his art, which he had described to the Japanese press as "a modified expressionist school—Kuniyoshism"—was "thought to be too European."[45] Kuniyoshi also recollected that he "had a hard time convincing my compatriots that there was such a thing as American art."[46] Certainly, these statements were made in an era of heightened American nativism, nationalism, and xenophobia, which limited and ultimately denied Japanese immigrants and Japanese American citizens their rightful liberties; Kuniyoshi had reason to avoid associations with the enemy government and to emphasize his American identification.[47] Even if self-serving, his characterizations of himself and his work index his agency as he sought control of his public image.

Kuniyoshi stocked his landscapes with legible emblems of nature. The stylized flora and fauna included in his 1920s productions reappear in later paintings, drawings, and prints: the flatly painted staffage inspired by colonial

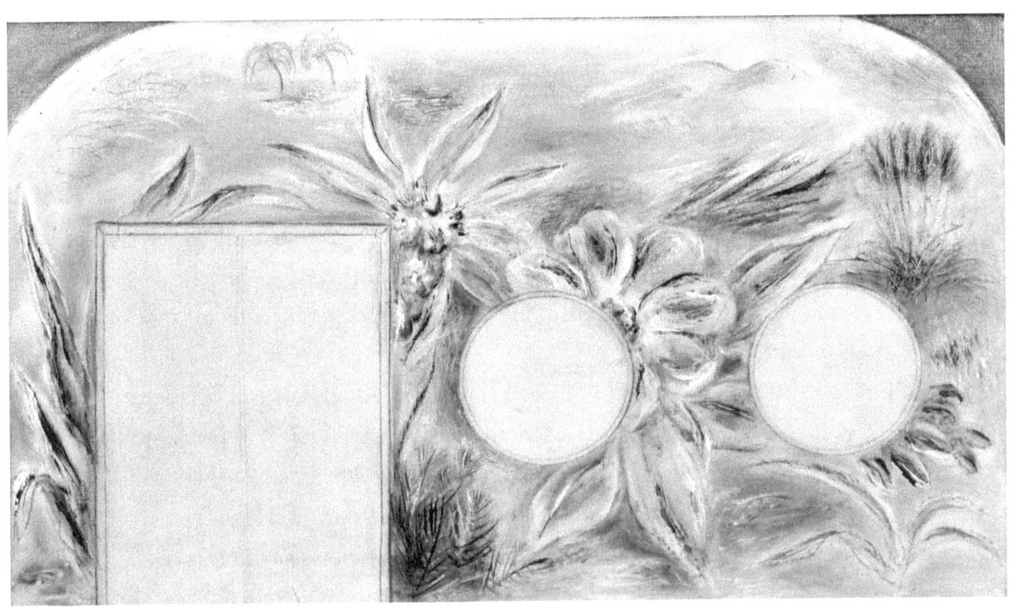

5.11 Yasuo Kuniyoshi, study for Mural for Radio City Music Hall, 1932. Gouache and watercolor on paper, 7 1/2 x 15 in. Courtesy of Owen Gallery, New York, New York

American and folk art motifs is transformed in the late 1920s and in the 1930s. Bounding horses, anthropomorphic cattle, and leafy plants—no longer icons of primitivist modernism—are incorporated into his expressionist tableaus as whimsical traces. A cow painted into his 1932 mural for Radio City Music Hall is a representative example. Like earlier renderings of such beasts, this one is geometric and resembles a simple parallelogram. It is small in scale, however, and overwhelmed by the leafless tree and a bending calla lily that buttress it. Overall, the mural's natural forms and the studies for them (figs. 5.10 and 5.11) retain their diffuse, symbolic power, and the project won Kuniyoshi new admirers.[48] The *New Yorker*'s critic Lewis Mumford praised "huge flowers in the women's powder-room," adding

> they are not merely very charming, but they make the room. Though his palette is not so somber as usual and therefore in a sense not so positively his own; his walls, which curve to meet the ceiling, do not attempt to recede: the motif is "ladies-powdering-their faces-among-Kuniyoshi's-lush-and-charming-and-possi-

> bly-symbolic-flowers." . . . it is, from my point of view, a sounder theory of modern mural painting. One school emphasizes the wall, the other the painting.[49]

The transgressive exaggeration of Kuniyoshi's early works, as dismayed observers considered them, have been forgotten. That this writer noted a difference between the primary color scheme of Kuniyoshi's paintings and the mural's delicate tints seems to signal approval for stylistic adjustments made to achieve the goals of mural decoration.

Just as Kuniyoshi recycled his chosen symbols of American and Japanese culture across his oeuvre, he also imported the signature subject of his genre portraits—monumental, fleshy and racially indeterminate females—into his landscapes. In *Between Two Worlds* (1939; fig. 5.12, plate 12), a trio of typical Kuniyoshi women strolls along a dirt path, a good distance away from a red-brick building atop a rise. Their presence and appearances are inexplicable in this setting: while their shorts and bralike tops are appropriate for warm-weather leisure activities, their environment is cheerless, and the edifice bespeaks the institutional character of a factory or prison. As Kuniyoshi had articulated his interest in painting cows, babies, women, and New England scenery, he also

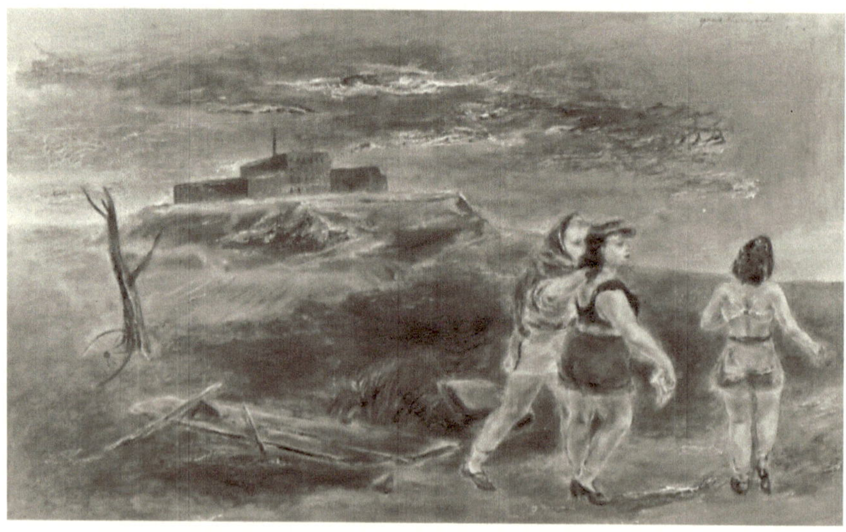

5.12 Yasuo Kuniyoshi, *Between Two Worlds*, 1939 (plate 12). Private collection

wrote of his attraction to open, desolate places. In his notes for a planned autobiography, he explained in 1944,

> Ever since I have had [sic] a trip to Southwest in 1935 and 1941 to New Mexico, Arizona, Colorado, Nevada, Utah, that something vastness and primitiveness which is different from Maine ruggedness, I thought it is more of a beginning of creation of earth. . . .
>
> I like these ghost towns, deserted places. Building [sic] still standing of 1870s. Their bigness of sky and earth react so much different than Eastern states. Sunrise and sunset is beyond human imagination.[50]

These scenes were different from Woodstock's pastoral views, which Kuniyoshi considered "magnificent" but "too beautiful to paint"; in contrast, he found the West as pictorial material "primitive" and the source for "real American painting," an ideal that had yet to be realized by him.[51] In chapter 4, I described Kuniyoshi's ambition of combining "reality and imagination" in his female genre portraits. Land, no less than the female form, was a familiar entity that Kuniyoshi wanted to defamiliarize while working within the confines of an accepted genre. If the women in *Between Two Words* are in liminal space, it is notable that Kuniyoshi makes the space an expansive one, in which figures and ground are passages displayed across the large canvas. Browned and grayed skin matches the dusty plateau's hues; thickened brushstrokes decorate the skies and roadway in the same way that attention-gathering cosmetics and headgear distinguish the thickened bodies. The women are matched symbols of Kuniyoshi—one wears a brimmed hat like those included in *Daily News, Relaxation* (1942) and on the artist in *At Work*—just as they are signs of his consistent interest in allusively rendering types and milieus only to place them outside the conventions of beauty and the picturesque.

The emptiness of the interiors in Kuniyoshi's figure studies of women in the 1930s parallels the vacuous spaces rendered in his landscapes of that decade and of the remaining years of his career. Responses to his landscapes were mixed, and yet critics ventured sincere readings of the imagery and style. In a 1936 review, a writer for the *American Magazine of Art* welcomed the "dynamic note" of two small, unspecified outdoor scenes that are distinguished for the

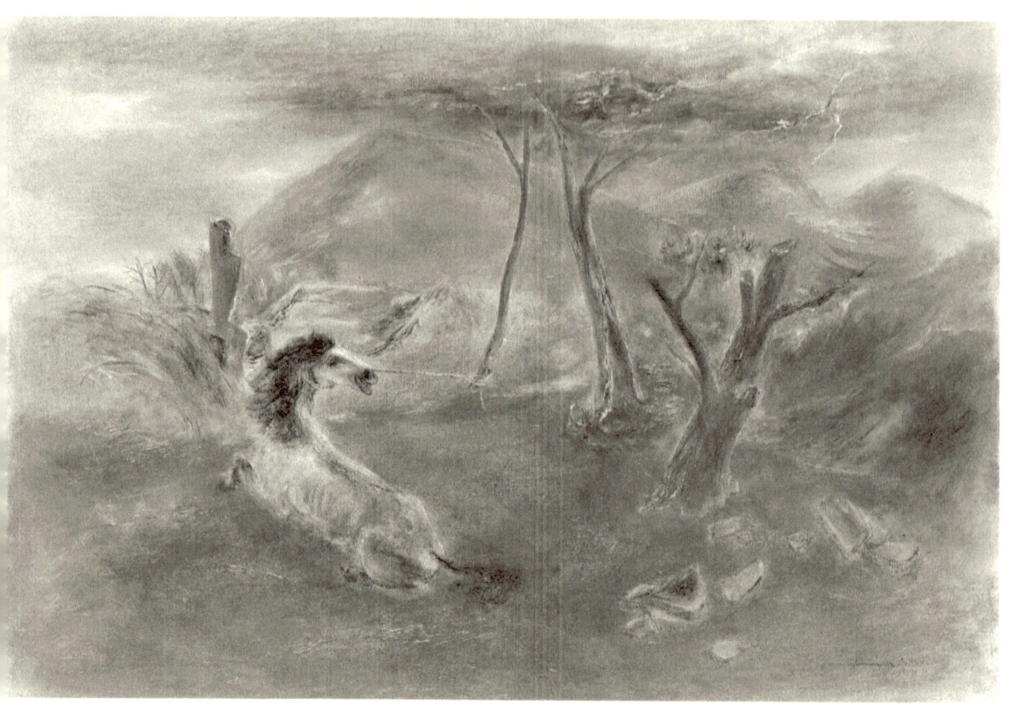

5.13 Yasuo Kuniyoshi, *Summer Storm*, 1938. Oil on canvas, 25 9/10 x 38 1/4 in. Gift of Dr. and Mrs. George Kamperman. Photograph © 1989 The Detroit Institute of Arts, Michigan

"active feeling of distance and landscape" that the artist has instilled in them.[52] A. D. Emmart cited, with reservations, "the real impact" of Kuniyoshi's work in Six Living American Artists, a Baltimore Museum of Art exhibition of 1939. Emmart, who preferred the artist's figure paintings and still lifes, nonetheless was intrigued by "the themes he develops with such graceful violence in his landscapes." Without naming the two landscapes on display, the painterly *Summer Storm* (1938; fig. 5.13) and *Stormy Weather* (circa 1938), Emmart judged Kuniyoshi to be the best artist in the exhibition, and yet one who "moves in a rather small orbit of romantic vision and technique and finds no way out."[53] Kuniyoshi's touch in these paintings is indeed painterly, and his interest was in representing deserted terrain, powerful animals, and nature's forces. Such content was not new to landscape painting in general, or to 1930s interpretations

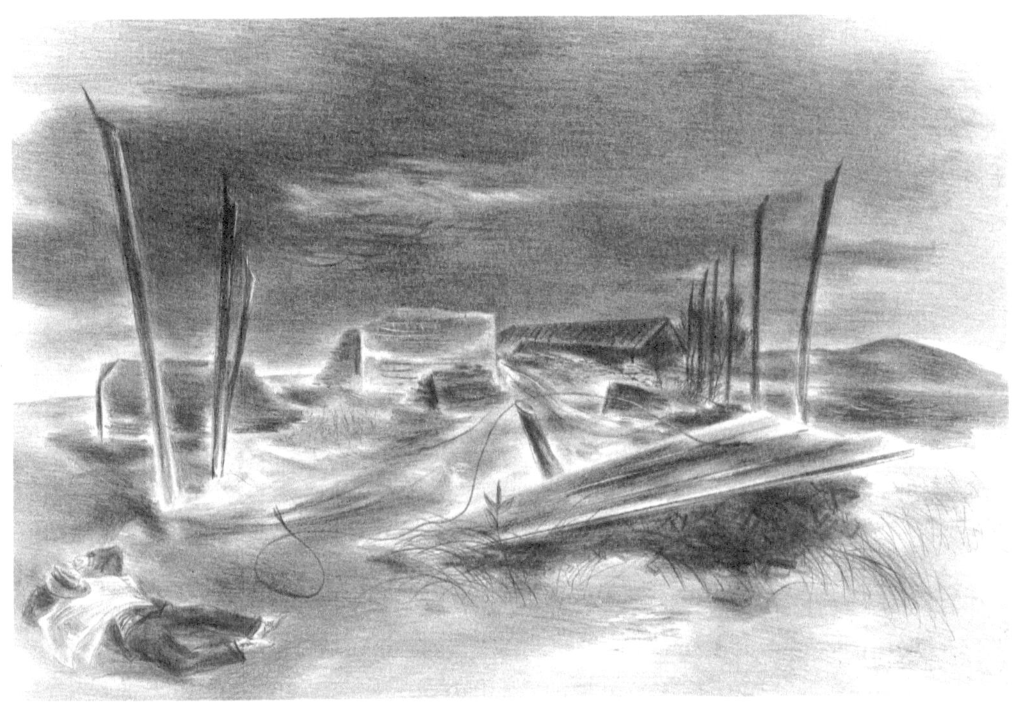

5.14 Yasuo Kuniyoshi, *Deserted Brickyard*, 1939. Lithograph on paper, sheet: 15 3/8 x 19 1/16 in., image: 10 5/8 x 15 5/8 in. Hirshhorn Museum and Sculpture Garden, Smithsonian Institution, gift of Joseph H. Hirshhorn, 1966. Photograph by Lee Stalworth

of the nation's open land in particular. But in Kuniyoshi's case, the anonymity of the pictured geography and its moody silences are in dialogue with his landscape photography of 1935–1941.

As Kuniyoshi scholar Tom Wolf has argued, Kuniyoshi made hundreds of "social" photographs until the time of the Pearl Harbor attack of 1941, when the U.S. government classified him as an enemy alien, confiscated his camera, and curtailed his movements and liberties.[54] Wolf's characterization covers the artist's black-and-white photos of his wife, Sara Mazo; friends at his Woodstock, New York, home; models captured in the nude; Coney Island beachgoers; and bustling city scenes. Amid this production are also outdoor photos of inanimate objects that refer to a human presence: abandoned barns, rusting farm machinery, a ruined chair, and a carousel horse installed like a piece of outdoor sculpture. Kuniyoshi's attention to their rugged textures, sinuous contours, and strong lines is the hallmark of realist photography, and their manner contrasts with the hazy rendering of these forms when they are imported into landscapes such as *Between Two Words* and *Deserted Brickyard* (1938; fig. 5.14). Kuniyoshi barred the crisp austerity of his photographs from his paintings, which he considered the sites for interpreting his emotion. Negotiating the cultural politics attached to his racialized body in wartime and his resulting feelings of isolation, depression, and alienation, Kuniyoshi wrote in 1944 that he found it difficult to focus on one painting at a time: working on six and seven canvases over several months, he often changed aspects of his paintings: "I may have to change the whole thing, because I depend on emotional creation. In other words, I have to feel everything instead of just looking at it. But I have found that even though I may have to change parts I gradually get back inside of this painting, and feel as I did when I started in months before."[55]

Kuniyoshi's stated desire was to develop representation based on reality and imagination. With his movements limited and his anxieties high in the 1940s, his landscapes must have depended more than ever before on his imagination, memories, sketches, and widely circulating symbols and visual conventions. Still lifes produced in this period better convey the impossibility of his subject position, for they are densely packed with pregnant symbols massed at the front of the picture plane. While his landscapes also include the motifs he favored, their pictorial significance and weight is dispersed, diffused, and absorbed into the expansive American imaginary.

SIX

CONCLUSION

"Racial art" is a term of the past, an old and limiting way of categorizing and conceptualizing figural images made by minority artists in the United States. No one uses the phrase anymore, and the majority of histories written about Malvin Gray Johnson, Yasuo Kuniyoshi, and Max Weber do not report on their era's racial art rhetoric, even though it was generated and sustained by these artists and their audiences. Grounded in essentialism, primitivism, and nationalism, racial art was a troubling chapter of early American modernism, and in this book I have tried to document and examine this significant historical discourse.

What retired the term "racial art"? One factor was that some gave up on the possibility of defining it. Russian-born Jewish American artist and writer Louis Lozowick (1892–1973) had long struggled with the concept in his work and in that of his coreligionists. Because he pursued a variety of approaches—cubism, constructivism, and realism—Lozowick neither expected a single Jewish art nor prescribed one. In 1924 he asserted, "There can be no Jewish art, unless there be a social need for it. Men like Max Weber who often mould their art out of Jewish material, because their soul is bound up in Jewish memories and interest, will remain exceptional."[1] With this statement Lozowick positioned "Jewish art" as a response to anti-Semitism and oppression against Jews and simultaneously contrasted it with artistic freedom. More than two decades later, reviewing Franz Landsberger's *A History of Jewish Art* in 1947, Lozowick questions this author's presumption of a distinct ethnoracial practice but happily praises the book's "admonition to Jewish artists to be true to themselves."[2]

An interest in racial art brought Johnson, Kuniyoshi, and Weber varying amounts of notoriety in the 1920s and 1930s, and yet these artists' conflicted comments about being set apart from their Anglo-American peers communicate unmistakable ambivalence. The ethnoracial and religious divide of racial art piqued Johnson—born in the United States and a proud World War I veteran—and the patriotic immigrants Kuniyoshi and Weber: all three embraced American national identity in word and deed. At the same time, they viewed creative challenges in terms of universals, for, like many in their generation who had lived through one or both world wars of the twentieth century, they believed that art could be a persuasive and unifying global language. As did Johnson, Kuniyoshi, and Weber, other artists and some art writers positioned universal expression as a worthy goal. African American painter Winifred Russell, quoted in the 1930 article "Art Not Racial, Negroes Tell Critic," rehearsed a series of questions and provided answers: "Can the Negro artist be immune to the dynamic influences of education and environment? No. Should he restrict himself in style and subject? No. Should the Negro become universal in conception, motive, manner, and appreciation? Yes."[3] The white American critic Edward Alden Jewell, in his 1939 book *Have We An American Art?*, rejected superficial formulas for nationalist art and, instead, promoted universalism, writing, "Wherever produced, all art should be, and all art must be, universal."[4] Today, we see the problematic, double-edged nature of universalism as put forth in Enlightenment writings: the promise of equality accorded to all humans sits side by side with the reinscription of Eurocentrism and its hierarchies.[5] But, in the post–World War II era, universalism impressed many as the way out of racism—a term first used to describe Nazi policy in the 1930s. Ethnic prejudice and oppression were increasingly dismissed in progressive, intellectual, scientific, and artistic circles as illogical and unreasonable.[6]

By the 1940s "universal expression" was an avant-garde buzz phrase preferred by many modernists who were moving away from identifications organized singly around racial, ethnic, national, and religious particularities. In African American artist Charles White's collage *Speakers Link Anti-Semitism, Anti-Negroidism . . .* of 1944, the medium rightly serves this artist's ambition to image the impetus for social justice and civil rights coalitions. Newspaper clippings pasted onto the picture board's surface connect oppressions and oppressed peoples, namely, the "Negroes," Jews, and workers divided by Nazis, all listed in boldface headlines. This text works like wallpaper set behind a single, foreground figure—pensive, variably shaded, androgynous, and prismatically rendered—embodying the challenge of making effective alliances, for it is resolutely inert. In this picture of different elements brought together, the left-leaning White (1918–1979) strategically confronts the hypostasis of single-issue identity politics and offers logic for cross-cultural alliances. The efforts of White and others to think universally was coincident with the aim of antiracist intellectual scholarly publications in the 1930s and 1940s to revise racial definitions that served scientific racism. Summarizing this turn, Matthew Frye Jacobson observed, "Strictly biological understandings of race as the key to the diversity of humanity gave way to cultural and environmental explanations."[7] On the subject of the human races, liberal writers outraged by eugenic pseudoscience and its influence on national policy and public consciousness argued that there were three: Caucasian, Mongoloid, and Negroid. Notably, in a 1943 pamphlet anthropologist Ruth Benedict emphatically asserted that "Aryans, Jews, Italians are *not* races," a pronouncement doubtlessly meant to undermine fascist ideations of race and their accompanying racism.[8] While this categorical shift placed national origins and ethnicity outside the lexicon of race, it also did little to generate questions about race in general, much less its historical hierarchies and sociocultural constructions, including its most prominent one, "Caucasian."

Writing a catalogue essay for the 1945 exhibition The Negro Artist Comes of Age, Alain Locke might have been thinking of White's ambitious agenda when he wrote, "Today the Negro artist is in the first instance an artist and only incidentally a Negro."[9] Similarly, the prominent African American artists Richmond Barthé (1901–1989), Romare Bearden (1911–1988), and Hale Woodruff (1900–1980) advised International Business Machines (IBM) to discontinue its annual exhibition Contemporary Art of the American Negro because, in Woodruff's words, it "hindered the acceptance of Negro art on a purely artistic basis."[10] Certainly, African American integration into the larger American artistic community was the primary goal of these artists and their supporters. In addition, by summoning a lofty standard of aesthetic purity (an ideal related to the pursuit of "art for art's sake"), Woodruff, Bearden, and Barthé signaled their investment in making art legible to and appreciable by many. Indeed, they situated black subjects and cultural themes in "the universal" that they hoped would interest a broad, popular audience.

African American artists' push for integration and assimilation into the dominant U.S. art market paralleled the moves of their Jewish American contemporaries in the New York School, which, famously advocated for art that was universal in its aesthetic appeal and phenomenological affect. Even as prominent Jewish American artists such as Barnett Newman (1905–1970) and Ben Shahn brought both nonobjective and figuratively representational strategies to bear on symbolically Jewish subjects, many American Jews, recent scholars have suggested, sought haven in secular positions in the aftermath of the Nazi holocaust and in the postwar climate of red baiting.[11] Kuniyoshi was also considered an artist who successfully produced symbols meant to be read as universal. In December 1948 *Look* magazine published the flattering layout "Kuniyoshi: One of America's Most Honored Artists Fuses East and West," and in the brief text accompanying the article, the unnamed journalist surmised that, for Kuniyoshi, "art is as universal as humanity; there are no arbitrary divisions."[12] Framed in terms of transcendence, Kuniyoshi's, Newman's, and Shahn's paintings moved beyond the conceptually narrow limitations of racial art while the work of other minority modernists with similar aspirations, such as Charles White and the gay, Philippines-born abstractionist Alfonso Ossorio (1916–1990), did not.[13]

Kuniyoshi and Weber anchored many modern and contemporary American art exhibitions of the 1940s and 1950s. In contrast to Johnson's production, which was posthumously circulated in all-black exhibitions and firmly tied to the Harlem Renaissance and the "Negro experience," Kuniyoshi's and Weber's art was occasionally uncoupled from racial affiliation in these decades. Thirteen Weber works—oil paintings, pen-and-ink drawings, and small sculptures that did not reference Jewish ceremony in their titles or imagery—were featured in the Whitney Museum's Pioneers of Modern Art in America exhibition of 1946. Separately, Kuniyoshi's 1950 painting *Fish Kite* was the third-prize winner in American Painting Today: 1950 at the Metropolitan Museum of Art, two years after he had been the subject of a Whitney retrospective exhibition. Yet the partial abandonment of racial art rhetoric in exhibition circles did not mean the end of presenting nonwhite artists as subjects apart in an emergent, sociologically influenced documentation of cultural production. Along with Landenberger's previously mentioned *History of Jewish Art*, the 1940s saw the publication of *100 Contemporary American Jewish Painters and Sculptors*, which included an overview essay by Louis Lozowick and artist statements presented in English and Hebrew.[14]

Although immigrant artists to the United States such as Kuniyoshi, Weber, and Shahn had earned the New York art establishment's respect by the 1940s, they were not accepted in all quarters, a fact made clear by reaction to their participation in the Advancing American Art project. A collection of seventy-nine oil paintings and seventy-three watercolors assembled by the U.S. State Department, Advancing American Art was exhibited in Paris, Prague, Port-au-Prince, and Havana in 1946–47. The selection of contemporary art produced in the United States was praised in those locales and was slated to travel elsewhere, but conservative press hostility to the representative artists and to modernist modes scuttled this diplomatic initiative. "Your Money Bought These Paintings" was the headline for a February 1947 *Look* magazine spread that included the reproductions of figurally abstract paintings by Kuniyoshi, Shahn, Robert Gwathmey (1903–1988), Louis Gugliemi (1906–1956), Gregorio Prestopino (1907–1984), Nahum Tschacbasov (1899–1984), and Karl Zerbe (1903–1972).[15] The article's text communicated utter skepticism about the quality and legibility of modernism, and other journalists went further by linking the art and the artists to anti-American and communist causes during the first half of 1947.[16] Stoked by such philistinism, the public and politicians responded with sarcasm and xenophobia. A letter writer complained to U.S. representative George Bates (D-Michigan) in 1947: "The names of the artists—Shahn, Zerbe, Prestopino,

Kuniyoshi, Gugliemi—do not seem to have the flavor of an American background but bring visions of a transplanted European hodgepodge at its worst."[17] Kuniyoshi's *Circus Girl Resting* (not dated) was a target of pointed abuse. As are many of the artist's female types of the 1920s, this subject was large and imposing, prompting one journalist to remark that this "typical American girl is better equipped to move a piano than to play one."[18] President Harry S. Truman's one-liner was equally dismissive: "If that's art, I'm a Hottentot."[19] Liberal artists and their supporters—painter Peppino Mangravite (1918–1992) and the critics Peyton Boswell, Ralph M. Pearson, and others—defended U.S. modernism and the right to freedom of expression in the press. Although Advancing American Art was recalled from exhibition halls in Prague and Port-au-Prince in June 1947 and its objects publicly auctioned in May 1948, a measure of amelioration was evident in a *Look* article of February 1948: "Are These Men the Best Painters in America Today?"[20] The question was asked of American curators and critics, and these experts produced a short list of artists deemed worthy of this honor, among them Kuniyoshi, Weber, Shahn, Stuart Davis, Philip Evergood (1901–1973), George Grosz (1893–1959), and John Marin.[21]

Still, essentializing Orientalist attitudes and xenophobia dogged U.S.-based artists of Asian descent in the post–World War II decades. Some, like Japanese American painter Henry Sugimoto (1900–1990), faced racist discrimination rooted in the belief that they were enemies "within."[22] Invited to teach at the Brooklyn Museum of Art's school in 1949, Japan-born painter (Léonard Tsugouharu) Foujita was also denounced as an unrepentant "fascist artist" in the same year by American artists who picketed his exhibition at the Mathias Komor Gallery in Manhattan.[23] For certain, some Asian American artists enjoyed measures of success. In the 1940s abstract painter Reuben Tam (1916–1991) began his association with the progressive Downtown Gallery in New York, where he exhibited with Kuniyoshi, Jacob Lawrence, Georgia O'Keeffe, and Ben Shahn. Tam also won a Guggenheim Foundation fellowship in 1948.[24] In 1947 the Japanese American Artists Group mounted a group exhibition at the Riverside Museum, a Manhattan venue that mounted contemporary art shows and collected historical Asian art. And, like Kuniyoshi, the New York–based artists Gyo Fujikawa (1908–1998) and Dong Kingman (1911–2000) were discussed in the national press in the 1940s and 1950s. In 1945 a *Time* magazine feature published soon after the opening of Kingman's solo exhibition at the M. H. de Young Memorial Museum in San Francisco offers two countervailing notes: the first is that "Dong is, and counts himself, All-American," and the second that "critics who look for Oriental innuendoes in Dong's bright colors and brash brushwork can trace his work back to China's 1,400-year-old tradition of sacrificing detail to get the 'rhythmic vitality' of a scene."[25] Fujikawa, a successful Japanese American illustrator, watercolorist, and children's book author who was detained during World War II years at the Rohwer Relocation Center in Arkansas, was favorably profiled in a three-page article in *American Artist* in 1954.[26] But even in the 1960s, the decade during which the umbrella term "Asian American" was coined to displace "Oriental," Kuniyoshi's life and career "inspired" a racist caricature in popular culture.[27] The 1961 movie *Breakfast at Tiffany's* featured the absurd character of I. Y. Yunioshi, a bespectacled, bumbling photographer played by white American actor Mickey Rooney, who, in broken English, repeatedly invited the story's heroine, Holly Golightly, to pose for him.[28]

Although the particularist, xenophobic language of the 1940s and 1950s is absent from our present art histories and criticism, multicultural politics and policies of the 1980s has produced a "racial art"–like space for difference that is both celebratory and delimiting. While we hail diversity as a positive and desired outcome, we ask all too few questions about the composition of "difference," or of sameness. As criticized by art historian James Meyer, the identity discourse that emerged in the 1980s confined "the subject to an essential identity or stereotype . . . [and leaves] traditional relations in tact." Rather than off-handedly cite an artist's engagement with race, class, gender, and sexuality, Meyer suggests that we acknowledge the construction of identities. Art historians, critics, and curators should examine the functional forms and operations of the artist's institutional critique: "We need to describe how these practices function, the readings they produce, how they situate themselves discursively and materially."[29] Meyer's terms—"function," "operation," "situate"—compel us to consider creative force and action, which matter not only in art but also in everyday acts of identification and identifying that we, as human beings, will never abandon.[30]

NOTES

CHAPTER 1. INTRODUCTION

1 Ralph M. Pearson, *The Modern Renaissance in American Art: Presenting the Work and Philosophy of 54 Distinguished Artists* (New York: Harper and Brothers, 1954), 40.

2 Alexander Calder, Stuart Davis, Edward Hopper, and Kuniyoshi represented the United States in 1952.

3 Writing about the need to examine ethnonational and cultural identifications with the same intensity as has been brought to the study of race, Alastair Bonnett has stated, "However reified their usage, constructs of the Chinese, the Jews, the Irish and so on are nearly offered as terms, as experiences, that must be 'respected.' Yet there is no more reason to respect the lie that such groups are natural formations with immutable attributes and clear boundaries, than there is to respect the fantasy of race. The engagement of antiracism with ethnicity contains the potential to extend and deepen the critique of the naturalization of

group difference into new and diverse areas." Bonnett, *Anti-Racism* (New York: Routledge, 2000), 171.

4 See David Bindman, *From Ape to Apollo: Aesthetics and the Idea of Race in the 18th Century*. (Ithaca, NY: Cornell University Press, 2002). In Johann Friedrich Blumenbach's eighteenth-century system of races, there were five races: Caucasian, Mongolian, Malayan, Negroid, and [Native] American. In this taxonomy, "Caucasian" referred to the Biblical narrative (for it was the place where Noah's Ark was said to have foundered) and described superior Indo-European peoples whose native lands stretched from Europe to the Middle East and the Asian subcontinent.

5 Zhou, "Are Asian Americans Becoming White?" in *Contemporary Asian America: A Multidisciplinary Reader*, 2d ed., ed. Min Zhou and J. V. Gatewood (New York: New York University Press, 2007), 354.

6 Kim, "Are Asians Black? The Asian American Civil Rights Agenda and the Contemporary Significance of the Black/White Paradigm," in *Contemporary Asian America* (see note 5), 337.

7 Matthew Frye Jacobson has criticized contemporary Jewish American scholars Michael Novak and Michael Lerner, who "disavow any participation in twentieth-century white privilege on the spurious basis of their parents' and grandparents' racial oppression." Jacobson, *Whiteness of a Different Color: European Immigrants and the Alchemy of Race* (Cambridge, MA: Harvard University Press, 1998), 7. Jacobson has surmised, "This disavowal of Whiteness has become pronounced in recent years, particularly around the question of affirmative action. The notion that Jews, Letts, Finns, Greeks, Italians, Slovaks, Poles, or Russians are not *really* white has become suddenly appealing in a setting where whiteness has wrongly become associated with unfair disadvantage." Jacobson, *Whiteness of a Different Color*, 280.

8 I take the term "auto-racialization" from Americanist historian David A. Gerber, who uses it in "Review: Caucasians Are Made and Not Born: How European Immigrants Became White People," *Reviews in American History* 27, no. 3 (September 1999): 440.

9 Norman L. Kleeblatt, "'Passing' into Multiculturalism," in *"Too Jewish"? Challenging Traditional Identities*, ed. Kleeblatt (New York: Jewish Museum; New Brunswick, NJ: Rutgers University Press, 1996), 3–38.

10 Specific to Jewish self-identification, Matthew Baigell has argued, in the early twentieth century, that some Jews living in the United States did not find racial

designation "threatening." Baigell contends, "Some even drew comfort from it considering the term, 'the Jewish race,' a mark of self-definition because it provided a sense of stability at a time when Jewish traditions and measures of identity were disappearing. It connoted a degree of communal awareness in a fluctuating, heterogeneous social situation." Baigell, *Jewish Art in America: An Introduction* (Lanham, MD: Rowman & Littlefield, 2007), 28.

11 Joy Weber, the artist's daughter and executor of his estate, rejected the request to reproduce his work in this book, writing that "to suggest 'race' as a basis for a book on artists and creativity is insulting to say the least and to include my Father—Max Weber—is totally unacceptable. My Father was a White Caucasian: his Religion was Judaism! The point of view to which the book seems to espouse is that of the Nazis who perpetuated such lies as perverted reasoning to give them the right to kill 6 million innocents guilty of only being of the Jewish faith! I thought such ideas were a thing of the past." Joy Weber to Kathy Zarur [research assistant to Jacqueline Francis], 11 February 2008.

12 "In the Galleries: The Museum of Modern Art," *The Arts* 16, no. 8 (April 1930): 568.

13 Phillips, "Max Weber," in *A Collection in the Making: A Survey of the Problems Involved in Collecting Pictures Together with Brief Estimates of the Painters in the Phillips Memorial Gallery* (New York: E. Weyhe; Washington, DC: Phillips Memorial Gallery, 1926), 62.

14 Two representative publications of the 1940s situate Weber within privileging discussions of American art and international modernism. See Milton W. Brown, "Max Weber, 'Jewish Artist': The Painting of This Pioneer of Modern Art and Its Supposed 'Jewish' Nature," *The Jewish Survey* 1 (May 1941): 18–19; and Max Osborn, "An American Jewish Artist," *Congress Weekly*, 19 May 1944, 9–10, in Max Weber Papers (hereafter cited as Weber Papers), Smithsonian Archives of American Art, Washington, D.C., roll NY 59-6, frame 593. Brown's rhetorical gesture indexes modernist claims to universalism and internationalism, Osborn's the promotion of a U.S. nationalism that recognized its hyphenated American citizens.

15 For representative examples, see a review of a Maurel Gallery (New York) exhibition of work by Tetsuzan Hori (ca. 1885– ?), "Japan's Way," *Art Digest* 6, no. 4 (15 November 1931): 2, 19; "Exhibitions in New York: Yun Gee, Elliot Orr (Balzac Galleries)," *Art News* 30, no. 33 (May 1932): 12; and Louis Lozowick, "Jewish Artists of the Season," *Menorah Journal* 10, no. 3 (June–July 1924): 282–84.

16 See, for instance, Paul Rosenfeld's assertion that Arthur Dove is the "man in the painting, precisely as Georgia O'Keeffe is the female." Rosenfeld, *Port of New York: Essays on Fourteen American Moderns* (New York: Harcourt, Brace, and Co., 1924; reprint, with introduction by Sherman Paul, Urbana: University of Illinois Press, 1961), 170.

17 In an undated, but likely contemporary review of Edwin Alden Jewell's book-length essay, *Americans* (New York: Alfred A. Knopf, 1930), an unnamed critic writes, "Perhaps as good a sign as any that there is such a thing as 'American art' is the increasing number of books which are being written about it. . . . our critics are gradually becoming more articulate, if as yet, somewhat timid and unconvincing." "The Riddle of What Is American Art," in Weber Papers, roll NY 59-6, frame 435.

18 Rosenberg, "Is There a Jewish Art?" *Commentary* 42, no. 1 (July 1966): 57–60. Among the notable publications of the last decade are Norman L. Kleeblatt, ed., *"Too Jewish"?: Challenging Traditional Ideas*; Matthew Baigell and Milly Heyd, eds., *Complex Identities: Jewish Consciousness and Modern Art* (New Brunswick, NJ: Rutgers University Press, 2001); Baigell, *Jewish Art in America*; Susan Chevlowe, *The Jewish Identity Project: New American Photography* (New York : Jewish Museum; New Haven: Yale University Press, 2005); Stacy Boris, *The New Authentics: Artists of the Post-Jewish Generation* (Chicago: Spertus Press, 2007).

19 *Afri-Cobra III* [exhibition, 7 to 30 September 1973] (Amherst: University of Massachusetts, 1973); Powell, *Black Art and Culture in the Twentieth Century* (New York: Thames and Hudson, 1997).

20 DeSouza, "Name Calling," in *Tradeshow: New Currents in Recent Asian American Art* (Shanghai: c2 Gallery at the Pottery Workshop, 2003), 2.

21 Machida, *Unsettled Visions: Contemporary Asian American Artists and the Social Imaginary* (Durham, NC: Duke University Press, 2008), 289n13.

22 Rogers Brubaker and Frederick Cooper discuss the cul-de-sac of multicultural discourse in "Beyond 'Identity,'" *Theory and Society* 29, no. 1 (February 2000): 1–47.

23 Ozawa, *Kuniyoshi Yasuo: Hyoden* (Tokyo: Shinchosa, 1974). I am grateful to Yasuo Watanabe for his translations of Ozawa's *Hyoden Kuniyoshi Yasuo: Genmu to Saikan* (Tokyo: Fukutake Shoten, 1991) and *Hisho to Kaiki: Kuniyoshi Yasuo no Seiyo to Toyo* (Okayama-Shi: Nihon Bukyo Shippan, Heisei 8 [1996]).

24 Goodrich, *Yasuo Kuniyoshi* (New York: Macmillan and Whitney Museum of American Art, 1948); Goodrich, *Yasuo Kuniyoshi* (New York: Whitney Museum of American Art at Philip Morris, 1986).

25 *Yasuo Kuniyoshi: 100th Anniversary of His Birth* (Kyoto: National Museum of Modern Art, 1989).

26 Wolf, *Yasuo Kuniyoshi's Women* (San Francisco: Pomegranate, 1993); Amon Carter Museum, *The Shores of a Dream: Yasuo Kuniyoshi's Early Work in America* (Fort Worth, TX: Amon Carter Museum, 1996).

27 North, *Max Weber: American Modern* (New York: Jewish Museum, 1982); and Susan Krane and Percy North, *Max Weber: The Cubist Decade, 1910–1920* (Atlanta: High Museum of Art, 1991). North also authored an essay for a 1996 Forum Gallery exhibition publication, *Max Weber's Women* (New York: Forum Gallery, 1996).

28 Rubinstein, *Max Weber: A Catalogue Raisonné of His Graphic Work* (Chicago: University of Chicago Press, 1980).

29 Goodrich, *Max Weber: Retrospective Exhibition* (New York: Macmillan; New York: Whitney Museum of American Art, 1949); Story, *First Comprehensive Retrospective in the West of Oils, Gouaches, Pastels, Drawings, and Graphic Works by Max Weber, 1881–1961* (Santa Barbara: Art Galleries, University of California at Santa Barbara, 1968); Werner, *Max Weber* (New York: Harry N. Abrams, 1975).

30 Jacqueline Francis, "Modern Art, 'Racial Art': The Work of Malvin Gray Johnson and the Challenges of Painting, 1928–1934" (PhD diss., Emory University, 2000).

31 Francis, "'Trying to Do What Artists of All Races Do': Malvin Gray Johnson's Modernism," in *Climbing Up the Mountain* (Durham: North Carolina Central University Art Museum, 2002), 52–84.

32 Francis, "Making History: Malvin Gray Johnson and Earle W. Richardson's Studies for Negro Achievement," in *The Social and the Real: Political Art of the 1930s in the Western Hemisphere*, ed. Diana Linden, Jonathan Weinberg, and Alejandro Anreus (State College: Pennsylvania State University Press, 2005), 116–31, 302–13; Francis, "Painting the South with a Northern Eye," *Mississippi Quarterly* 56, no. 4 (Winter 2004): 597–617.

33 Baigell, "Max Weber's Jewish Paintings," *American Jewish History* 88, no. 3 (September 2000): 342.

34 Braufman, "Max Weber's Judaic Themes" (master's thesis, San Jose State University, 1981).

35 Levin, "Between Two Worlds: Folk Culture, Identity, and the American Art of Yasuo Kuniyoshi," *Archives of American Art Journal* 43, nos. 3–4 (2003): 2–17.

36 Bloodgood, *At Woodstock: Kuniyoshi* (Woodstock, New York: Woodstock Artist Association, 2003).

37 Levin, "Between Two Worlds," 2.

38 Ichikawa, "A Study on Yasuo Kuniyoshi and the Problems of the Japanese-American Painters," in *Japanese Artists Who Studied in the U.S.A. and the American Scene* (Tokyo: National Museum of Art, 1982), 174–80; Munroe, "The War Years and Their Aftermath," in *Yasuo Kuniyoshi: 100th Anniversary* (see note 25), 38–44; Shi-Pu Wang, "Becoming American? Asian Identity Negotiated through the Art of Yasuo Kuniyoshi" (PhD diss., University of California at Irvine, 2006).

39 Munroe, "The War Years and Their Aftermath," in *Yasuo Kuniyoshi: 100th Anniversary* (see note 25) 43.

40 Richard Delgado, "Introduction," *Critical Race Theory: The Cutting Edge*, ed. Delgado (Philadelphia: Temple University Press, 1995), xiii–vxi. Kimberlé Crenshaw et al., *Critical Race Theory: The Key Writings That Formed the Movement* (New York: New Press, 2005), xiii–xxxii.

41 Here, I follow artist and cultural studies scholar Coco Fusco, who has written that photographs did not merely record the existence of racialization, but that "photography *produced* race as a visualizable fact" (emphasis in original text). Fusco, "Racial Time, Racial Marks, Racial Metaphors," in *Only Skin Deep: Changing Visions of the American Self*, ed. Fusco and Brian Wallis (New York: International Center of Photography; New York: Harry N. Abrams, 2003), 16.

42 Jacobson, *Whiteness of a Different Color*, 174.

43 Berlant and Warner, "Introduction to 'Critical Multiculturalism,'" in *Multiculturalism: A Critical Reader*, ed. David Theo Goldberg (Cambridge, MA: Basil Blackwell, 1994), 107.

44 Mercer quoted in Joan Kee, "Who's Afraid of Asian American Art?" in *Tradeshow* (see note 20), 35.

45 Gibson, *Abstract Expressionism: Other Politics* (New Haven: Yale University Press, 1997).

46 Pinder, ed., *Race-ing Art History: Critical Readings in Race and Art History* (New York: Routledge, 2002); Ferguson, "Race-ing Homonormativity: Citizenship, Sociology, and Gay Identity," in *Black Queer Studies: An Anthology*, ed. E. Patrick Johnson and Mae G. Henderson (Durham, NC: Duke University Press, 2005), 52–67.

47 Alistair Bonnett's explanation of antiracist politics is a useful guide: "Anti-racism is, after all, widely associated with not merely wanting to abolish racism but with placing race itself under scrutiny, of disturbing the foundations upon which racial knowledge and experience are built." Bonnett, *Anti-Racism*, 171.

48 Early, "A Place of Our Own," *New York Times*, 14 April 2002, national edition, "Educational Life," section D, 35.

49 See Jacqueline Francis, "Writing African-American Art History," *American Art* 17, no. 1 (Spring 2003): 2–10.

50 For example, see Alice Yang, "Asian American Exhibitions Reconsidered," in *Why Asia? Contemporary Asian and Asian American Art* (New York: New York University Press, 1998), 97; Harold Rosenberg, "Is There a Jewish Art?" *Commentary* 42, no. 1 (July 1966): 57–60.

51 Whiteness is a historical construction that requires maintenance and renovation. Among the important publications that have advanced my thinking are Richard Dyer, *White* (New York: Routledge, 1997); John R. Hartigan, *Odd Tribes: Toward a Cultural Analysis of White People* (Durham, NC: Duke University Press, 2005); Jacobson, *Whiteness of a Different Color*; and David R. Roediger, *Working Toward Whiteness: How America's Immigrants Became White—The Strange Journey from Ellis Island to the Suburbs* (New York: Basic Books, 2005).

52 Anreus, *Orozco in Gringoland: The New York Years* (Albuquerque: University of New Mexico Press, 2001); Baskind, *Raphael Soyer and the Search for Modern Jewish Art* (Chapel Hill: University of North Carolina Press, 2004); Cassidy, *Marsden Hartley: Race, Region, and Nation* (Hanover, NH: University of New England Press, 2005); Hutchinson, "Modern Native American Art: Angel DeCora's Transcultural Aesthetics," *Art Bulletin* 83, no. 4 (December 2001): 740–56; Lee, *Yun Gee: Poetry, Writings, Art, Memories* (Pasadena : Pasadena Museum of California Art; Seattle: University of Washington Press, 2003); Weinberg, *Speaking for Vice: Homosexuality in the Art of Charles Demuth, Marsden Hartley, and the First American Avant-Garde* (New Haven: Yale University Press, 1993); and Wolff, *Anglo Modern: Painting and Modernity in Britain and the United States* (Ithaca, NY: Cornell University Press, 2003).

53 The estate of Max Weber declined to co-operate with this project and denied permission to reproduce any of the artist's work in this publication.

54 Pearson, *Modern Renaissance in American Art*, 40, 41.

55 See the exhibition catalogue *Max Weber: The Cubist Decade, 1910–1920* by Krane and North.

56 North, *Max Weber*, 19.

57 Hoeber, *New York Globe* review, reprinted in *Camera Work* 36 (October 1911): 31, and quoted in North, "Max Weber: The Cubist Years," in Krane and North, *Max Weber* (see note 55), 25. Weber's shift toward greater abstraction in the teens espe-

cially provoked critics such as Hoeber, who, North notes, had previously admired Weber's work.

58 Carey quoted in Krane and North, *Max Weber* (see note 55), 25.

59 Krane, "Introduction," in Krane and North, *Max Weber* (see note 55), 18.

60 A version of the following has been published in Francis, "'Trying to Do,'" 52–84.

61 An untitled Johnson drawing accompanied James Weldon Johnson's article "The Making of Harlem" in a special "Harlem" issue of *Survey Graphic*. Many of this issue's articles, including "The Making of Harlem" (re-titled "Harlem: The Cultural Capital"), appeared in Alain Locke's 1925 anthology *The New Negro*. Johnson's drawing was not reproduced in the anthology, and "The Making of Harlem" was paired with German artist Winold Reiss's geometric abstractions.

62 K. G. S., "Exhibition at Church," *New York Times*, 6 July 1932, 22.

63 See Gary A. Reynolds and Beryl J. Wright, *Against the Odds: African American Artists and the Harmon Foundation* (Newark, NJ: Newark Museum, 1989).

64 The Foundation also mounted exhibitions for the white American portraitist Betsy R. Graves and Chinese American painter Dong Kingman. See Tuliza N. Fleming, *Breaking Racial Barriers: African Americans in the Harmon Foundation Collection* (Washington, DC: Smithsonian Institution; San Francisco: Pomegranate, 1997).

65 Calo, "African American Art and Critical Discourse between World Wars," *American Quarterly* 51 (September 1999): 595.

66 Kuniyoshi scholar Tom Wolf's reading of *At Work* slightly differs from mine, for he writes that "There is no communication between the two [figures]." Wolf, *Kuniyoshi's Women* (San Francisco: Pomegranate, 1993), xvi.

67 Interestingly, Kuniyoshi, Miyamoto, Nakamizo, and Tamatzu were discussed together in Ruth L. Benjamin, "Japanese Painters in America," *Parnassus* 7, no. 5 (October 1935): 12–15. This article is a rare example of Japanese or Japanese American racial grouping, for in a climate where the binaries of "Oriental" style and disposition and of independent American art still preoccupied the critical body, the notion of Asian American artists must have threatened a fixed and stable understanding of both identifications. Also see Tom Wolf, "The Tip of the Iceberg: Early Asian American Artists in New York," in Gordon H. Chang, Mark Dean Johnson, and Paul J. Karlstrom, ed. *Asian-American Art: A History, 1850–1970* (Stanford: Stanford University Press, 2008), 83–109.

68 "The World of Art," *New York Times Book Review and Magazine*, 15 January 1922, 18.

69 "Studio and Gallery," *Sun* (New York), 7 January 1922, 9; Dudley Poore, "Yasuo Kuniyoshi," *The Arts* 7, no. 2 (February 1925): 114.

70 In 1926 a *Time* magazine writer sarcastically referred to "the Jap-Manhattan school" in a review of the Society of Independent Artists' open exhibition. After disparaging the work of painters Eitaro Ishikagi and Noboru Foujioka, the unnamed journalist added, "And another member of the Jap-Manhattan School showed evolution as a tree with the body of an ape, burrowing worms for roots, a fruit of masks against a sky studded with glass diamonds." "Independent Artists," *Time*, 15 March 1926, available at http://www.time.com/time/magazine/article/0,9171,736643,00.html (accessed 11 June 2006).

71 In an exhibition review of Weber's art in 1956—sixty-five years after he had emigrated to the United States—Margaret Breuning quoted an earlier writer and surmised: "Many innate gifts contributed to his development; born in Russia, he inherited the Russian delight in color, and just as Russia seems in many respects 'an Oriental nation, looking to the West,' so he seems to possess a native affiliation with the East, particularly of China and Japan." "Metropolitan Shows Feininger, Kuhn, Kuniyoshi, Marin, and Nordfeldt," *Arts Magazine* 30 (April 1956): 9.

72 Salpeter, "Yasuo Kuniyoshi: Artists' Artist," *Esquire* 7, no. 4 (April 1937): 216.

73 Elsie McElroy, "Yasuo Kuniyoshi—The Fist and the Shadow of the Fist," 1942, typescript in Kuniyoshi Artist File, Archives of the Whitney Museum of American Art, 11.

74 "Universality in Art," *The League Quarterly* (Spring 1949): 6–7.

75 Krauss, "In the Name of Picasso," *October* 16 (Spring 1981): 7–22.

CHAPTER 2. THE MEANINGS OF MODERNISM

1 Watson, "The Universal Diplomat," *Parnassus* 5 (January 1933): 2.

2 Janet Wolff has astutely observed that "the divide between modernism and non-modernism (realism) is far from clear. . . . Modernism is not necessarily abstract—the figure appears in cubist and Futurist work—which makes the opposition of modernism/figurative work suspect. As many critics have also pointed out, the definition of 'realism' is by no means fixed." Wolff, *Anglo Modern: Painting and Modernity in Britain and the United States* (Ithaca, NY: Cornell University Press, 2003), 12.

3 Lisa Tickner has written about "local modernisms" that are distinguished by "local inflections to the web of relations that makes up the cultural field." Tickner,

Modern Life and Modern Subjects: British Art in the Early Twentieth Century (New Haven: Yale University Press, 2000), 193.

4 McBride, "Art News and Reviews: Both Amuses and Confuses: Works of Modernist Creates a Wide Difference of Opinion," *New York Sun*, 18 February 1923, n.p., in Max Weber Papers (hereafter cited as Weber Papers), Smithsonian Archives of American Art, Washington, D.C., roll NY 59-6, frame 416.

5 Cortissoz, *American Art* (New York: Charles Scribner's Sons, 1923), 18. A 1927 *Chicago Evening Post* review of exhibitions by Emil Ganso and Yasuo Kuniyoshi noted that "neither is of the despised French practitioners of the 'degenerate new art.'" C. J. Bulliet, "On Trying to Smile in Front of Kuniyoshi's Babies: Ganso, Kuniyoshi Create Excitement," *Chicago Evening Post*, 3 May 1927, *Magazine of the Art World*, section, 1, 6. An earlier review of several exhibitions in 1922 bore the headline "Exhibitions That Forecast an Epidemic of Modernism," *New York World*, 15 January 1922, in Yasuo Kuniyoshi Papers (hereafter cited as Kuniyoshi Papers), Smithsonian Archives of American Art, Washington, D.C., roll D-176, frame 87.

6 Clark, *History of the National Academy of Design, 1825–1953* (New York: Columbia University Press, 1954), 178–79. Clark's language resonates with Madison Grant's *The Passing of the Great Race*, in which Grant argues that American blacks and European immigrants had diminished American racial stock in the post–Civil War era. Published in 1916, Grant's book was popular and influential in racial-science circles for decades.

7 Geographer David Lowenthal has argued, "Historical texts embellish all heritage. History co-opted by heritage exaggerates or denies accepted fact to assert a primacy, an ancestry, a continuity. It underwrites a founding myth meant to exclude others." Lowenthal, "Identity, Heritage, and History," in *Commemorations: The Politics of National Identity*, ed. John R. Gillis (Princeton, NJ: Princeton University Press, 1994), 53.

8 Art critics and historians have also argued from the opposite end of the spectrum. Joshua C. Taylor has written that in nineteenth-century American art "style was itself content." Taylor, "The Religious Impulse in American Art," *Papers on American Art*, ed. John C. Milley, 121 (Maple Shade, NJ: Edinburgh Press for the Friends of Independence National Historical Park, 1976).

9 The form, content, and particularity of American art were concerns, of course, before the twentieth century. In the 1878 essay "Originality in American Art," an anonymous author writes, "A new country is exactly the wrong place to look for

originality in any pursuit which is the fruit of development and special training, most of all in art. . . . So far as we see, only two kinds of originality are possible in art. One is the originality which begins with no acquirement or habit; develops in its own forms and methods in native experimental ways. This is the originality of barbarous art; it is simple, naïve, and in the hands of an apt people always has a charm of its own. . . . The other kind of originality, the only kind which is possible or desirable in a high civilization, is that of thoroughly trained artists, whose skill is cumulative, advancing step by step from the mastery of old forms to the development of the new. . . . To a young nation then, as to a young artist, one may safely say: It is much more important that your art should be good in its kind that it should be original." "Originality in American Art," *American Architect and Building News* 3, no. 106 (5 January 1878): 3.

10 Established in 1825, the National Academy of Design was the premier American art institution through the mid-twentieth century. In the early twentieth century, many of its members vehemently opposed the antinaturalist trajectory of modernism; yet the school of the NAD faculty included painters who aimed to make their work au courant by cautiously adopting modernist strategies, and who likely imparted such techniques to their students.

11 Wolff, *Anglo Modern*, 5.

12 Edward Alden Jewell, "On Being National and On Being Universal," in Jewell, *Have We an American Art?* (New York: Longmans, Green, 1923), 121–23.

13 Alfred Werner took a representatively sanguine view of U.S. art history in the late 1940s, the years following the Nazi holocaust and the years of American red-baiting: "In this country the realm of plastic arts has been conspicuously free of poisonous prejudice. Here the American Negro, Henry Ossawa Tanner, has been honored for his artistic accomplishments, and due credit has been given to the talents of the Japanese-born Yasuo Kuniyoshi as well as to the craftsmanship of the German anti-Fascist, George Grosz, and the Russian Jew, Max Weber. . . . But while there is here little or no bias against an artist's racial comment or religious background, there exists a tendency to watch new styles and ideas with caution, if not with hostility." Werner, "Max Weber's Triumph," *Opinion: A Journal of Jewish Life and Letters* 19, no. 8 (May–June 1949), 12.

14 Locke, "Deeper River: Deeper Sea," *Opportunity: Journal of Negro Life* (January 1936): 6, 7, quoted in Paul Anderson, *Deep River: Music and Memory in Harlem Renaissance Thought* (Durham, NC: Duke University Press, 2001), 155.

15 Locke's enthusiasm for European modernism and modernist developments in the

United States distinguished him from other American observers' tentative, and frequently hostile, engagements with the new art. See his praise for the figural abstraction in African sculptural traditions and for the work of Aaron Douglas, Jacob Epstein, the German Expressionists, Henri Matisse, Archibald J. Motley Jr., and an idiosyncratic list of others in Locke, "The Legacy of the Ancestral Arts," in *The New Negro: Voices of the Harlem Renaissance* (New York: Albert Boni and Sons, 1925; reprint, New York: Atheneum, 1992), 254–70.

16 Anderson, *Deep River*, 155.

17 Analyzing New York critic Mary Austin's veiled attacks on the Jewish cultural entrepreneurs Waldo Frank and Louis Untermeyer in the early twentieth century, Matthew Baigell has written, "Austin reminded these New Yorkers of their triple outsider status: urban, foreign, and Jewish." Baigell, "From Hester Street to Fifty-Seventh Street: Jewish American Artists in New York," in *Painting a Place in America: Jewish Artists in New York, 1900–1945* (New York: Jewish Museum; Bloomington: Indiana University Press, 1991), 40.

18 Davis to McBride, quoted in Grace Glueck, "Art Review: European Influences on Americans' Views." *New York Times*, 3 September 2004, national edition, section B, 27.

19 Motley, "The Negro in Art" (1928), quoted in Jontyle T. Robinson, "The Life of Archibald J. Motley, Jr.," in Robinson, Wendy Greenhouse, and Archibald John Motley, *The Art and Life of Archibald J. Motley, Jr.* (Chicago: Chicago Historical Society, 1991), 15.

20 Woodruff, "Local Negro Artist Finds Painters Hard to Classify," quoted in Therese Leininger-Miller, "African American Artists in Paris, 1922–1934" (PhD diss., Yale University, 1995), 216.

21 Craven, *Men of Art* (New York: Simon and Schuster, 1931), 502.

22 *New York Tribune*, 15 January 1922, in Kuniyoshi Papers, roll D-176, frame 78.

23 Craven, *Men of Art*, 510, 12. In his final chapter, "Conclusion: Hopes and Fears for America," Craven also named Thomas Hart Benton, John Sloan, Boardman Robinson, Charles Burchfield, Preston Dickinson, John Marin, William Yarrow, and Georgia O'Keeffe as painters "who have looked beyond their studio walls into the fascinating American environment" (511–12).

24 Jewell, "Modern Art Museum: Contemporary American: Debating Inclusion of Certain Artists, a Show That, However, Has Many Pinnacles," *New York Times*, 22 December 1929, 14. Critic Margaret Breuning expands the point of Jewell's off-hand remark: "Assembling a group of paintings, by accredited artists whose oeuvre

has long been accepted and widely acclaimed is merely getting an open sesame to collections and forming a well related ensemble. It is a straight away performance, involving no connoisseurship or needing no particular discrimination. Yet the first exhibit comprising works by artists who have long basked in a refulgent aura of reputation consumed the energies of the museum for a long period of time, while this American exhibition appears to have sprung up with both the mushroom's proclivities of swift growth and lack of roots. [It] bespeaks haste in its assembling." Breuning, "Museum of Modern Art Holds Exhibition of Work of American Artists: American Art Rather Faultily in New Museum," *New York Evening Post*, 14 December 1929, in Kuniyoshi Papers, roll D-176, frame 317.

25 Kootz, *Modern American Painters* (New York: Brewer and Warren, 1930), 3–24.

26 Porter, "Roots of Culture," letter to the editor, *New York Times*, 27 December 1931, section 8, 12. Porter's statement is among the many instances of black subscription to a pluralist ideal of the American nation, conceived of as the union of many unique peoples. Equally important, as a painter Porter demanded the right to artistic agency and individuality. Porter argues against racial art in *Modern Negro Art* (New York: Dryden Press, 1943; reprint, Washington, DC: Howard University Press, 1992).

27 "The Art Galleries: Nineteen Who Are Living," *New Yorker* 5 (21 December 1929): 72. Helen Read of the *Brooklyn Eagle* noted that much of the displayed work had been executed long before 1929, making the show less contemporary. "Modern Museum's New Show," 15 December 1929, in Kuniyoshi Papers, roll D-176, frame 314. The *New Yorker* review's headline was perhaps the only description that could be applied to all the exhibition's participants, reflecting the magazine editors' opinion about the heterogeneity of the works displayed, a description that fit all of its participants. Kuniyoshi Papers, roll D-176, frame 318.

28 The *New Yorker* critic found Kuniyoshi's *Nude (Reclining)* to be among the exhibitions' best works. In a pointed contrast, Edward Alden Jewell compared Kuniyoshi's success to the failure of Bernard Karfiol's exhibited works: "Kuniyoshi on the other hand has arrived at the fullest command of his resources. The great sprawled nude—so artistically integrated, nevertheless with all the other features of the canvas—leaves nothing that is essential to the design unsaid." Jewell, "Modern Art Museum," xi.

29 New York critic Margaret Breuning bluntly articulated this view, writing that Feininger, Pascin, and Kuniyoshi took up space that should have been reserved for Americans. Feininger's was a "foreign idiom" and "negligible talent"; Pas-

cin's School of Paris mode was most "alien to American art"; and Kuniyoshi's was "an Oriental endowment and psychology with no appreciable relation to Occidental art, except in subject matter." Breuning, "Museum of Modern Art." Henry McBride, who defended Kuniyoshi's inclusion, nonetheless disapproved of Feininger's, and named George Luks, Childe Hassam, Joseph Stella, Florine Stettheimer, and Alexander Brooks as being among those who could have taken the German painter's place. McBride, "The Palette Knife," *Creative Art* 6, no. 1 (January 1930): supplemental page 9.

30 McBride, "The Palette Knife," supplemental page 9.

31 Ciolkowska, "Absolutism in Modern American Art," *Artwork* (January–March 1926): 94. Ciolkowska offered more than a dozen exceptions to her assessment of American art, naming artists from the Stieglitz circle, the Ashcan School, and others from the heterogeneous circles of New York–exhibiting artists, such as realist Mahonri Young and expressionist Charles Burchfield. She noted, nonetheless, that most of these praiseworthy artists were "not represented in their own museums let alone those in Europe."

32 In the American press, visiting German scholar Julius Meier Graefe praised the watercolors of Arthur Davies and John Marin, and singled out Dickinson's work because it "struck a particular nerve," while that of George Bellows did not. Meier-Graefe, "A Few Conclusions on American Art," *Vanity Fair* 31, no. 3 (November 1928): 83, 134, 136, 138.

33 Weber, "Max Weber's Startling Accusation," letter, published in *The Sun* (1919), in Weber Papers, roll NY 59-7, frame 133.

34 Weber, "Max Weber's Startling Accusation," published letter to [Henry] McBride, *The Sun*, 1919, in Weber Papers, roll NY 59-7, frame 137.

35 Jacob T. Levy has written "that—like ethnic pluralism—cultural hybridity, mélange, metissage, mestizaje, the processes of blending and melding and change under whatever description, are facts of the world, facts of our condition, and they always have been. They are not new; they are not distinctively modern—much less distinctively post-modern—and most important, they do not somehow offer a solution to the problems associated with life in a multiethnic world." Levy, *The Multiculturalism of Fear* (New York: Oxford University Press, 2000), 7.

36 Brace, "Yasuo Kuniyoshi," *Creative Art* 11 (November 1932): 188.

37 Jewell, "Art in Review: Kuniyoshi in New One-Man Exhibit at Downtown Gallery, Shows Considerable Progress," *New York Times*, 8 February 1933, Art and Books section, 15.

38 Certainly, the sanctity and purity of races, cultures, and other identity positions were widely held notions. Isamu Noguchi, urging mid-twentieth-century Japanese painters to tamp their enthusiasm for foreign modernist styles, confidently asserted, "To be authentic and original is to be modern. Therefore if something in Japan is authentic and original it is even more modern than anything imported from abroad." Quoted in Ian Buruma, "Between Two Words," review of *The Orientalist: Solving the Mystery of a Strange and Dangerous Life*, by Tom Reiss, and *The Life of Isamu Noguchi: Journey without Borders*, by Masayo Duus, *New York Review of Books* 52, no. 10 (9 June 2005): 42.

39 Kuniyoshi, "What Is an American Art?" talk at the Museum of Modern Art, New York, February 1940, Whitney artists' records, microfilm reel N670, frame 17, quoted in Gail Levin, "Between Two Worlds: Folk Culture, Identity, and the American Art of Yasuo Kuniyoshi," *Archives of American Art Journal* 43, nos. 3–4 (2003): 15.

40 Kwame Anthony Appiah has written about the "romantic fascination with difference" and "spectatorship identity" in *The Ethics of Identity* (Princeton, NJ: Princeton University Press, 2005), 142.

41 Baskind, *Raphael Soyer and the Search for Modern Jewish Art* (Chapel Hill: University of North Carolina Press, 2004), 41.

42 See Christopher M. Mott's essay, which explores the initial diversity of black images in the interwar black press and the gradual move toward a singular black identity. "The Art of Self-Promotion; or Which Self to Sell? The Proliferation and Disintegration of the Harlem Renaissance," in *Marketing Modernisms: Self-Promotion, Canonizing, and Rereading*, ed. Kevin Dettmar and Stephen Watt (Ann Arbor: University of Michigan Press, 1996), 253–74.

43 Schuyler, "The Negro-Art Hokum," *Nation* 122 (16 June 1926): 662–63.

44 Hughes, "The Negro Artist and the Racial Mountain," *Nation* 122 (23 June 1926): 692–94.

45 Hutchinson, *The Harlem Renaissance in Black and White* (Cambridge, MA: Belknap Press of Harvard University Press, 1995), 221, 222.

46 Anderson, *Deep River*, 175–76.

47 Even toward the end of the twentieth century, African American artists' work remained outside of discussions of modernist influences and exchange. For example, the authors of the survey text *American Art* have written, "Not unreasonably, apart from their attraction to primitivism, the black artists of the twentieth century tended to identify with American Scene painting, rather than with mod-

ernism in its European and formally sophisticated examples." Milton W. Brown, Sam Hunter, and John Jacobus, *American Art* (New York: Harry N. Abrams, 1988), 450.

48 The essay is the introduction to *Cézanne* (New York: Montross Gallery, 1916); a portion of the essay appears in John Rewald, *Cézanne in America: Dealers, Collectors, Artists, and Critics, 1891–1921* (Princeton, NJ: Princeton University Press, 1989), 290.

49 James A. Porter, "Malvin Gray Johnson, Artist," *Opportunity: Journal of Negro Life* (April 1935): 117–18.

50 Kuniyoshi, "East to West," *Magazine of Art* 33, no. 2 (February 1940): 75. After Kuniyoshi returned from a year-long visit to France in 1926, most critics found French influence in his new work. An *Art News* writer inventoried the influence of Matisse, Vlaminck, "Braque maybe and Picasso and possibly Toulouse-Lautrec" in his work, adding, "But he cannot be said to have fallen under their spell. Rather, they seem to have suggested to his imagination new and exciting angles from which to the world may be viewed, new poses, subtleties of line, subtleties and contrasts of tone." "Yasuo Kuniyoshi—Daniel Gallery, till March 27," in Kuniyoshi Papers, roll D-176, frame 181. In "Yasuo's French Art at Daniel Gallery," the critic for the *New York American* judged that "he appears to be following a Parisian school, of which we had reflections here a dozen years ago, but which is now, and very happily outmoded." Kuniyoshi Papers, roll D-176, frame 182.

51 Craven, *Men of Art*, 477, 489. In addition to his caustic comments about Cézanne's "limited intelligence," Craven described the artist's portraits as "forms in a state of paralysis, with inert crusts for heads, and thick clubs for arms and legs." Peninah R. Y. Petruck writes that Craven considered modernism "the exclusive investigation of painting's formal preoccupations" that was all too often divorced from the representation of "literal subject matter." Petruck, *American Art Criticism, 1910–1939* (New York: Garland, 1981), 195.

52 Brace, "Henry Lee McFee," *American Magazine of Art* 27 (July 1934): 375. Murdock Pemberton, "One Hundred 'Important' Paintings," *Creative Art* 4 (May 1929): supplemental page 38.

53 Holger Cahill's measure of American folk art in 1932 was that "Folk art cannot be valued as highly as the work of our greatest painters and sculptors, but it is certainly entitled to a place in the history of American art. . . . The folk artists tried to set down not so much what they saw as what they knew and what they felt. Their art is an authentic expression of American experience." Cahill, "American

Folk Art," in *American Folk Art: The Exhibition of 1932* (Williamsburg, VA: Abby Aldrich Rockefeller Folk Art Collection, 1932), 12.

54 "In the Galleries: The Museum of Modern Art," *The Arts* 16, no. 8 (April 1930): 568.

55 In the teens, most American reviewers denounced Weber's cubist practices as grotesque, refusing to consider it art. By the twenties, his detractors, who still found him "too stylistic, too intensely personal, to 'get over' to the public" and his work antihumanist and too primitive, reminded their readers that he was an academically trained artist, and a talented one respected by his peers. Increasingly, these critics judged him a poet or an artist who expressed a poetic sensibility that was tied to his Jewishness. See the reviews for Weber's 1923 New York exhibition: "Art Announcements: Max Weber at Montross," *Brooklyn Daily Eagle*, 18 February, 1923, n.p.; review, *New York World*, 17 February 1923, n.p.; *New York Times* review, 25 February 1923, n.p.; and Henry McBride, "Art News and Reviews: Both Amuses a Confuses: Work of Modernist Creates a Wide Difference of Opinion," *New York Herald*, 18 February 1923, n.p.; all in Weber Papers, roll NY 59-6, frame 416.

56 Sally Price has written of the "single-object focus" of an ad promoting an exhibition of Surinam art: the copy accompanying a Suriname cape with geometric design states, "If we didn't tell you it came from the Suriname Rain Forest, you'd think it was modern art." Price, *Primitive Art in Civilized Places* (Chicago: University of Chicago Press, 1989), 121. Such single-theme focus indexes the assumption that "modern" describes the art of a Western civilization while "primitive" is the province of nonliterates elsewhere.

57 Mark Antliff and Patricia Leighten, "Primitive," *Critical Terms for Art History*, ed. Robert S. Nelson and Richard Shiff (Chicago: University of Chicago Press, 1996), 170–84.

58 Of the lesser-known painter Hedda Sterne, the only woman pictured in Nina Leen's 1951 group portrait of the New York School, Judith Wilson notes that her pose on a ladder "perfectly illustrates the feminist critique of pedestalling as a form of immobilisation." Wilson, "Will the 'New Internationalism' Be the Same Old Story? Some Art Historical Considerations," in *Global Visions: Towards a New Internationalism in the Visual Arts*, ed. Jean Fisher (London: Kala Press; London: Institute of International Visual Arts, 1994), 62.

59 Martin, "Painting and Primitivism: Hart Crane and the Development of an American Expressionist Esthetic," *Mosaic* 14, no. 3 (Summer 1981): 60. Artist Marsden Hartley's summation is representatively primitivist: "The Redman in the

aggregate is an example of the peaceable and unobtrusive citizen; we would not presume to interfere with the play of children in the sunlight. They are among the beautiful children of the world in the matters of ethics, morals and etiquette." Hartley, "The Scientific Esthetic of the Redman, Part I," *Art and Archaeology* 13, no. 3 (March 1922): 113–19.

60 Wolff, *Anglo Modern*, 143, 145.

61 See W. Jackson Rushing, *Native American Art and the New York Avant-Garde: A History of Cultural Primitivism* (Austin: University of Texas, 1995).

62 Marion Bussang, "An Artist Ahead of His Time: They Pay Attention to Max Weber Now" (circa 1941), in Weber Papers, roll NY 59-6, frame 655. W. Jackson Rushing has written about Weber's interest in Native American art in *Native American Art and the New York Avant-Garde: A History of Cultural Primitivism.*

63 Robert J. Goldwater, *Primitivism in Modern Art*, rev. ed. (New York: Vintage Press, 1967), 9, 38.

64 One exception was artist, educator, and illustrator Hinook Mahiwi Kilinaka (also known as Angel DeCora), who was active in early twentieth-century cultural circles. Kilinaka/DeCora's career is discussed in Elizabeth Hutchinson, "Modern Native American Art: Angel DeCora's Transcultural Aesthetics," *Art Bulletin* 83, no. 4 (December 2001): 740–56.

65 See Elazar Barkan and Ronald Bush. eds., *Prehistories of the Future: The Primitivist Project and the Culture of Modernism* (Stanford: Stanford University Press, 1995).

66 Quoted in John Lahr, "A Critic at Large: King Cole: The Not So Merry Soul of Cole Porter," *New Yorker*, 12 and 19 July 2004, 103.

67 Addressing the essentialism of Orientalism, Arif Dirlik has posed questions that are useful to my consideration of culturalist epistemology and primitivism. Dirlik asks, "Is Orientalism an autonomous product of Euro-American development, which is then projected upon the 'orient,' or is it rather the product of an unfolding relationship between Euro-Americans and Asians, that required the complicity of the latter in endowing it with plausibility? . . . How Euro-American images of Asia may have been incorporated into the self-images of Asians in the process may in the end be inseparable from the impact of 'Western' ideas per se. One fundamental consequence of recognizing this possibility is to call into question the notion of Asian 'traditions' which may turn out, upon closer examination, to be 'invented traditions,' the products rather than the preconditions of contact between Asians and Europeans, that may owe more to Orientalist perceptions of

Asia than the self-perceptions of Asians at the point of contact." Dirlik, "Chinese History and the Question of Orientalism," *History and Theory* 35, no. 4 (December 1996): 99, 104.

68 Johnson quoted in Martin Puryear, "Introduction," in Powell, *Homecoming: The Art and Life of William H. Johnson* (Washington, DC: National Museum of American Art, Smithsonian Institution, 1991), xix. Johnson's 1932 remarks about "his family of primitivism and tradition" were preceded by his acknowledgment that he had "studied for many years and all over the world." In sum, Johnson's influences were numerous and broad, despite his claim in a 1930s interview that he had rejected an intellectual lifestyle: "Words, unfortunately, are often only a smoke-screen which life hides behind. . . . All of these many ideas and points of view one eventually forgets when one lives." Powell himself concludes, "It did not matter to Johnson that his own life and career contradicted his claims to a primitive heritage." Powell, *Homecoming,* 75, 68, 78.

69 Foster, *Prosthetic Gods* (Cambridge, MA: MIT Press, 2004), 344n6. Foster cites Sander Gilman's research on norms and deviance in *Difference and Pathology: Stereotypes of Sexuality, Race, and Madness* (Ithaca, NY: Cornell University Press, 1985).

70 Museum of Modern Art, *Max Weber: Retrospective Exhibition, 1907–1930* (New York: Museum of Modern Art, 1930), 8.

71 Barr invokes spirit in his essay's last paragraph as well: "But it is scarcely by his still life paintings or by the drenched blue of his landscapes that Weber most clearly commands our study, nor by any external or purely aesthetic quality of paint or of arrangement; it is rather by the penetrating, pathetic sentiment of his more intimate and personal compositions—by a quality of spirit." Museum of Modern Art, *Max Weber,* 12.

72 A judge for the 1952 Arts of Oregon exhibition, Weber also examined precolonial Pacific Northwest sculpture in the collection of the Portland Art Museum. "My heart goes out to these beautiful, pure primitives, which are the beginning of art. . . . We go to these primitive people because we've come on so much fear, so much intellectualism in art. We must get back to a little more emotionalism. . . . That's what's so wonderful about these primitives. I almost feel as though I were that primitive Indian, as though I made that art. It incorporates the thunder and nature, and that's what we must include in our art." "Museum's Stone Sculpture Draws Praise from Artist," *Oregonian,* 1 April 1952, in Weber Papers, roll NY 59-6, frame 654.

73 "The World of Art," *New York Times Book Review and Magazine*, 15 January 1922, section 3, 18.

74 McBride, "Yasuo Kuniyoshi's New Work Exhibited," in Kuniyohsi Papers, roll D-176, frame 97.

75 Bulliet, "On Trying to Smile," *Chicago Evening Post*, 6.

76 Although the prominence and the survival of racial signs—the Jewish nose, black buttocks, "Oriental eyes"—contradict Walter Benn Michaels's assertion that "race cannot be reduced to any of its representations," Michaels is correct in his estimation that "anything and everything can be understood as a representation of it [race]. It is only because the thing itself is invisible that everything can be imagined as a way of seeing it." Michaels, "Autobiography of an Ex-White Man: Why Race Is Not A Social Construction," *Transition* 73, vol. 7, no. 1 (1998): 130.

77 Hugh S. Chandler has written, "Essentialism is belief in a more exotic sort of modality, one that does not derive meaning in this direct and simple way. . . . Some necessary truths about individuals are simply consequences of the background system for the individual in question. But some systems of this sort interact with certain contingent facts to yield hybrid necessary truths. When our devices for referring to such individuals do not depend upon knowledge of the relevant contingent facts, those hybrid truths become exotic." Chandler, "Sources of Essence," *Midwest Studies in Philosophy* 11 (1986): 379, 388.

78 "Ugly or Beautiful, New York Sees the Art of Diego Rivera," *Art Digest* 6, no. 7 (1 January 1932): 12. The writer's mention of Jacques Élie Faure (1873–1937) is provocative, for the French art historian argued that each ethnoracial and national group manifested its racial character in its artistic practices. See Margaret C. Flinn, "The Prescience of Élie Faure," *SubStance* 34, no. 3, issue 108 (2005): 47–61.

79 Following Louis Dumont, anthropologist Richard Handler has concluded that "collectivities in Western social theory are imagined as though they are human individuals writ large. The attributes of boundedness, continuity, uniqueness, and homogeneity that are ascribed to human persons are ascribed as well to social groups." Handler, "Is 'Identity' a Useful Concept?" in *Commemorations* (see note 7), 33.

80 In *Black Skin, White Masks* (1967), Fanon's pithy charge is "The Negro is determined from without." In *Anti-Semite and Jew* (1948), Sartre asserts, "The Jew is one whom other men consider a Jew." Both quoted in Michaels, "Autobiography of an Ex-White Man," 139.

81 David R. Roediger, *Working toward Whiteness: How America's Immigrants Became White; The Strange Journey from Ellis Island to the Suburbs* (New York: Basic Books, 2005); Karen Brodkin, *How Jews Became White Folks and What That Says About Race in America* (New Brunswick, NJ: Rutgers University Press, 2000); Matthew Frye Jacobson, *Whiteness of a Different Color: European Immigrants and the Alchemy of Race* (Cambridge, MA: Harvard University Press, 1998); and Noel Ignatiev, *How the Irish Became White* (Cambridge, MA: Harvard University Press, 1995). Roderick A. Ferguson, with respect to Jewish immigrants and native U.S. citizens, has asserted that religion became a more private matter in the twentieth century, which nurtured "the conditions for participation and recognition of the Jew." Ferguson's assessment is part of his critique of "sociology's designation of sexuality as a social phenomenon" and the way it fails to acknowledge its investment in "social formations of racial exclusion and practice." Ferguson, "Race-ing Homonormativity: Citizenship, Sociology, and Gay Identity," in *Black Queer Studies: A Critical Anthology*, ed. E. Patrick Johnson and Mae G. Henderson (Durham, NC: Duke University Press, 2005), 53, 56.

82 Park, "Racial Assimilation in Secondary Groups," *American Journal of Sociology* 19 (1914): 610, quoted in Roderick A. Ferguson, "Race-ing Homonormativity: Citizenship, Sociology, and Gay Identity," in Johnson and Henderson, *Black Queer Studies*, 56.

83 McBride quoted in "Noguchi's Double Life," *Art Digest* 6, no. 11 (1 March 1932): 18.

84 Ethnoracial essences informed critical assessment even at midcentury. Critic Margaret Breuning, writing about the modernist painter B. J. O. Nordfelt confidently proclaimed that he "seems always to be near the sea, perhaps because of his Nordic origin. But the development of his themes moves from realistic fidelity to seizure of essentials in abstract designs, not in seascapes, but in renderings of the intrinsic qualities of moving waters, jagged forms and masses of rocks, the dynamic struggle of tide and wave on a Maine coast." Breuning, "Metropolitan Shows Feininger," 46.

85 In its title, Arturo Schomburg's 1925 essay "The Negro Digs Up His Past" suggests a recovery operation akin to those undertaken by contemporaneous white intellectuals who were fascinated with colonial and early American culture and history. However, Schomburg's aim was historical revision aimed at recognition of black achievement across the ages; for him, digging up a past was an intellectual project rather than an atavistic one. Schomburg, "The Negro Digs Up His Past," in Locke, *The New Negro*, 231–37.

86 William Auerbach-Levy, "Negro Painters Imitate Whites," *New York World*, 5 January 1930, "Sunday Magazine," Metropolitan section, 1M. Johnson quoted in Lester A. Walton, "Art Not Racial: Negroes Tell Critic; Leaders Reply to Charge That Works Lack Individuality," *New York World*, 2 February 1930, editorial section, 6. I will discuss this debate in depth in chapter three.

87 Malvin Gray Johnson application transcript, 1930, Guggenheim Fellowship Archives, New York.

88 Harvard alumnus Harold Stearn, a non-Jew, characterized Jews in this way in 1916. Stearn quoted in Baskind, *Raphael Soyer* (see note 41), 31. Also see Matthew Frye Jacobson's comparative study of European immigrants' collective identifications and nationalist identities in the United States: *Special Sorrows: The Diasporic Imagination of Irish, Polish, and Jewish Immigrants in the United States* (Cambridge, MA: Harvard University Press, 1998).

89 Of the Russian-born Maurice Sterne, Duncan Phillips wrote that "the Oriental Semitic from Russia has made an exceptionally good record in art since his transplantation to our shores." Phillips, "Personality in Art: III," *American Magazine of Art* 28 (April 1935): 217–18.

90 Kuniyoshi in Baltimore Museum of Art, *Six Living American Artists* (Baltimore, MD: Baltimore Museum of Art, 1939), n.p.

91 This is Noguchi's description of his goal: "I am a fusion of both East and West, but I want to transcend both worlds." Quoted in Ian Buruma, "Between Two Words" (see note 38), 42.

92 McBride, "Robust Art of Yasuo Kuniyoshi," undated, in Kuniyoshi Papers, roll D-176, frame 167.

93 The purity of Oriental and Occidental bodies arguably garnered respect for perceived transparency and genetic saturation. In contrast, the mixed-race body represented not a more potent amalgamation but rather the hybrid's weakness. Daniel Boyarin has cited the trope of the Jew as mulatto. Boyarin, *Unheroic Conduct: The Rise of Heterosexuality and the Invention of the Jewish Man* (Berkeley: University of California Press, 1997), 263.

94 Salpeter, "Yasuo Kuniyoshi: Artist's Artist," *Esquire* 7, no. 4 (April 1937): 216.

CHAPTER 3. MAKING RACE IN AMERICAN RELIGIOUS PAINTING

1 McBride, "Art News and Reviews: Both Amuses and Confuses: Work of Modernist Creates a Wide Difference of Opinion," *New York Sun*, 18 November 1923, n.p.,

in Max Weber Papers (hereafter cited as Weber Papers), Smithsonian Archives of American Art, Washington, D.C., roll NY 59-6, frame 521. Holger Cahill quotes part of McBride's statement in *Max Weber* (New York: Downtown Gallery, 1930), 35. Curiously, Cahill chooses not to excerpt McBride's contention that Weber's early work was addressed to American Christians, i.e., non-Jewish Americans.

2 McBride was raised in his parents' Quaker household until the age of fifteen, when his mother died and his widowed father sent to him to live a Quaker boarding house. McBride's support of Jewish artists—some of whom were his students at the Educational Alliance during the late nineteenth and early twentieth century—must be noted alongside the anti-Semitism evident in his letters of the 1930s. Cultural historians Steven Watson and Catherine Morris attribute this development to McBride's political conservatism and "lifelong pro-German sympathies." Watson and Morris, eds., *An Eye on the Modern Century: Selected Letters of Henry McBride* (New Haven: Yale University Press, 2000), 17–18, 23, 246.

3 For instance, Matthew Baigell has written, "Among the early modernists, such as Weber and Walkowitz, one senses a schizoid or revolving-door pattern. Committed as they were to secular and American themes, they also exhibited in Lower East Side shows and even found subject matter there." Baigell, "From Hester Street to Fifty-Seventh Street: Jewish-American Artists in New York," in *Painting a Place in America: Jewish Artists in New York, 1900–1945*, ed. Norman L. Kleeblatt and Susan Chevlowe (New York: Jewish Museum; Bloomington: Indiana University Press, 1991), 35–36.

4 Hartley positioned himself as a Maine native capturing New England archetypes, from white steeple churches to white American spinsters, and, more narrowly, the Maine coast and the French-Canadian, North Atlantic fishermen who made their livelihood from its waters. Donna Cassidy, *Marsden Hartley: Race, Region, and Nation* (Hanover, NH: University Press of New England, 2005).

5 Matthew Baigell estimates that there were "perhaps as many as 60 paintings, prints and at least one sculpture devoted to religious subject," a number he states is hard to fix because "some paintings were exhibited or published at different times with different names." Baigell, "Max Weber's Jewish Paintings," *American Jewish History* 88, no. 3 (September 2000): 342.

6 Malvin Gray Johnson to Hannah Moriarty, 26 April 1931, in "Johnson" folder, Harmon Foundation Papers (hereafter cited as Harmon Foundation Papers), Library of Congress, Washington, D.C.

7 Weber, "Painting: A Note on the 'Talmudists,'" *Menorah Journal* 23 (April–June 1935): 100; recounted in Goodrich, *Max Weber: Retrospective Exhibition* (Minneapolis: Walker Art Center; New York: Whitney Museum of American Art, 1949), 47, 49.

8 *New York World* review, 25 February 1923, in Weber Papers, roll NY 59-6, frame 416; "Weber Show Strong, Varied," *American Art News* 21, no. 19 (17 February 1923): 5. In these and other reviews, *Invocation* is referred to as *Adoration*. As Matthew Baigell and Sheila B. Braufman have noted, Weber did not routinely date and title his work, and when he did, there were discrepancies, i.e., variable titles and dates for some individual works.

9 McBride, "Joseph Stella and Max Weber," *Dial* 74 (April 1923): 424–25. McBride makes no mention of Stella's Italian heritage or immigration to the United States.

10 Rainey, "Negro Art Exhibit Has Merit," *Washington Post*, 19 May 1929, section 2, 9.

11 Calo, "African American Art and Critical Discourse between the World Wars," *American Quarterly* 51 (September 1999): 595.

12 See Rosenfeld's remarks in "American Painting," *Dial* 1 (December 1921): 660, and their citation and Baigell's comment in *Jewish Art in America: An Introduction* (Lanham, MD: Rowman and Littlefield, 2007), 34.

13 McBride, "Joseph Stella and Max Weber," 425.

14 Melquist, *The Emergence of American Art* (New York: Charles Scribner's Sons, 1942), 260.

15 Appiah, "Identity, Authenticity, Survival," in Charles Taylor et al., *Multiculturalism: Examining the Politics of Recognition* (Princeton, NJ: Princeton University Press, 1994), 155.

16 Bordner quoted in Gary A. Reynolds, "American Critics and the Harmon Foundation," in Reynolds, Beryl J. Wright, and David C. Driskell, *Against the Odds: African American Artists and the Harmon Foundation* (Newark, NJ: Newark Museum, 1989), 111.

17 Morgan, *Visual Piety: A History and Theory of Popular Religious Images* (Berkeley: University of California Press, 1998); and Morgan and Promey, *Exhibiting the Culture of American Religions* (Valparaiso, IN: Brauer Museum of Art, Valparaiso University, 2000).

18 In title, three more of Johnson's works appear to be religious subjects: an extant portrait, *Ezekiel* (1930), and the unlocated *Spiritual Singers* (1930) and *Come, Sinner* (1934).

19 Elizabeth Broun has contended that Ryder was held in high regard by different

and otherwise adversarial New York circles of the era, offering "something to the conservatives, the vanguard, the nativists, the internationalists, the formalists, and the romantics." Broun, *Albert Pinkham Ryder* (Washington, DC: Smithsonian Institution Press, 1989), 145.

20 One of Johnson's patrons and friends, John Wilson Lamb, an African American vocalist and Methodist choral director, might have encouraged the artist to interpret spirituals. From the artist Lamb purchased *Swing Low, Sweet Chariot*; *Roll Jordan, Roll*; *Climbing Up the Mountain*; and six other Johnson paintings. In addition, publications by secular and Protestant groups hoping to better interracial relations—the *Crisis*, the Congregational Church's *Wellspring*, and the *Christian Advocate*—reproduced *Swing Low, Sweet Chariot* in 1929 and 1930. During these years, and even after Johnson's death in 1936, the Harmon Foundation responded to requests from organizations, including the American Red Cross, Boston University's School of Religious Education, and the American Baptist Society, for reproductions of *Swing Low, Sweet Chariot* and *Roll Jordan, Roll* for publication and informative purposes. See these files in the Harmon Foundation Papers: "Judges General Correspondence, Harmon Awards, 1929" folder, box 29; "Correspondence Exhibitions, Negro Art Exhibits, 1930" folder, box 65; Miles W. Smith to Marry Beattie Brady, 26 November 1940, in "Johnson" folder, box 76; Mary Louise Fagg to M. Hobson 14 November 1946, letter, box 76; Miss Gillette to Mrs. Ellis, 20 November 1929, Harmon Foundation memo, in "Johnson" folder, box 76.

21 See Emily Genauer (1958), Weber Papers, roll NY 59-7, frame 682; Alfred Werner, *Max Weber* (New York: Harry N. Abrams, 1975), 56; Sheila B. Braufman, "Max Weber's Judaic Themes" (master's thesis, San Jose State University, 1981), 37; Daryl R. Rubinstein, *Max Weber: A Catalogue Raisonné of His Graphic Work* (Chicago: University of Chicago Press, 1980), 40–41. In 1951 Weber told interviewer Paul Bird that a friend suggested that he take up Jewish and rabbinical themes in 1919. Bird, "A Weber Profile," *Art Digest* 25, no. 18 (1 July 1951): 6.

22 After interviewing the artist's daughter, Sheila B. Braufman reported Ms. Joy S. Weber's belief that her father's Judaic works were not done on commission, nor did Weber use a model. "Instead," Bronfman writes, "they came from an inner necessity which caused him to reach back to the past and create these expressions of spirituality in an age of disillusionment." Braufman, "Max Weber's Judaic Themes," 46.

23 Weber, quoted in Weber Papers, roll NY59-6, frame 008.

24 Weber quoted in Braufman, "Max Weber's Judaic Themes," 80.

25 Cahill wrote, "In his woodcuts—*Prayer, Profile*—in his figure paintings—*The Worshipper, At Evening, A Solo, Tranquility*—and in his small sculptures, there is a fusion of what has been called Weber's Hebraic quality with the qualities of Maya and Aztec sculpture. The spirit of Chac-Mool lives again in many of Weber's most powerful figure compositions." Cahill, *Max Weber*, 35–36.

26 Cahill, *Max Weber*, 36.

27 Norman L. Kleeblatt and Susan Chevlowe have cited Jewish modernists' interest in suffering as a subject. Calling it an "ironic iconographic twist," Kleeblatt and Chevlowe have asserted that Mark Rothko's and Adolph Gottlieb's chiliastic depictions are means to "represent Jewish suffering in the modern era." Kleeblatt and Chevlowe, "Painting a Place in America: Jewish Artists in New York, 1900–1945," in *Painting a Place in America* (see note 3), 126. Baigell theorizes that Weber's Jewish works were the outcome of "the growing anti-Semitism in America and the recent pogroms in Eastern Europe." Baigell, "From Hester Street to Fifty-Seventh Street," in *Painting a Place* (see note 3), 45.

28 Percy North relates the 1916 *Adam and Eve* to Weber's marriage that year and the painting's form to a preceding one, *The Geranium* (1911). North finds problems in *Adam and Eve*: "In an iconographically inconsistent and confusing composition the melancholy couple seem to be archetypes of all men and women isolated from their past and forced to establish new identities in a hostile and unfamiliar environment." North, *Max Weber: American Modern* (New York: Jewish Museum, 1982), 47.

29 *Mother and Child* appears to be one of two images Weber used for Rosh Hashanah (Jewish New Year); "Happy New Year" greetings are printed on it as well. Weber also used a woodcut of a bearded male reader, made sometime between 1918 and1920, for a New Year missive to artist Abraham Walkowitz in 1934. The print is reproduced in Baigell, "From Hester Street to Fifty-Seventh Street," in Kleeblatt and Chevlowe, *Painting a Place in America* (see note 3), 48. Ellen Smith has written, "Jewish New Year postcards thus give a unique opportunity to examine images of Jews as they were created, acquired, and distributed by and for the Jewish community itself. No outsiders aimed to capture the 'exotic' or the 'other' in these images. Rather, the postcards help us gain insight into how the Jewish community saw itself: how it chose to depict its members and its behaviors and further encode itself through the printed labels and written messages integral to the meaning to of the cards." *The Visual Culture of American Religions*, ed. David Morgan and Sally M. Promey (Berkeley: University of California Press, 2001),

230. Considering Weber's bold primitivist rendering in both these examples, it is hard to entirely dismiss the exoticization of the figural subjects, whether he meant them to be Jewish or not.

30 Of Weber's rabbis, art historian Percy North has asserted, "His concentration on the head emphasized the intellectual nature of Judaism." North, *Max Weber*, 48.

31 Writing about *Invocation* (1919), which was displayed as *Adoration* at Weber's solo exhibition at the Montross Gallery in 1923, an unnamed critic located monumentality in the painting's subjects—three Jewish men at religious study and in prayer—and praised Weber's skill in interpreting it: "It is an impressive work, strong in emotional power and imparting the feeling of reverence that actuated the artist." In "Weber Show Strong, Varied," *American Art News* 21, no. 19, (17 February 1923): 5.

32 Matthew Baigell has noted that contemporary, non-Jewish critics grappled with "what was for them an exotic group of artists and an unknown and unknowable subject matter." Baigell, "From Hester Street to Fifty-Seventh Street," in Kleeblatt and Chevlowe, *Painting a Place in America* (see note 3), 45.

33 Goodrich, *Max Weber*, 49.

34 Goodrich, "Collecting and Collective Memory: German Expressionist Art and Modern Jewish Identity," in *Jewish Identity in Modern Art History*, ed. Catherine Soussloff (Berkeley: University of California Press, 1999), 118.

35 "In 1936, when he was asked to submit a new print to the American Artists' Congress, for which he was a juror, he was forced to reach back to earlier material for a suitable subject since he had not made any prints in at least three to four years. Choosing a small basswood cut, which had been originally executed with a Rabbi or religious theme in mind, he renamed it 'Pensioned' for purposes of the socially conscious catalogue and exhibition." Rubinstein, *Max Weber*, 56.

36 For example, an unnamed critic for the *New York Times* reviewing Weber's 1923 exhibition at the Montross Gallery rejects the artist's embrace of primitivism: for this writer, Weber's figures, "the human symbol," lack agency, and "resilience of power to move, to defend oneself, to attack, to resist, to sit up." The critic advises Weber's audience to "implore him to confine himself to still life where he is superb, or to the city streets where something of the emotion of the gothic building is contributed to the New York skyscraper, or to the landscapes brooding alone, or to all these things without the intrusion of man, woman or child into his house of art." "Max Weber's Exhibition," *New York Times*, 18 February 1923, x7.

37 Adlow, "Works Shown by Established and Young Contemporaries," *Christian Science Monitor* 49, no. 163 (7 June 1957): 5.

38 Cheney, *Modern Art in America* (New York: Whittlesey House, McGraw-Hill, 1939), 180.

39 Sweeney, "Art Chronicle." *Partisan Review* 11 (Spring 1944): 175–76.

40 Watson, "Max Weber," *Magazine of Art* 34, no. 2 (February 1941): 79–80.

41 Pearson, *The Modern Renaissance in American Art: Presenting the Work and Philosophy of 54 Distinguished Artists* (New York: Harper and Brothers, 1954), 24.

42 Pearson, *Modern Renaissance in American Art*, 31.

43 Cahill, *Max Weber*, 36–37.

44 Museum of Modern Art, *Max Weber: Retrospective Exhibition*, 1907–1930. Text by Alfred H. Barr Jr. (New York: Museum of Modern Art, 1930), 21.

45 "New York Artist Wins $250 Prize at Exhibit of the Work of Negro Artists" was a Harmon Foundation authored document, released on 7 January 1929 to the press. "Publicity Releases, Negro Art Exhibit, 1929" folder, Harmon Foundation Papers, box 66. Johnson's statement and other facts about the painting in this document are reprinted with little adaptation in "*Swing Low, Sweet Chariot* Will Be Popular," *Art Digest* 8 (mid-January 1929): 1–2.

46 Irving Howe, "'Americanizing' the Greenhorns" (1976), reprinted in Kleeblatt and Chevlowe, *Painting a Place in America*, 14–21. Marlon B. Ross has written about the early twentieth-century articles in the African American press, advising Southern migrants to adopt the urban sophisticate's habits. Ross, *Manning the Race: Reforming Black Men in the Jim Crow* (New York: New York University Press, 2004), 173.

47 Weber, "Painting: A Note on the 'Talmudists,'" 100. Recounted in Goodrich, *Max Weber*, 55–56. Goodrich, *Max Weber* (New York: Whitney Museum of American Art and Macmillan, 1949), 47, 49.

48 Baigell, "Max Weber's Jewish Paintings," 349.

49 Weber's paintings of rabbis and religious scholars generated a debate in the "Reader's Comment" section of *Art Digest* in early 1946. In a letter to the publication's editors, Henry P. Pina of Los Angeles, who self-identified as an Orthodox Jew, proclaimed that these Weber works had "no semblance of truth neither realistic nor emotional." Pina's concluding remark was "Mr. Weber has insulted me." In Pina, "Protest Against Weber," *Art Digest* 20, no. 9 (1 February 1946): 4. In a letter published two weeks later, Ralph Bagley of Washington described these Weber works as "aesthetic abortions." In Bagley, "Question of Religion," *Art Digest* 20,

no. 10 (15 February 1946): 4. Finally, in a letter published a month later, Evelyn Thornber praised Weber's works in this vein for their "terrible intensity," which she likened to El Greco's art. In Thornber, "Weber and El Greco," *Art Digest* 20, no. 12 (15 March 1946): 4.

50 "Rattlesnake," the subtitle for Johnson's painting *Negro Soldier*, is likely a nickname for the U.S. Army regiment to which the sitter belonged.

51 New York's Educational Alliance advanced its program for Jewish assimilation and uplift by sponsoring well-attended exhibitions at its lower-east-side offices in 1895 and 1896. Norman Kleeblatt and Susan Chevlowe quote from the Alliance's 1896 annual report, in which the organization's intent to encourage assimilation is clear. They write, "As one 'aged Jew' commented after seeing the 1896 show and having it explained to him: 'Oh! That is grand! It will keep many away from vice,' a grandiloquent translation from what Alliance's report referred to as 'jargon,' the pejorative term for Yiddish." Kleeblatt and Chevlowe, "Painting a Place in America," in *Painting a Place in America*, 95.

52 I am indebted to Johannes Fabian's *Time and the Other: How Anthropology Makes Its Object* (New York: Columbia University Press, 1983), the groundbreaking critique of that discipline's shaping of "difference." Fabian writes of nineteenth- and twentieth-century Western anthropologists' determination to deny their coevalness with their non-Western contemporary subjects and to make them "primitive ancestors" on pages 105–9.

53 Kleeblatt and Chevlowe usefully map out the differing positions on assimilation and cultural retention at the Educational Alliance Art School in its post-1917 years. While its founder, painter Abbo Ostrowsky, "had little interest in avant-garde styles," he nonetheless hired Louis Lozowick (1892–1973), who made machines the principle motifs of his clean modernist drawings and maintained connections to Europe's avant-garde, to teach at the Alliance. Kleeblatt and Chevlowe contrast "Lozowick's secular and cultural orientation" with turn-of-the-century Alliance director Julia Richman's "conviction that Jewish identity was to be nurtured solely . . . through 'family traditions and congregational life.'" Kleeblatt and Chevlowe, "Painting a Place in America," in *Painting a Place in America*, 99–101.

54 Roditi, "Master of Emotions," in Weber Papers, roll NY 59-6, frame 689.

55 Baigell quotes Mumford, who wrote, "The wistfulness and melancholy born of the old ghetto now pass[es] into [Weber's] image. In that sense, Weber is our Chagall. He speaks with his own voice. Is it the voice of his race, too? Yes, in its

obvious images. Yes, even more in its grave inwardness." Baigell does not provide the citation for Mumford's remarks. Baigell, *Jewish Art in America*, 35. In these remarks, Mumford (1895–1990), born to a Jewish father and a Protestant mother, makes no reference to the Jewish heritage he shared with Chagall and Weber.

56 Unnamed British critic quoted in "Epstein's Bible," *Art Digest* 6, no. 12 (15 March 1932): 7

57 Edward Alden Jewell was among the first critics to explicitly connect Weber's work to caricature, and he did so tentatively in "Zorn, Weber, O'Keeffe and Others," *New York Times*, 16 January 1944, in Weber Papers, roll NY 59-6, frame 591. Elizabeth Sacaratoff does not use the word "caricature" in her praising review of a 1941 Weber exhibition; nonetheless, she writes, "Weber's people always move about—and usually toward you. In his *Exotic Dance*, a half-dozen Martian-looking abstract creatures speed around and around in mad ecstasy." Sacaratoff, "Max Weber's Show Is Important and Moving," *PM's Weekly*, 16 February 1941, n.p., in Weber Papers, roll NY 59-6, frame 553.

58 Landsberger, *A History of Jewish Art* (reprint, Port Washington, NY: Kennikat Press, 1973), 337–38.

59 Although neither Kuniyoshi nor his work has figured in this chapter's discussion of religious representation, I include him here because of his documented personal and political struggles in the years leading to World War II. Kuniyoshi was not interned; still he was treated as an enemy alien and for a period deprived of his civil liberties.

60 Locke, "The Negro Spirituals," in *The New Negro: Voices of the Harlem Renaissance* (New York: Albert Boni and Sons, 1925; reprint, New York: Atheneum, 1992), 199. Barnes Foundation administrator Laurence Buermeyer concurred with Locke's estimation in "The Negro Spirituals and American Art," *Opportunity: Journal of Negro Life* 4 (1926): 158–59. As art historian Helen Shannon has written, the Berlin-trained Locke was almost certainly familiar with German Gottfried von Herder's (1744–1803) nationalism: "A perfect congruence existed between Herder's emphasis on folk literature and Locke's emphasis on the centrality of spirituals in African-American culture." Shannon argues that both Locke and Du Bois knew the work of Herder from their training in philosophy in Germany. Shannon, "Toward the Harlem Museum of African Art: New Negroes, the Primitive, and the Folk," unpublished paper (1998), 240–41.

61 On Tamiris, see Jennifer Dunning, *Alvin Ailey* (Reading, MA: Addison-Wesley, 1996), 70.

62 Robeson gave a fund-raising recital at Town Hall for Alain Locke's planned Harlem Museum of African Art, which had been founded in 1927 and dissolved circa 1930. His program was "Negro Folk-Music." Shannon, "Toward the Harlem Museum of African Art."

63 Johnson, "Dictation of Malvin Gray Johnson," 3, in "Johnson" folder, Harmon Foundation Papers, box 76. Also see "Plates with Dictation from Brightwood, Virginia," in Rodgers, *Climbing Up the Mountain: The Modern Art of Malvin Gray Johnson* (Durham: North Carolina Central University Museum of Art, 2002), 90–110.

64 Rodgers, "Climbing Up the Mountain: The Modern Art of Malvin Gray Johnson," in Rodgers, *Climbing Up the Mountain* (see note 62), 10–51.

65 Jackson, "Genesis of the Negro Spiritual," *American Mercury* 26 (June 1932): 243–55. Also see Guy B. Johnson, *Folk Culture on St. Helena Island, South Carolina* (Hatboro, PA: Folklore Associates, 1931).

66 Hurston, "Characteristics of Negro Expression," in *Negro: An Anthology*, ed. Nancy Cunard (London: Cunard and Wishart, 1934). Boas's presence in this discourse was significant: antiracist in word and deed, he advanced both cultural relativism as an ideological approach and cultural assimilation as a solution for ending racial prejudice and fomenting racial cooperation. George Hutchinson argues that Boas's relationships with colleagues and students comprised a practical extension of his scholarly methodologies in *The Harlem Renaissance in Black and White* (Cambridge, MA: Harvard University, 1997), 61–77

67 R. Emmet Kennedy identified these black, Southern song forms in *Mellows: A Chronicle of Unknown Singers* (New York: Albert and Charles Boni, 1925), n.p. In the decades following the Emancipation Proclamation, African Americans devised different strategies for the related projects of cultural construction and revision. Stark contrasts can be drawn between the activities of those recovering "folk," ancestral, and heritage identifications and those preferring assimilation into the ideal of a homogeneous, American identity. For the former, the interest was in the spiritual, the legend, and African history and cultural production: cultural renaissance manifestoes such as Langston Hughes's "The Negro Artist and the Racial Mountain" (1926) would fall in the first category, and George Schuyler's response to it, "The Negro Art-Hokum" (1926), into the second.

68 William Isles, musical director of Marcus Garvey's Universal Negro Improvement Association, cautioned against the institutionalization of "slave songs" in contemporary African American Culture. Isles, "The Negro in Music," in *Negro World*

(1922), quoted in Tony Martin, *Literary Garveyism: Garvey, Black Arts and the Harlem Renaissance* (Dover, MA: Majority Press, 1983), 110–11.

69 J. Martin Favor has brilliantly discussed the folk concept in New Negro literature and its elevation in African American literary criticism. See Favor, *Authentic Blackness: The Folk in the New Negro Renaissance* (Durham, NC: Duke University Press, 1999).

70 Du Bois, *The Souls of Black Folk* (Chicago: A. C. McClurg, 1903; reprint, New York: Penguin, 1996); Alain C. Locke, "The New Negro," in *The New Negro*; Hughes, "The Negro Artist and the Racial Mountain"; and Hurston, "Characteristics of Negro Expression." James Clifford discusses the Negrophile in "Negrophilia," *New History of French Literature*, ed. Denis Hollier (Cambridge, MA: Harvard University Press, 1989), 901–8

71 Lamb also owned six other Johnson pieces: two genre portraits, *Meditation* (1931) and *African Fruit Vendor* (circa 1929); two landscapes, *Old Road* (circa 1930) and *Harlem Bridge* (1930); a Lamb portrait (1929); and a still life (circa 1930). These titles come from Johnson's "biographical data" form for the Harmon Foundation in 1933 (19 January), in which he stated that Lamb's Musical Art Forum of Orange, New Jersey, owned twelve of his oil paintings and one watercolor drawing. The artist described this body of work as "mostly spirituals." "Johnson" folder, Harmon Foundation Papers, box 76.

72 Lamb, who met Johnson in 1925 or 1926, enthusiastically supported the artist. He wrote two references for Johnson, who was a candidate for a William E. Harmon Foundation Award for Distinguished Achievement in Fine Art in 1927 and in 1929. In the first reference (1 August 1927), Lamb stated that he had known Johnson for a year; in the second, Lamb said he had known Johnson for five years. Lamb praised the artist's "great imagination" and "creative ability" as manifested in the color and the "warmth of feeling" in his work. Valuing his Johnson collection at more than $2,200, Lamb deemed him "one of the greatest artist [sic] of my race" and asserted that "among Negro artists in this country he has no peer." Both letters in "Johnson" folder, Harmon Foundation Papers, box 48. Furthermore, Lamb, a Norfolk, Virginia native, may have been Johnson's connection to the Blue Ridge Mountain hamlet of Brightwood, where the artist spent the summer of 1934.

73 See Keith Marshall, *John McCready, 1911–1965* (New Orleans: New Orleans Museum of Art, 1931); also "Loneliness Stirred His Brush to Activity," *Art Digest* 12 (15 October 1937): 15.

74 Gilmer, "Malvin Gray Johnson," to Harmon Foundation, 7 September 1958, attached to letter, in "Johnson" folder, Harmon Foundation Papers, box 76.

75 In 1931 Johnson asked the Harmon Foundation to return his copy of *The Utica Jubilee Songbook*, illustrated with reproductions of his spiritual paintings and submitted to the Foundation as a document of his accomplishments. "I am at work on a new group of paintings now and often refer to the music to aid me," he wrote to Foundation assistant Hannah Moriarta. Johnson, to Moriarta, 26 April 1931, in "Johnson" folder, Harmon Foundation Papers, box 48.

76 Auerbach-Levy, "Negro Painters Imitate Whites," *New York World*, 5 January 1930, "Sunday Magazine," Metropolitan section 1M.

77 Barbara E. Johnson's critique of "the paradoxes of Western mimesis," binary models, and exclusionary constructions of vernacular theory have influenced my thinking. See Johnson's response to Henry Louis Gates Jr., "Canon Formation, Literary History, and the Afro-American Tradition: From the Seen to the Told," in *Afro-American Literary Study in the 1990s*, ed. Houston A. Baker Jr. and Patricia Redmond (Chicago: University of Chicago Press, 1989), 39–44.

78 Transcript, Malvin Gray Johnson application, 1930, Guggenheim Foundation Archives, New York. Johnson's application for a 1930 award was submitted before 31 January 1930. Harmon Foundation files tell us that Johnson took his paintings *Mighty Day, I Know the Lord Laid His Hands on Me*, and *Climbing Up the Mountain* to the Guggenheim Awards Committee on 20 January 1930. "Correspondence, Negro Art Exhibit, 1930–1931" folder, Harmon Foundation Papers, box 65.

79 Du Bois's *The Gift of Black Folk: The Negro in the Making of America* (Boston: Stratford, 1924; reprint, Millwood, NY: Kraus Thomson, 1975) is a treatise whose purpose is evident in its subtitle.

80 Transcript, Malvin Gray Johnson application, 1930, Guggenheim Foundation Archives, New York.

81 Wassily Kandinsky's "Concrete Art" (1938) is a representative statement of the shared roots of musical and artistic creativity. *Theories of Modern Art*, ed. Herschel B. Chipp (Berkeley: University of California Press, 1968), 346–48.

82 Johnson quoted in Lester A. Walton, "Art Not Racial, Negroes Tell Critic; Leaders Reply to Charge that Their Works Lacks Individuality," *New York World*, 2 February 1930, editorial section, 6.

83 Johnson's friends, the painters O. Richard Reid and Winifred Jonathan Russell, also were quoted in the article "Art Not Racial," and they echoed Johnson's senti-

ments. While Reid and Russell referenced the symbolic significance of "Negro subjects" for African American artists, each argued for freedom of choice in terms of content and form.

CHAPER 4. TYPE/FACE/MASK

1 As Shearer West has pointed out, artists and theorists could not easily reconcile portraits' "mimetic associations" with modernist abstraction. Clive Bell summarily placed portraiture (and landscape, history, and narrative painting) outside the category of "art" because it did not emanate from significant form that stimulated the viewer but instead from the pictorial information it presented, which could be checked against the living source. West, *Portraiture* (New York: Oxford University Press, 2004), 187–88.

2 Edward Said summarized this taxonomic discourse thusly: "In the writing of philosophers, historians, encylopedists, and essayists we find character-as-designation appearing as physiological-moral classification: there are, for example, the wild men, the Europeans, the Asiatics and so forth. These appear in Linnaeus, but also in Montesquieu, in Johnson, in Blumenbach, in Soemmering, in Kant. Physiological and moral characteristics are distributed more or less equally: the American is 'red, choleric, erect,' the Asiatic is 'yellow, melancholy, rigid,' the African is 'black, phlegmatic, lax.'" Said, *Orientalism* (New York: Vintage Books/Random House, 1994), 119. English eugenicist Sir Francis Galton (1822–1911) opined that Native Americans were "melancholic," blacks without "patience, reticence, nor dignity," the post–potato famine Irish "low and coarse," and "the upper-class Victorians near the top, surpassed only by the ancient Greeks." Dick Teresi, "Eminent Victorian, Alas: Sir Francis Galton, Famous Polymath, Was in Reality a Blockhead," review of Martin Brookes, *Extreme Measures: The Dark Visions and Bright Ideas of Francis Galton, New York Times Book Review*, 24 October 2004, section 7, 34.

3 According to Alain Locke, "The characteristic African art expressions are rigid, controlled, disciplined, abstract, heavily conventionalized; those of the Aframerican—free, exuberant, emotional, sentimental, and human. Only by the misinterpretation of the African spirit, can one claim any emotional kinship between them—for the spirit of African expression, by and large, is disciplined, sophisticated, laconic, and fatalist. The emotional temper of the American Negro is exactly opposite." Locke, "The Legacy of the Ancestral Arts," in *The New Negro* (New York:

A. and C. Boni, 1925; reprint, New York: Atheneum, 1992), 254. F. A. Whiting Jr. states, "As you would expect of a people predominantly Latin, Argentine artists have a classic regard for the human figure." "Argentine Artists at Richmond," *Magazine of Art* 33, no. 2 (February 1940): 124. Matthew Frye Jacobson presents the breadth of the nineteenth- and early twentieth-century racial lexicon in *Whiteness of a Different Color: European Immigrants and the Alchemy of Race* (Cambridge, MA: Harvard University Press, 1998).

4 Siobhan Somerville, "Scientific Racism and the Emergence of the Homosexual Body," *Journal of the History of Sexuality* 5, no. 2 (October 1994): 243–65.

5 See William Stott's discussion of social documentary in *Documentary Expression and Thirties America* (New York: Oxford University Press, 1973), 18–25. In "Black Representation and Western Survey Textbooks," Kymberly N. Pinder has identified this tendency to contextualize African American artistic production "within the confines of racialized attitudes" and to discuss the work in sociological terms. Pinder notes that to survey text authors, the value of African American art, like that of African American literature, is not aesthetic but illustrative. Pinder, "Black Representation and Western Survey Textbooks," *Art Bulletin* 81, no. 3 (September 1999): 533.

6 Writing about stereotype, cultural historians Elizabeth Ewen and Stuart Ewen usefully note that "the link between media and stereotype is found in the origin of the word": "stereotype" was the name French printer Fermin Didot gave to the process he invented in 1794 of using molded plates to print duplicate pages of press. Ewen and Ewen, *Typecasting: On the Arts & Sciences of Human Inequality* (New York: Seven Stories Press, 2006), 3.

7 Snyder and Zurier, "Picturing the City," in Zurier, Snyder, and Virginia M. Mecklenburg, *Metropolitan Lives: The Ashcan Artists and Their New York* (New York: Norton, 1995), 115–30.

8 Kalpana Seshadri-Crooks's analysis of the structured logic of racial meaning, especially her consideration of difference, is invaluable: "We *believe* in the factuality of difference in order to *see* it, because the order of racial difference is an order that promises access to an absolute wholeness to its subjects—white, black, yellow or brown. . . . Thus, visuality in the realm of race should be understood as functioning in support of *and* as a defence against the fantasy of the totalized subject" (emphasis in original). See Seshadri-Crooks, *Desiring Whiteness: A Lacanian Analysis of Race* (New York: Routledge, 2000), 5.

9 T. J. Jackson Lears has written of the wide circulation and increased production

of racist and nostalgic imagery in "Packaging the Folk: Tradition and Amnesia in American Advertising, 1880–1940," in *Folk Roots, New Roots: Folklore in American Life*, ed. Jane S. Becker and Barbara Franco (Lexington, MA: Museum of Our Natural Heritage, 1989), 103–40.

10 Sloan quoted in C. V. [Claudia Vess], "John Sloan," in Guy C. McElroy, *Facing History: The Black Image in American Art, 1710–1940* (Washington, DC: Corcoran Gallery of Art; San Francisco: Bedford Arts, 1990), 109.

11 The illustrator for Mark Twain's *The Adventures of Huckleberry Finn: Tom Sawyer's Comrade* and *Pudd'nhead Wilson* (1899), Kemble also provided drawings for African American poet Paul Laurence Dunbar's *Folks from Dixie* (1898) and for popular magazines such as *Life* and the *Century*. See Kemble, "Illustrating *Huckleberry Finn*," *Colophon: A Book Collector's Quarterly* (February 1930): n.p.

12 "The Negro in Art: How Shall He Be Portrayed?" was the title for responses to questions posed by the Crisis editors in 1926. See *Crisis* 31, no. 5 (March 1926): 219–20; *Crisis* 32, no. 6 (April 1926): 278–80; *Crisis* 32, no. 1 (May 1926): 219–20; *Crisis* 32, no. 2 (June 1926): 71–73; *Crisis* 32, no. 4 (August 1926): 193–94; *Crisis* 32, no. 5 (September 1926): 238–39; *Crisis* 33, no. 1 (November 1926): 28–29.

13 In "The Negro in Art," *Crisis* 32, no. 5 (September 1926): 238, 239.

14 In "The Negro in Art," *Crisis* 32, no. 4 (August 1926): 194.

15 African American writer Wallace Thurman protested the expectation that black writers and artists had to present "the best of the race." In 1927 he sarcastically surmised that the encouragement given to black writers and artists "to exhibit specimens from the college rather than the kindergarten, specimens from the parlor rather than the pantry" was tied up in and bound by African American desires to represent themselves "butter side up." Thurman, "Negro Artists and the Negro," *New Republic* 52 (31 August 1927): 37–39.

16 In this body of production were *Flying Dutchman* (1926), *The Model (Egyptian*; 1927), *Study of a Negro* (1927), *Study in the Nude* (1927), *Head of an Irishwoman* (1927), *Head of a Negro* (1928), *Portrait of Wilson Lamb* (1928), *The Moroccan* (1928), *Washington* (1928), *Lincoln* (1928), and *The Slave* (1927). These titles are taken from Johnson's registration cards, Archives of the National Academy, New York. *Study of a Head* is reproduced in Kenneth G. Rodgers's essay "Climbing Up the Mountain: The Modern Art of Malvin Gray Johnson," in *Climbing Up the Mountain: The Modern Art of Malvin Gray Johnson* (Durham: North Carolina Central University Museum of Art, 2002), 21.

17 See, for example, Milton W. Brown, Sam Hunter, et al., *American Art* (New York:

Harry N. Abrams, 1988), 488. In their discussion of "Social Realism and the Depression," the authors write, "Social content overrode any other objective aesthetic criteria . . . this new art turned its back with impartial disdain on American Scene painting and modernism." Similarly, Cécile Whiting asserted that leftists and progressive artists of the 1930s eschewed modernism in favor of spare representation that carried their political message. Whiting, *Antifascism in American Art* (New Haven: Yale University Press, 1989), 24–27. Confronted with a panoply of styles in the 1930s, contemporary art historians have focused on thematic content—regionalism, social protest, and antifascism among them—that are easier to manage and, importantly, provide a foil to the dominant, modernist narrative, i.e., a steady march toward figural abstraction and nonobjectivity as methods for a progressive visual language.

18 Reiss, *My Models Were Jews: A Painter's Pilgrimage to Many Lands* (New York: Gordon Press, 1938).

19 "Antwerp to See Foujioka's California Types," *Art Digest* 6, no. 20 (1 September 1932): 11.

20 Silverman, "Re-figuring 'the Jew' in France," in *Modernity, Culture, and "The Jew,"* ed. Bryan Cheyette and Laura Marcus (Cambridge, England: Polity Press, 1998), 197.

21 "Like all races, the Caucasian race is a fabrication, a fact made tragic by the inflexible brevity of the color line and the profound social and political consequences at stake in the public caprice of classification." Jacobson, *Whiteness of a Different Color*, 125.

22 Based on his careful readings of nineteenth-century statements by American politicians, intellectuals, and jurists, Jacobson concludes that "the ascendant view among native-born Americans in the 1890s . . . was . . . that Southern European, Semitic, and Slavic immigrants held as *poor* a claim to the color 'white' as the Japanese, and therefore ought to be turned away at once." Jacobson, *Whiteness of a Different Color*, 76–77.

23 See Martin A. Berger, *Sight Unseen: Whiteness and American Visual Culture* (Berkeley: University of California Press, 2005), 109–12. Jacobson, *Whiteness of a Different Color*, 177–87.

24 Brilliant, "Portraits as Silent Claimants: Jewish Class Aspirations and Representational Strategies in Colonial and Federal America," in *Facing the New World: Jewish Portraits in Colonial and Federal America* (New York: Jewish Museum; New York: Jewish Theological Seminary of America; Munich: Prestel, 1997), 6.

25 Jacobson, *Whiteness of a Different Color*, 173.

26 The narratives of Weber's career consistently suggest that he was once modern and then he was not. Goodrich writes that the artist had been interested in contemporary art but then returned to his "racial background." Goodrich, *Max Weber: Retrospective Exhibition* (Minneapolis: Walker Art Center; New York: Whitney Museum of American Art, 1949), 40.

27 Sheila B. Braufman has cited Weber's goal to "humanize geometry" in the artist's 14 November 1919 letter to his friend Leonard Von Noppen. Braufman, "Max Weber's Judaic Themes," (master's thesis, San Jose State University, 1981), 28. Weber also said retrospectively, "In my early days I discovered the geometry in the work of God; now I felt the need to return to the works of God themselves." Quoted in Werner, *Max Weber* (New York: Harry N. Abrams, 1975), 29.

28 Jonathan Rosen, "Books: The Fabulist: How I. B. Singer Translated Himself into American Literature," *New Yorker*, 7 June 2004, 88.

29 Braufman identified twenty-six Weber images—fifteen oil paintings, six gouaches, two drawings, one lithograph, one woodcut, and one linoleum print—with "Rabbi" in the title. See her appendix, "List of Judaic Works," in "Max Weber's Judaic Themes," 142–44.

30 Does Gertler's inscription also serve as identification with the rabbi figure, an ethnoracial or religious common denominator? Importantly, this signatory flourish exists alongside Gertler's 1912 proclamation, one that stakes claim to a middle ground defined by negations: "I shall be neither Jew nor Christian." Quoted in Janet Wolff, *AngloModern: Painting and Modernity in Britain and the United States* (Ithaca, NY: Cornell University Press, 2003), 129.

31 Cohen, *Jewish Icons: Art and Society in Modern Europe* (Berkeley: University of California Press, 1998), 116.

32 Brilliant, "Portraits as Silent Claimants," 4.

33 These prints are reproduced in Rubens's *History of Jewish Costume* (London: Vallantine, Mitchell, 1967), 192–93, which also offers a rare full-body-length unidentified lithographic portrait of a clean-shaven German Reform rabbi (1843–47) thought to be Hamburg's Napthali Frankfurter.

34 Rubens, *History of Jewish Costume*, 3.

35 Exodus 20:4, Deuteronomy 5:8 quoted in Cohen, *Jewish Icons*, 286n11.

36 My evocation of the picturesque body of difference is informed by Anthony W. Lee's discussion of picturesque images of San Francisco's Chinatown in the nine-

teenth century. Lee, *Picturing Chinatown: Art and Orientalism in San Francisco* (Berkeley: University of California Press, 2001), 59–99.

37 "National Academy Makes Another Gesture Toward Liberalization," *Art Digest* 6, no. 13 (1 April 1932): 3–4.

38 Louis Lozowich, *100 American Jewish Artists* (New York: YKUF Art Section, 1947).

39 Dan Kurzman, *No Greater Glory: The Four Immortal Chaplains and the Sinking of the Dorchester in World War II* (New York: Random House, 2004); and Suzanne Schwimmer, "The Four Chaplains Stamp: The Story of the Original First Design by Louis Schwimmer," available at http://www.schwimmer.com/fourchaplains (accessed 11 June 2007).

40 Braufman, "Max Weber's Judaic Themes," 74.

41 Museum of Modern Art, *Max Weber: Retrospective Exhibition, 1903–1970*. Text by Alfred H. Barr Jr.

42 Kootz, *Modern American Painters* (New York: Brewer and Warren, 1930), 57–58.

43 "Max Weber," *Magazine of Art* 34, no. 2 (February 1941): 82. Of course, Weber is among the legions of artists—visual and literary—to make such claims of identification with their practice and represented subjects.

44 McBride, quoted in Werner, *Max Weber*, 56.

45 "Introduction," Wolf and Myers, *Shores of a Dream: Yasuo Kuniyoshi's Early Work in America* (Fort Worth, TX: Amon Carter Museum, 1996), vi.

46 Autobiographical texts, 8 November 1944, unmicrofilmed, in Yasuo Kuniyoshi Papers (hereafter cited as Kuniyoshi Papers), Smithsonian Archives of American Art, Washington, D.C., quoted in Tom Wolf, untitled essay, *Yasuo Kuniyoshi's Women* (San Francisco: Pomegranate, 1993), vi.

47 Wolf, *Yasuo Kuniyoshi's Women*, viii.

48 According to Richard Dyer, "A person is deemed visibly white because of a quite complicated interaction of the elements, of which flesh tones within the pink to beige range are only one: the shape of the nose, eyes, and lips, the colour and set of hair, even body shape may be mobilized to determine someone's 'colour.'" Dyer, *White* (London: Routledge, 1997), 42.

49 Corn notes the folk art–influenced experiments of Marguerite and William Zorach and Kuniyoshi; regarding *Boy Stealing Fruit*, she concludes, "The results were never very satisfying." Corn, *The Great American Thing: Modern Art and National Identity, 1915–1935* (Berkeley: University of California Press, 1999), 332.

50 Richard Dyer says, "Whites must be seen to be white, yet whiteness as race resides

in invisible properties and whiteness as power is maintained by being unseen. To be seen as white is to have one's corporeality registered, yet true whiteness resides in the non-corporeal." Dyer, *White*, 45.

51 For example, Tom Wolf and Jane Meyers write, "Early works appear to embody a uniquely multicultural quality. " in "Introduction, *Shores of a Dream*, vii. In contrast, Kuniyoshi works of the 1930s and after are said to contain "torpid, erotic figures," as characterized by John Clark in Munroe, *Japanese Art after 1945: Scream Against the Sky* (New York: Harry N. Abrams, 1994), 56.

52 Illustrating his assertion with a reproduction of Weber's *Adoration of the Moon* (1944), Matthew Baigell writes that in the late 1920s, the "authentic Weber finally emerged. . . . In his figure studies, images finally appeared as spiritualized beings, fluctuating between material and ghostlike presences, as if Weber, at last, could possess both the tactility of their bodies and the intangibility of their souls. Especially in his paintings of Jewish themes, one senses both the physical closeness and the psychic elusiveness of the figures. They never quite emerge from the welter of open-ended planes and independent linear inventions, nor do they fully dissolve into inexplicable spaces." Baigell, *A Concise History of American Painting and Sculpture* (New York: Harper and Row, 1984), 221–22.

53 Anonymous, "Yasuo Kuniyoshi," *Six Living American Artists* (Baltimore, MD: Baltimore Museum of Art, 1939), n.p.

54 I am not suggesting, however, that the Jewish rabbi was a masculine ideal in the manner of the American cowboy. Daniel Boyarin has argued that the rabbinic Jewish man was considered feminine, the very opposite of the European male. Boyarin, *Unheroic Conduct: The Rise of Heterosexuality and the Invention of the Jewish Man* (Berkeley: University of California Press, 1977).

55 Kuniyoshi explained, "I was interested in the cow because I thought in decorative as well as ugly and so I painted cows constantly until I was exhausted. Following that I turned to babies. People think babies are beautiful, but I thought otherwise and so I painted babies and babies." Kuniyoshi, "East to West," *Magazine of Art* 33, no. 2 (February 1940): 77.

56 Kuniyoshi, "East to West," 80.

57 The consideration of representation that shores up race's claims to stability, legibility, and authority is an analysis that is long overdue. We are, presently, at the important and encouraging juncture of recognizing racial strategies. For example, Petrine Archer-Shaw has proposed that photographer Man Ray, in *Portrait of Nancy Cunard* (1926), made this white female sitter "primitive" by presenting

her in "external signifiers" meant to be read as "a shorthand for the exotic": outré animal-skin clothing and jewelry made of tusks, metal, and wood. Archer-Shaw concludes that Cunard "projects not 'otherness,' but difference." Archer-Shaw, *Negrophilia: Avant-Garde Paris and Black Culture in the 1920s* (New York: Thames and Hudson, 2000), 93. I would argue, more emphatically than Archer-Shaw does, that the covering of Cunard's white skin in cloth and baubles and the transformative eye makeup she wears compromise and undermine previous ideals of white female beauty. Cunard's look, as observed Lauren Graber (a student in a University of Michigan graduate seminar I taught in 2006), is also machinelike. As do Kuniyoshi's female genre subjects, Cunard's body as composition betrays the problem of visualizing otherness.

58 Keen observers recognized the transgressiveness of such actions. In 1927 Wallace Thurman praised Aaron Douglas and Richard Bruce Nugent: he lauded the former for "advanced modernism and raw caricatures of Negro types," the latter for "his interest in decadent types and the kinks he insists on putting upon the heads of his almost classical figures." Thurman, "Negro Artists and the Negro," 37.

59 This quote was published in a feature article about Alston and sculptor Henry Bannarn's "306," a New York City workshop and meeting place for black artists and writers in the 1930s. Referencing his Harlem Hospital mural, *Magic and Medicine*, Alston described "African" faces in this way: "You see the faces of those Negroes in the sketches for the murals are angular, different from the conventional concept of beauty. But when you paint Negroes who look like Greek gods, you're just faking." "Creative Negroes: Harlem Has Its Artists, Working under Difficult Conditions," *Literary Digest*, 1 August 1936, n.p., in "Negroes-Art," volume 2, Microfilm R-707, reel 12, Schomburg Center for Research in Black Culture. In his 1925 essay "The Legacy of the Ancestral Arts," Alain Locke railed against "Nordicized transcription" in European American and African American representations of blacks. It is understandable that Alston's opinion mirrored that of his mentor.

60 Mainly known for his sculpture, Sargent Claude Johnson also produced paintings and drawings for exhibitions in the 1920s and 1930s. His painting *Vera* (circa 1931) is also reproduced in the 1931 Harmon Foundation publication *Exhibition of the Work of Negro Artists* (New York: Harmon Foundation). Quoted in the *San Francisco Chronicle* in October 1935, Johnson offered remarks that demonstrate his embrace of a primitivist racial art: "I am producing a strictly Negro Art, studying not the culturally mixed Negro of the cities, but the more primitive slave type as

it existed in this country during the period of slave importation. . . . It is the pure American Negro I am concerned with, aiming to show the natural beauty and dignity in that characteristic lip, that characteristic hair, bearing and manner. . . . I am concerned with color not solely as a technical problem, but also a means of heightening the racial character of my work. The Negroes are a colorful race. They call for an art as colorful as can be made." Quoted in "San Francisco Artists," *San Francisco Chronicle*, 6 October 1935, D3.

61 U.S.-produced images of mixed-race people as political metaphor date at least to mid-nineteenth century. A famous image in American art, Eastman Johnson's *Old Kentucky Home (Life in the South)* of 1859 presents a range of black types, including an undoubtedly mixed-race woman. Other examples are Thomas Satterwhite Noble's *The Price of Blood* (1868) and Harry Watrous's *The Drop Sinister* (circa 1914). The latter painting garnered significant attention when exhibited at the National Academy of Design in 1914. A copy of the painting, reproduced in a 1915 issue of *Crisis*, presents a light-skinned African American husband and wife and their golden-haired, lighter-skinned daughter. In the text accompanying the image, an anonymous writer protested the prejudice that awaited the child: "The United States Census says she is a 'Negro.' . . . 90,000 of her neighbors, good Christian, noble, civilized people, are going to insult her, seek to ruin her and slam the door of opportunity in her face the moment they discover *The Drop Sinister.*" "The Drop Sinister," *Crisis: A Record of the Darker Races* 10 (October 1915): 286–87.

62 The nationally distributed black weekly newspaper the *Pittsburgh Courier* reported that the *Quadroon Madonna* attracted "much attention" when exhibited in Nashville, Tennessee, where the painting traveled along with selected works from the 1928 Harmon Foundation exhibition in New York City. According to the anonymous writer, "People ask more questions about this picture than any other one of the collection." *Pittsburgh Courier*, 23 June 1928, n.p., in "Publicity" folder, Harmon Foundation Papers (hereafter cited as Harmon Foundation Papers), box 66, Library of Congress, Washington, D.C.

63 In his survey *Negro Art: Past and Present*, Locke placed artists in the categories "traditionalists," "modernists," and "extreme modernists." An earlier scheme of 1931 included "Africanists" or "Neo-Primitivists" as well. Dawson, Locke wrote, belonged to the "academic vein . . . of younger traditionalists," along with Arthur Diggs, William Farrow, John Wesley Hardrick, William A. Cooper, Robert Savon Pious, O. Richard Reid, Henry Bozeman Jones, Allan Freelon, James A. Porter,

and Dan Terry Reid. *Negro Art: Past and Present* (Washington, DC: Associated Publishers, 1936), 66.

64 According to a Dawson biography, the painting was sold to "the Negro Art Salon at Roosevelt High School," Gary, Indiana. "Charles Dawson," In Gary A. Reynolds, Beryl J. Wright, and David C. Driskell, *Against the Odds: African-American Artists and the Harmon Foundation* (Newark, NJ: Newark Museum, 1985), 172. In other words, *Quadroon Madonna,* which does not proclaim its subjects' names, was not retained in a family collection. Hence it is unlikely that it was a commission; it is probably a genre portrait.

65 For a consideration of class privilege and skin color chauvinism among African Americans, see Michael D. Harris's readings of Archibald J. Motley Jr.'s paintings in *Colored Pictures: Race and Visual Representation* (Chapel Hill: University of North Carolina, 2003).

66 Waring, letter to William E. Harmon, quoted in Tuliza K. Fleming, "Breaking Racial Barriers," *Breaking Racial Barriers: African Americans in the Harmon Foundation Collection* (Washington, DC: Smithsonian Institution; San Francisco: Pomegranate, 1997), 15.

67 Waring, letter to Du Bois, 1929, quoted in Fleming, *Breaking Racial Barriers* (see note 64), 15.

68 An alternative reading is that the "Anno Domini" (In the Year of Our Lord) inscribed on the painting is a homonymic play on the subject's name, "Anna Derry" (also written on this image). Although Waring was not known for incorporating textual whimsy into her imagery, she often made use of potent symbols. See her oil painting *Marian Anderson* (1944), in which distant crosses on a hilltop—the sign of the Crucifixion on Mount Calvary—are visible behind the singer and reference the spirituals in her concert repertoire. *Marian Anderson* is reproduced in Fleming, *Breaking Racial Barriers*, 32.

69 Richard J. Powell has identified Derry as "the elderly mother" of one of Waring's friends. *Black Art and Culture in the Twentieth Century* (London: Thames and Hudson, 1997), 49. Hall's portrait is still in the collection of Cheyney University, a rural Pennsylvania college community where both women lived and worked.

70 Locke, *Negro Art*, 65.

71 Motley's Bronzeville paintings are case studies of this phenomenon. These bawdy tableaux have been seen as an insider's record of his own milieu. However, such a view is reductive, for it fails to account for Motley's position as a light-skinned,

middle-class, male voyeur painting lower-class and predominantly darker-skinned blacks.

72 Dennis Barrie, "Interview with Archibald Motley" (1967), quoted in Amy J. Mooney, "Representing Race: Disjunctures in the Work of Archibald J. Motley, Jr.," *Art Institute of Chicago Museum Studies* 24 (1999): 167.

73 Amy J. Mooney has argued that Motley saw his black genre portraits (of groups and individuals) as a reparative response to denigrating stereotypes. Her essay is the first to broach the possibility of paradoxical results emanating from Motley's reliance on stock, stereotypical characters. Mooney, "Representing Race," 163–79.

74 Motley, "How I Solve My Painting Problems (1947)," quoted in Jontyle T. Robinson and Wendy Greenhouse, "Catalogue of the Exhibition," in *The Art of Archibald J. Motley, Jr.* (Chicago: Chicago Historical Society, 1991), 71.

75 Motley quoted in Robinson and Greenhouse, "The Life of Archibald J. Motley, Jr.," in *The Art of Archibald J. Motley, Jr.* (see note 73), 8–9.

76 Motley, "How I Solve My Painting Problems," in *The Art of Archibald J. Motley, Jr.* (see note 73), 9.

77 Tuttle, "The Negro in the Field of Art," part 5, *Argus*, 12 October 1928, n.p., in "Archibald J. Motley" folder, Harmon Foundation Papers, box 44. In preparation for writing this five-part series, Tuttle wrote to the Harmon Foundation for information on its exhibitors. Worth Tuttle to Harmon Foundation, 25 April 1928, in "Miscellaneous, Negro Art Exhibit, 1928–1930" folder, Harmon Foundation Papers, box 66.

78 Of the paintings Motley exhibited at the New Gallery, his Africa series, including the primitivist *Kikuyu, God of Fire* (1927), garnered the most critical attention.

79 Locke's response to Winold Reiss's controversial genre portrait *Two Public School Teachers* (1925) is also illuminating, for Locke, a Howard University professor, identified with the subjects' professional and racial identities as rendered by the German artist. Locke had published his response in the special "Harlem" issue of the monthly *Survey Graphic* and defended the portrait as "good type portraiture of its sort, a professional ideal, that particular seriousness, that race redemption spirit, that professional earnestness and even a sense of burden which I would be glad to think representative of both my profession and especially its racial aspects." Locke, "To Certain of Our Philistines," *Opportunity: Journal of Negro Life* 3 (May 1935): 156. Other African Americans had deemed

the sharply linear drawing of two African American women unflattering. Locke's colleague Elise McDougald reported that "a Mr. Williams" suggested that it was a "piece of subtle propaganda to prejudice the white reader." Elise McDougald to Locke, undated letter, "Survey Graphic" box, Locke Papers, Howard University, Washington, D.C, quoted in *To Color America: Portraits by Winold Reiss* (Washington, DC: Smithsonian Institution Press, 1989), 50.

80 Locke, "The American Negro as Artist," 217.

81 MacLeish to Yasuo Kuniyoshi, 24 June 1942, quoted in Alexandra Munroe, "The War Years and Their Aftermath: 1940–1953," in *Yasuo Kuniyoshi: 100th Anniversary of His Birth* (Kyoto: National Museum of Modern Art, 1989), 39.

82 Thomas D. Mabry to Yasuo Kuniyoshi, 10 September 1942, quoted in Munroe, "The War Years and Their Aftermath," in *Yasuo Kuniyoshi* (see note 79), 39.

83 Munroe, "The War Years and Their Aftermath," in *Yasuo Kuniyoshi* (see note 79), 39.

84 Africanist historian Jan Vansina has written that the "process of translating the form of one medium into another is called skeuomorph development." Critical to the concept of the skeuomorph is that the object "carried out in another medium than the usual one [is different], just as an engraving differs from a drawing." Vansina, *Art History in Africa* (London: Longman, 1984), 56.

85 Henderson, "Negro Art Exhibit," *Southern Workman* 63 (July 1934): 216.

86 As is the case with the named Malvin Gray Johnson subjects, the sitters in William H. Johnson's 1930 portraits *Girl in a Green Dress* and *Jim* bear a striking resemblance to each other. Both paintings were executed during Johnson's two-month visit to his hometown of Florence, South Carolina, in February–April 1930. The identity of the female subject is unknown, but Jim was the name of one of the artist's younger brothers. Using his neighbors and family as subjects, Johnson wrote that he was "hoping to abstract something of their [—] and putting it on canvas." Quoted in Powell, *Homecoming: The Art and Life of William H. Johnson* (Washington, DC: National Museum of American Art, 1991), 44. In light of Johnson's statement (however incomplete), I situate *Jim* and *Girl in a Green Dress* as pendant portraits that are in dialogue with each other.

87 As Joanna Woodall has noted, Western artists' portraits of friends and family date to the fifteenth century or earlier; by the late nineteenth century, the uncommissioned portrait was an important genre for the avant-garde for it "enhanced the authority of the artist by making worthiness to be portrayed dependent upon

one's relationship to him or her." Woodall, "Introduction," *Portraiture: Facing the Subject* (Manchester, England: Manchester University Press, 1997), 7.

88 See Margaret Breuning, "Art World Events," *New York Evening Post*, 27 February 1933, 11; Evelyn S. Brown, "The Harmon Awards," *Opportunity: Journal of Negro Life* 11 (March 1933): 79; unnamed writer, "Art—Harmon Awards," *Crisis: A Record of the Darker Races* 40 (May 1933): 111; unnamed writer, "Harlem Library Shows Negro Art," *Art News* 31 (20 May 1933): 14.

89 Jewell, "Art in Review: Sargent Johnson Wins Chief Prize at Exhibition by Negro Artists, Sponsored by the Harmon Foundation," *New York Times*, 21 February 1933, 22.

90 Henderson, "Negro Art Exhibit," 68.

91 Locke, *Negro Art*, 66.

92 Jost Hermand, "Artificial Atavism: German Expressionism and Blacks," in *Blacks and German Culture*, ed. Hermand and Reinhold Grimm (Madison: University of Wisconsin Press, 1986), 64–86. Leading up to the 1937 Degenerate Art exhibition in Munich, German critics denounced expressionist art: Nazi-identified critic Alfred Rosenberg deemed German artists' adaptations of African art to be dangerous "mestizoism" in 1930. Nazi racism was entwined against with anti-Semitism as well, for cultural consumption of non-German art was termed "Niggerization" or "Jewification" of the nation. Significantly, Alain Locke was an enthusiastic admirer and defender of Pechstein and other European modernists. See Locke's essay, "To Certain of Our Philistines," *Opportunity: Journal of Negro Life* 3 (May 1925): 155–56. German expressionist art was exhibited in New York City at J. B. Neumann's New Art Circle (also known as the Living Art Gallery), the site of Locke's Blondiau-Theater Arts Collection of Primitive African Art show of 1927 and of several Cézanne exhibitions.

93 Brandford, "Harmon Foundation Announces Awards to Negro Artists," *New York Age*, 25 February 1933, 7. On Boykin, see Mary Ann Calo, *Distinction and Denial: Race, Nation, and the Critical Construction of the African American Artist, 1920–1940* (Ann Arbor: University of Michigan Press, 2007), 77–87.

94 Johnson's correspondence indicates his knowledge of Boykin and his downtown studio-workshop at the end of the 1920s. The latest possible date for Johnson's exposure to African art was 1927: in that year he attended a Town Hall fundraiser for Alain Locke's Harlem Museum of African Art and presumably he was familiar with the objects Locke sought to preserve and display. See Helen Shannon, "Toward the Harlem Museum of African Art: New Negroes, The Primitive,

and The Folk," unpublished paper, 1988. Johnson may have visited Locke's 1927 Blondiau-Theater Arts Collection of Primitive African Art exhibition (7 February to 5 March) at the New Art Circle in New York. Moreover, as a contributor to the "Harlem" issue of *Survey Graphic*, Johnson likely was acquainted with "The Legacy of the Ancestral Arts," one of Locke's contributions to the issue, and the subsequently published *The New Negro*. Locke's exhortations for African Americans to study African art and the modernist styles it had inspired may have prompted Johnson's investigations. Lastly, the 135th Street Branch of the New York Public Library in Harlem was a source for Johnson, not only for its black art and cultural texts but also for its displayed objects: realistic busts of black heroes, allegorical statues, black portraiture in painting and drawing, and African masks. Indeed, an undated photo of a literary gathering at the library shows a mask that strongly resembles one in Johnson's *Negro Masks*. The photo, in the collection of the Schomburg Center for Research in Black Culture, is reproduced on the cover of the paperback edition of J. Martin Favor's *Authentic Blackness: The Folk in the New Negro Renaissance* (Durham, NC: Duke University Press, 1999). The origin, maker, and current whereabouts of the pictured mask remain unknown.

95 Johnson's drawing of a Gelede-like mask with a snakelike upper region is undoubtedly based on a mask presented in the outtakes for the Harmon Foundation film "A Study of Negro Artists" (circa 1937), National Archives, College Park, Maryland, 200 HF 214X.

96 The Pierce portrait was published in Elmer A. Carter, "He Smashed the Color Line: A Sketch of Billy Pierce," *Opportunity: A Journal of Negro Life* 8, no. 5 (May 1930): 148. One of the pastels especially pleased the galleries' director, Juliana Force, who purchased two of them.

97 "Hotel Worker Wins First Prize in Art Exhibition," *Amsterdam* (New York) *News*, 5 March 1930, 7.

98 T. T. F., "Grotesque Exaggeration Dominates Art Sketches and Paintings at New Exhibit," *Amsterdam News* (New York), 14 May 1930, 11.

99 T. T. F., "Grotesque Exaggeration Dominates Art Sketches," 11.

100 Delaney studied with Lloyd Branson, a white portraitist and landscapist, in the early 1920s. Sponsored by Branson, he moved to Boston in 1923 and enrolled in classes at the Copley Society, the South Boston School of Art, and the Lowell Institute. In New York from November 1929, Delaney was almost certainly known to Malvin Gray Johnson: both painters socialized in Harlem and Greenwich Vil-

lage circles, and both were connected to Cloyd Boykin's "Primitive Art Group," a loose contingent of African American artists.

101 T. T. F., "Grotesque Exaggeration Dominates Art Sketches," 11.

102 T. T. F., "Grotesque Exaggeration Dominates Art Sketches," 11.

103 David Leeming, *Amazing Grace: A Life of Beauford Delaney* (New York: Oxford University Press, 1998), 39. Nonetheless, Locke's writings of the 1930s only once mention Delaney: he is described as "another promising portraitist and folk-type painter," a group that includes Allan Crite, Grayson Walker, Richard Bruce Nugent, Henry Bannarn, Samuel Countee, Georgette Seabrook, Sara Murrell, James A. Porter, Henry Hudson, and Lois M. Jones. Locke, *Negro Art*, 80.

104 Quoted in Leeming, *Amazing Grace*, 37. Among Delaney's drawings from his New York days are *Portrait of a Boy* (1934) and *Portrait of a Man* (circa 1943), both published in *Against the Odds*. Both could be described as delicately drawn, naturalistic renderings, although the later work's ethereal quality imbues it with counternaturalistic realism.

105 Delaney quoted in Leeming, *Amazing Grace*, 36–37.

106 *A Man* is reproduced in Leeming, *Amazing Grace*, 38.

107 See praise for George Murray's marine landscapes and the genre portraits by Edna Rabouin, Jacob Adams, and Richard Lindsey in "Art Students Hold Exhibit," *Amsterdam News* (New York), 22 November 1930, in L. S. Alexander Gumby Papers (hereafter cited as Grumby Papers), Amistad Research Center, reel 9; and "Students' Exhibit Begins at Gumby's," *Amsterdam* (New York) *News*, 26 November 1930, in Gumby Papers, reel 9. It is worth noting the difference between black Americans' expectations for art and for other fields of culture in the interwar period: figural exaggeration and abstraction that were not accepted in painting and sculpture were unproblematically consumed in comic strips published in black newspapers and magazines.

108 Lewis, "The Harlem Sketch Book," *Amsterdam* (*News* (New York), 22 January 1930, 9. For an introduction to this incisive cultural critic's career, see Theodore Kornweibel Jr., "Theophilus Lewis and the Theater of the Harlem Renaissance," in *The Harlem Renaissance Remembered*, ed. Arna Bontemps (New York: Dodd, Mead, 1972), 171–89.

109 Harmon Foundation, "Exhibition to Be Held of the Work of Negro Artists," press release, 4 January 1930, 2, in "Publicity" folder, in Harmon Foundation Papers, box 64.

110 "Harmon Foundation, "Exhibition to Be Held," 2.

111 *Art Digest* 4 (15 January 1930): 13.

112 Woodall, "Introduction," in *Portraiture*, 7.

113 In the 1930 review discussed in chapter two, "Negro Painters Imitate Whites," William Auerbach-Levy wrote that William H. Johnson "still has to achieve greater originality. His latest work shows a distinctive break away from his American training but is too much influenced by the French moderns." "Negro Painters Imitate Whites," *The New York World*, 5 January 1930, metropolitan section, 1M.

114 Lewis, "The Harlem Sketch Book," 9.

115 Fleming, *Breaking Racial Barriers*, 14.

116 Brilliant, *Portraiture* (Cambridge, MA: Harvard University Press, 1991), 30. Nevertheless, even when contemporary historians recognized the creative effort in black portraits of the 1920s and 1930s, they still devoted great energy to positioning the work as an illustrative transcript of the ongoing Harlem Renaissance spirit and as an authoritative visual documentation of "the New Negro." For an example, see Richard J. Powell's discussion of Archibald J. Motley's "Bronzeville" paintings in "Re/Birth of a Nation," in Hayward Gallery, *Rhapsodies in Black: Art of the Harlem Renaissance* (London: Hayward Gallery, 1997), 20–21.

117 In her exhibition catalogue essay on the artist, Ala Story writes, "Weber's maternal relatives were only lawyers and men of business. However it was of consequence that he was born a Russian, responding in childhood to the exposure of its folk art, its religious processions marking the days of worship, its churches filled with Byzantine art and decorations, its colorful costumes and flamboyant ceremonial robes, its synagogues with their carvings and paintings of lions, draperies, musical instruments and statuary interwoven with the faith they served." Story, *Max Weber* (Santa Barbara: Art Galleries, University of California, 1968), 5.

118 Goodrich, *Max Weber*, 31–32.

119 Percy North notes Weber's criticism of Fauvism in the artist's "Chinese Dolls and Modern Colorists," *Camera Work* 31 (July 1910): 51, where he writes, "No smear of Veronese green, juxtaposed with one vermillion, or other formless complementary daubs or splashes, however brilliant in color, can ever take the place of even the dullest toned or moderately colored painting that has form." North, "Max Weber: The Cubist Decade," in North and Susan Krane, *Max Weber: The Cubist Decade, 1910–1920* (Atlanta: High Museum of Art, 1991), 23.

120 Barr's assertion follows this introductory statement: "His mind is complexly furnished with an intimate knowledge of the art of our day and of past and exotic periods; the development of his style is a compendium of the problems of early

twentieth-century painting; and his career is rich in contrasts with the important artistic personalities of the last three decades in France and in America." Barr, *Max Weber*, 7.

121 Barr, *Max Weber*, 8.

122 Goodrich, *Max Weber*, 40.

123 Wolf, "Kuniyoshi in the Early 1920s," in Amon Carter Museum, *Shores of a Dream*, 22.

124 The January 1930 statement is found in a transcript, Malvin Gray Johnson application, 1930, Guggenheim Foundation Archives. The second statement is a quote from Lester A. Walton, "Art Not Racial, Negroes Tell Critic," *New York World*, 2 February 1930, editorial section, 6.

125 West, *Portraiture*, 178. Paul de Man, "Autobiography as De-facement," in *The Rhetoric of Romanticism* (New York: Columbia University Press, 1984), 69.

126 My thinking has been influenced by Rosalind Krauss, *Cindy Sherman, 1975–1993* (New York: Rizzoli, 1993), 17; and Michael Camille, "Simulacrum," in Nelson and Shiff, *Critical Terms for Art Historians*, 31–44 (Chicago: University of Chicago Press, 1996).

CHAPER 5. THE RACE OF LANDSCAPE

1 Bohn, "In Pursuit of the Fourth Dimension: Guillaume Apollinaire and Max Weber," *Arts Magazine* 54 (June 1980): 166–69; Henderson, *The Fourth Dimension and Non-Euclidean Geometry in Modern Art* (Princeton, NJ: Princeton University Press, 1983)

2 Weber, *Camera Work* 31 (July 1910): 25, reproduced in Susan Krane and Percy North, *Max Weber: The Cubist Decade, 1910–1920* (Atlanta: High Museum of Art, 1991), 95.

3 North, *Max Weber: American Modern* (New York: Jewish Museum, 1983), 52.

4 Weber, like most artists, considered his market, and his concerns heightened in the Depression years. His work found buyers—institutional and individual—during this era, and Weber apparently did not qualify for the artist relief employment administered by the Works Project Administration. Nonetheless, he was aware of the dire predicament facing artists in the constricted art market of the 1930s and noted it in his 1936 speech to the American Artists' Congress. Weber, "The Artist, His Audience, and Outlook," in Matthew Baigell and Julia Williams, *Art-*

ists against War and Fascism: Papers of the First American Artists' Congress* (New Brunswick, NJ: Rutgers University Press, 1986), 121–29.

5 As my discussion of Kuniyoshi's nudes in chapter 4 indicates, the nude, whether isolated in figure studies or situated in idylls, was a risk-laden motif to present to conservative U.S. audiences. Two Chicago press reviews preserved in Weber's scrapbooks reference the exhibition of his nudes painted in gouache at the Art Institute of Chicago. While they are undated, the reviews likely refer to his participation in a 1941 group show there. Marguerite B. Williams praises these works, noting that they are "made so tiny and so delicate in color that all the rawness and vulgarity found in his larger bacchanals in oil have disappeared." Williams, "World Showing of Water Colors Is Modern Riot," in Max Weber Papers (hereafter cited as Weber Papers), Smithsonian Archives of American Art, Washington, D.C., roll NY 59-6, frame 439. In "Throwing a Thunderbolt," an unnamed reviewer also cites the small scale of these works and concludes, "They get away with so much because in order to be seen they must be peered at." Weber Papers, roll NY 59-6, frame 435.

6 Watson, "Max Weber," *Magazine of Art* 34, no. 2 (February 1941): 81. Weber told Watson that he had made more than a thousand figure drawings while living and working in Paris (1905–8), obviating the need for models. Landscapes were based on his pencil sketches annotated with color notes. Watson reported, "To him they were, despite their small size and comparatively few lines, treasures of information." Once he had started his canvas, Weber would revisit "the site itself and again study the color."

7 Phillips, A *Collection in the Making: A Survey of the Problems Involved in Collecting Pictures Together with Brief Estimates of the Painters in the Phillips Memorial Gallery* (New York: E. Weyhe; Washington, DC: Phillips Memorial Gallery, 1926), 62.

8 See, for example, Percy North's assessment of Weber's post-1919 production: "His work became lyrical and romantic albeit rough-hewn and expressive. He painted familiar and comforting pictures, not the startlingly awkward figures of his cubist paintings. His work lost its hard edge and its difficult stance." North, "Max Weber: The Cubist Decade," in Krane and North, *Max Weber* (see note 2), 43.

9 As I noted in chapter 2, a New York critic reviewing Weber's 1923 exhibition at the Montross Gallery preferred the artist's still-life and scene paintings, deeming his figural interpretations primitive and antihumanist. "Max Weber's Exhibition," *New York Times*, 18 February 1923, section 7, 7. In his 1930 monograph, Holger

Cahill also looked to solidify Weber's reputation in landscape art, asserting, "Arthur B. Davies used to say that Weber was the greatest landscape painter in America and the greatest painter of trees in the world." Cahill, *Max Weber* (New York: Downtown Gallery, 1930), 39.

10 The MoMA publication appeared first but was indebted to Cahill's insights. Barr's single footnote for his introduction to the illustrated catalogue is an acknowledgement: "The writer wishes to thank Mr. Holger Cahill for much of the information included in these notes. A book on Max Weber by Mr. Cahill is about to be published." Barr, *Max Weber,* 7.

11 Museum of Modern Art, *Max Weber: Retrospective Exhibition*, 1903–1970. Text by Alfred H. Barr Jr.

12 Barr, *Max Weber,* 11 (emphasis in the original).

13 Ibid., 12.

14 Cahill, *Max Weber,* 37, 38.

15 Ibid., 38.

16 Ibid., 39–40.

17 Ibid., 44. A few paragraphs before this conclusion, Cahill states unequivocally, "Weber has never forgotten nature. He has always adhered to the grand advice of his paternal friend, Henri Rousseau. And he understands the primitives as few other understand them." Ibid., 43.

18 Weber's description for *Eight Figures,* displayed in his 1930 MoMA exhibition: "In this study subject matter, attitude and gesture were entirely subsidiary to the problem of form, balance of volume, and sculpturesque special values. The seat and back of a long bench within the boundaries of the rectangle make up an arrangement of several horizontal spaces in which the figures are placed. The postures and structure of the figures were ordained more by a plastic necessity than by merely emotional, ideal or decorative interest." Quoted in Barr, *Max Weber,* 22.

19 In his 1930 monograph, Holger Cahill reported, "During the years between 1915 and 1924 Weber literally retired to one small room where he took stock of the universe." Cahill, *Max Weber,* 34. Nonetheless, Cahill also cites a lack of interest in American art during World War I and the years following, and Weber's occasional participation in group shows in the same period as well.

20 Jewell, "Zorn, Weber, O'Keeffe and Others," *New York Times*, 16 January 1944, x9.

21 Malvin Gray Johnson to Harmon Foundation, September 1934; in "Malvin Gray Johnson" folder, Harmon Foundation Papers (hereafter cited as Harmon Foundation Papers), box 76, Library of Congress, Washington, D.C.

22 See Robert B. Stepto, *From Beyond the Veil: A Study of Afro-American Narrative* (Urbana: University of Illinois Press, 1991), 167–68. Stepto maps north-to-south journeys in African American novels and narratives in which a literary protagonist travels to real and symbolic rural homes in order to solve a life dilemma.

23 In September 1934 Johnson approached Herman Baron about exhibiting the Virginia works in his ACA Gallery in Greenwich Village. Like Baron, enthusiastic Harmon Foundation officials also hoped to mount a solo exhibition of Johnson's art.

24 Betty Johnson to [Evelyn] Brown, 26 March 1934 [sic], in "Malvin Gray Johnson" folder, Harmon Foundation Manuscripts, box 76. The correct date for this letter is almost certainly 26 March 1935, for it arrived at the Harmon Foundation 27 March 1935.

25 Among Johnson's remarks to his patrons at the Harmon Foundation, who recorded his descriptions of the Virginia work, is this comment about *Untitled (Red Road)*: "I happened to be walking around looking for some subject matter to do in the way of landscape, and go on one of the so-called Thoroughfare roads where traffic goes through, and hit this muddy spot. This painting is my impression." "Dictation of Malvin Gray Johnson," in "Johnson" folder, Harmon Foundation Papers, Library of Congress, Washington, D.C., box 76. Unlike a prospectus of his intentions or a faithful journal of his daily accomplishment, this document is comprised of retrospective assessments. Johnson dictated his commentary to a Harmon Foundation staffer, and it was subsequently transcribed, typed, and perhaps edited. In other words, "Dictation" is a mediated text that permits some contextualization of the Virginia work.

26 This painting was referred to as *Untitled (Red Road)* in a Hampton University Museum exhibition of 1999. It was published as *Southern Landscape* in Romare Bearden and Harry Henderson, *A History of African-American Artists from 1792 to the Present* (New York: Atherton, 1993), 184. It was first exhibited as *Red Road* at the Delphic Studios in New York in April–May 1935.

27 "Dictation of Malvin Gray Johnson," 2–4.

28 "Dictation of Malvin Gray Johnson," 2. In this statement the painting was called *First Sunday with Dinner on the Ground*. The checklist for the Harmon Foundation's November 1934 exhibition of Johnson's work (along with that of Richmond Barthé and Sargent Claude Johnson) titled the painting as *All Day Meetin'—Dinner on the Ground;* in "Johnson" folder, Harmon Foundation Papers, box 77. It was exhibited as *First Sunday Dinner on the Ground* in 2002.

29 British film critic Judith Williamson has argued, "The more power any group has to create and wield representation, the less it is required to be representative." Quoted in Isaac Julien and Kobena Mercer, "De Margin and De Center," in *Black British Cultural Studies*, ed. Houston A. Baker Jr., Manthia Diawara, and Ruth H. Lindeborg (Chicago: University of Chicago Press, 1996), 197.

30 "Yasuo Kuniyoshi," *New York Post*, 10 January 1924, in Yasuo Kuniyoshi Papers (hereafter cited as Kuniyoshi Papers), Smithsonian Archives of American Art, Washington, D.C., roll D-176, frame 168.

31 "Yasuo Kuniyoshi," 184, in Kuniyoshi Papers, roll D-176, frame 11.

32 Breuning, "Art World Events," *New York Evening Post*, 10 February 1933, n.p., in Kuniyoshi Papers, roll D-176, frame 5.

33 Kuniyoshi, "East to West," *Magazine of Art* 33, no. 2 (February 1940): 75, 77.

34 According to the Chinese lunar-solar calendar used by the Japanese until 1872, Kuniyoshi was born in the year of the ox. In 1873 the Japanese government adopted the Gregorian calendar, and most Japanese used both systems in the nineteenth century.

35 Masanori Ichikawa has read similar intentions behind Kuniyoshi's allusive representations, i.e., that the artist tried to undermine stereotypes by parodying them. "A Study on Yasuo Kuniyoshi and the Problems of the Japanese-American Painters," in National Museum of Art, *Japanese Artists Who Studied in the U.S.A. and the American Scene* (Tokyo: National Museum of Modern Art, 1982), 176. Adam Greenhalgh has argued that Kuniyoshi claimed the cow as an American symbol—of the national agrarian tradition and of the dairy industry and its marketing to Greenhalgh, "Yasuo Kuniyoshi's *Cows in Pasture*," *Gastronomica* 9, no. 3 (Summer 2009): 15–21.

36 In "Between Two Worlds: Folk Culture, Identity, and the American Art of Yasuo Kuniyoshi," Gail Levin initially argues that the artist's "work exemplifies cultural hybridity and cross-fertilization." Levin, *Archives of American Art Journal* 43, nos. 3–4 (2003): 2. Yet the article makes Japanese folklore and art central to Kuniyoshi's vision and technique. Levin's research supports this claim, yet it bears out the thesis that the artist sought to connect himself to the United States through his collection of colonial and early American art as well. Levin also muses about the *piñata*-like object in Kuniyoshi's *Two Babies* (1923), divulging that Kuniyoshi collected Mexican toys when traveling in Mexico in 1935 and that he tried glass painting, a European practice that was studied and taken up by Marsden Hartley, Wassily Kandinsky, and other modernists interested in the *volk* and their arts.

37 Wolf quoted in Meyers and Walf, *The Shores of a Dream: Yasuo Kuniyoshi's Early Work in America* (Fort Worth, TX: Amon Carter Museum, 1996), 31–32. Like their patron Hamilton Easter Field and many of their artist-peers in the New York's Whitney Studio Club, Kuniyoshi and his first wife, artist Katherine Schmidt, collected colonial American and U.S. folk art in the 1920s. The *New York Herald* named Kuniyoshi among the artists summering in Maine in 1923 who "went mad on the subject of American primitives . . . and stripped all the cupboards bare of primitives in the Maine antique shops." In "Show at Whitney Studio Galleries, Early American Art," *New York Herald*, 17 February 1924, n.p., in Kuniyoshi Papers, roll D-176, frame 147. Invited to guest curate an exhibition for the Whitney Studio Club, Kuniyoshi mounted Portraits and Religious Works in April 1924.

38 In a note dated 8 November, 1944, Kuniyoshi writes about the found objects—detritus and antique—that inspired his work. "When I walk out into the street, if I see anything interesting in shape and color, even stones, I pick them up and bring them home. If I see an interesting antique in a window, I go in and buy it. I gather together all these materials and gradually get used to them until they are a part of me. When I am thoroughly acquainted with these objects, I fit them together to suit my feeling and construct material for a still life. I know exactly what it is all about because I have felt it, because I love it, because I feel the shape and color." Kuniyoshi, "Kuniyoshi Writing: Notes for Autobiography" (1944) folder, unmicrofilmed, Kuniyoshi Papers, box 1.

39 Levin, "Between Two Worlds," 4. Levin cites Wanda M. Corn's conclusion about early twentieth-century folk art collecting: "The appetite for an indigenous folk, while primitivizing and romanticizing, expressed a desire for an imagined blood relationship to a national past." Corn, *The Great American Thing: Modern Art and National Identity, 1915–1935* (Berkeley: University of California Press, 1999), 326–27

40 "Sunday, 27 August 1944 [?]," in "Kuniyoshi Autobiography" folder, unmicrofilmed, Kuniyoshi Papers, Smithsonian Archives of American Art, Washington, D.C., box V29F7, quoted in Susan Lubowsky, "From Naïveté to Maturity, 1906–1939," *Yasuo Kuniyoshi: 100th Anniversary of His Birth* (Kyoto: National Museum of Modern Art, 1989), 32.

41 Aline B. Louchheim, "Yasuo Kuniyoshi, Look At My Past," *Art News* 47 (April 1948): 46.

42 Kuniyoshi's biographical entry for the 1939 Baltimore Museum of Art's exhibition Six Living American Artists lists his noted "preferences" among artists: "Seshu,

Korni, Chinese sculptors, Courbet, Signorelli, Daumier, and Delacroix" and his interest in "French architecture and early Italian brick buildings as well." "Yasuo Kuniyoshi," Baltimore Museum of Art, *Six Living American Artists* (Baltimore, MD: Baltimore Museum of Art, 1939), n.p. Every artist's entry, except Millard Sheets's, offers information on influences: Morris Kantor (Courbet), Bernard Karfiol (Ingres, Renoir, Picasso, Derain, and the early Picasso), Karl Knaths (Cézanne, Matisse, Braque, Klee, de Chirico, Mondrian, Miro, Chagall, and Campendonk), and Henry Varnum Poor (Walter Sickert).

43 Shi-Pu Wang, "Japan against Japan; U.S. Propaganda and Yasuo Kuniyoshi's Identity Crisis," *American Art* 22, no. 1 (Spring 2008): 28–51.

44 Kuniyoshi quoted in "An Accumulation of Sadness," *PM*, 27 November 1944, 17, in Gail Levin, "Between Two Worlds: Folk Culture, Identity, and the American Art of Yasuo Kuniyoshi," *Archives of American Art Journal* 43, nos. 3–4 (2003): 3.

45 The English-language Japanese newspaper *Sake* reported Kuniyoshi's description of his art: "Briefly, mine is a modified expressionist school—Kuniyoshism, if I may say so." "Kuniyoshi, Noted Artist Developed in U.S., Visiting Fatherland For Exhibition," *Sake*, 16 October 1931, n.p., in Kuniyoshi Papers, roll D-176, frame 342. In "East to West" Kuniyoshi writes that an exhibition of his art was "very well received, although it was thought to be too European." Kuniyoshi, "East to West," 81. That Kuniyoshi's displayed work was not considered Japanese is, of course, telling. Art historian John Clark's research of interwar art discourse in Japan has revealed debates centered upon nationalism, modernism, and newly emerging definitions of the artist's role in society and relationship to the art object. Clark, "Artistic Subjectivity in the Taisho and Early Showa Avant-Garde," in *Japanese Art after 1945: Scream Against the Sky*, ed. Alexandra Munroe (New York: Harry N. Abrams, 1994), 41–53.

46 Kuniyoshi, "East to West," 81

47 The U.S. government imprisoned more than 110,000 Japanese immigrants and citizens in rural "camps" in Arizona, Arkansas, California, Colorado, Idaho, Utah, and Wyoming from 1942 to 1945. After the Japanese attack on Pearl Harbor in 1941, Kuniyoshi was required to request government permission to travel. Subsequently, he was among the artists asked by the U.S. Office of War Information to produce anti-Japan propaganda; Kuniyoshi complied by making posters following the OWI request for images of "the recent Japanese atrocities—the water cure, for example." He also wrote propaganda speeches for broadcast to Japan. See Munroe, *Yasuo Kuniyoshi*, 38–39; and Wang, "Japan Against Japan," 28–51.

48 Radio City commissioned Georgia O'Keeffe for this mural project; she accepted and then declined. Tom Wolf, citing O'Keeffe scholars, has written that "Kuniyoshi's scheme of enlarged flowers [might be] related to O'Keeffe's famous floral images." See Wolf, "Kuniyoshi in the Early 1920s," in Meyers and Wolf, *The Shores of a Dream: Yasuo Kuniyoshi's Early Work in America* (Fort Worth, TX: Amon Carter Museum, 1996), 40.

49 Mumford, "The Art Galleries: The Rockefeller Collection," *New* Yorker 8, no. 7 (7 January 1933): 53, 56.

50 In "Kuniyoshi Autobiography" folder, unmicrofilmed, Kuniyoshi Papers, box V29 F57.

51 Kuniyoshi variably described Woodstock, New York, where he had built a summer home in 1929. In 1936 Henry McBride quotes him as saying that he was "bored stiff with the 'too nice' landscape." Quoted in Lubowsky, "From Naïveté to Maturity," 26. Writing to friends in Japan in 1936, Kuniyoshi described the view from his property thusly: "The view is magnificent to look at, but too beautiful to paint." Quoted in Bloodgood, *At Woodstock*, 16. Kuniyoshi writes in notes dated 18 November 1944, "My experience traveling all over the continent has made me feel very deeply about the Southwest, more than any other place in America. Many people think New England and the Middle West are America, both for the landscape and the inhabitants, but the Southwest, or rather a little north of there (states like Nevada, Colorado, Utah and Wyoming) goes farther back. It is much more primitive, and somehow I feel that if ever a real American painting is produced it must come from these sources." "Kuniyoshi Autobiography" folder, unmicrofilmed, Kuniyoshi Papers, box V29 F57.

52 E. M. Benson, "Yasuo Kuniyoshi Exhibits at the Downtown Gallery," in *American Magazine of Art* 29 (May 1936): 332.

53 Emmart, "Art . . . U.S. Art Still Far From Epic," 10. Six Living American Artists presented the work of Kuniyoshi, Morris Kantor, Bernard Karfiol, Karl Knaths, Henry Varnum Poor, and Millard Sheets.

54 Wolf, "Kuniyoshi as Photographer," in *Yasuo Kuniyoshi: 100th Anniversary of His Birth* (Kyoto: National Museum of Modern Art, 1989), 164. His binoculars and radio also were confiscated.

55 Notes for 8 November 1944, in Kuniyoshi, "Kuniyoshi Writing: Notes for Autobiography," Kuniyoshi Papers.

CONCLUSION

1 Lozowick, "Jewish Artists of the Season," *Menorah Journal* 10, no. 3 (June–July 1924): 282.

2 Lozowick, "What, Then, Is Jewish Art?" *Menorah Journal* 35, no. 1 (January–March 1947): 110.

3 Lester A. Walton, "Art Not Racial, Negroes Tell Critics: Leaders Reply to Charge That Works Lack Individuality." *New York World*, 2 February 1930, editorial section, 6.

4 Jewell, *Have We an American Art?* (New York: Longmans, Green, and Company, 1939), 145.

5 Alastair Bonnett surmises that "the universalist tradition may be seen as, at one and the same time, an emancipatory force and part and parcel of the colonial and neocolonial imposition of Western values and norms. . . . Comte's and Marx's universalism relied on according Europe the position of civilising centre, of the cockpit of history, the place where human liberation and equality are defined and from where they are disseminated. The universalist promise of equality demands the submission, the self-obliteration, of those to who it is 'offered.' 'We can all be one', 'we can all be equal,' it is suggested, 'if you become like me.'" Bonnett, *Anti-Racism* (New York: Routledge, 2000), 20, 24.

6 Jan Nederveen Pieterse credits Magnus Hirschfeld's 1938 book, *Racism*, on Nazi race policy as a key text that brought the term into the popular lexicon. *White on Black: Images of Blacks in Western Popular Culture* (New Haven: Yale University Press, 1992), 50. Bonnett writes that "the increasing association . . . of racial thinking with unreason led many who wished to align themselves with the authentic spirit of science to position 'real science' as *inherently* anti-racist." Bonnett, *Anti-Racism*, 20.

7 Jacobson, *Whiteness of a Different Color: European Immigrants and the Alchemy of Race* (Cambridge, MA: Harvard University Press, 1998), 99.

8 Benedict quoted in Jacobson, *Whiteness of a Different Color*, 100. Jacobson faults Benedict and other liberal white intellectuals for failing to recognize that their campaigns against anti-Semitic racializations did nothing to question the construction of race and its hierarchies. Jacobson favorably contrasts Benedict's approach to George Schulyer's, whose 1931 satirical novel *Black No More* presciently "apprehended the shift that was just taking place in the reconsolidation of whiteness": Schuyler, Jacobson writes, "drew upon the power of that observation to

further his argument about the general fabrication of races—*all* races." Jacobson, *Whiteness of a Different Color*, 124.

9 Locke, "Up Until Now," in *The Negro Artist Comes of Age: A National Survey of Contemporary American Artists* (Albany, NY: Albany Institute of History and Art, 1945), vii.

10 Woodruff quoted in Richard J. Powell, *Black Art and Culture in the Twentieth Century* (New York: Thames and Hudson, 1997), 105; Ann Eden Gibson, *Abstract Expressionism: Other Politics* (New Haven: Yale University Press, 1997), 71.

11 Maurice Berger situates the Rosenbergs' trial and execution and "the disenchantment with leftist politics" among the factors that influenced secular and conservative stances among Jewish intellectuals in the post–World War II decades. Berger, "Museum Without Walls," in Maurice Berger and Joan Rosenbaum, *Masterworks of the Jewish Museum* (New York : Jewish Museum; New Haven: Yale University Press, 2004), 31n6. Discussing Clement Greenberg's and Harold Rosenberg's statements and writings, art historian Margaret Olin has contended that their "use of the rhetoric of individuality to justify the rejection of an explicit Jewish identity may conceal a fear of identifying openly as a Jew. Fear of espousing Jewish identity may have been justified. " Olin, *The Nation without Art: Examining Modern Discourses on Jewish Art* (Lincoln: University of Nebraska Press, 2001), 175. In *How Jews Became White Folks and What That Says About Race in America* (New Brunswick, NJ: Rutgers University Press, 2000), anthropologist Karen Brodkin discusses the shifts in American Jewish identity and identification in the twentieth century through autobiographical narrative and interdisciplinary meditation on cultural, historical, national, and social phenomena.

12 *Look* 12, no. 25 (7 December 1948): 94–96.

13 Gibson's book-length consideration of abstract expressionism's "other politics," as regards to race, gender, sexuality and ethnicity, is invaluable and follows her groundbreaking research on the problem of universality in "Two Worlds: African-American Abstraction in New York at Mid-Century," in Kenekleba Gallery, *The Search for Freedom: African-American Abstract Painting, 1945-1975* (New York: Kenkeleba Gallery, 1991), 11–53; and Gibson, "Universality and Difference in Women's Abstract Painting: Krasner, Ryan, Sekula, Piper, and Streat," *Yale Journal of Criticism* 8, no. 1 (Spring 1995): 103–32.

14 100 *Contemporary American Jewish Painters and Sculptors* (New York: Yiddisher Kultura Farband Art Section, 1947).

15 *Look* 29 (18 February 1947): 80–81.

16 “It’s Striking, but Is It Art or Extravagance?” *Newsweek* 30, no. 8 (25 August 1947); “Eyes to the Left: Modern Painting Dominates State Department and Pepsi-Cola Sections,” *New York Times*, 6 October 1946, section 2, 8.

17 Henry Collidge Learned to Representative Bates, 10 February 1947, Records Group for Assistant Secretary of State for Public Affairs William Benton, Art, box 7, National Archives, Washington, D.C., quoted in Margaret Lynne Ausfeld, “*Circus Girl* Arrested: A History of the ‘Advancing American Art’ Collection, 1946–1948,” in *Advancing American Art: Politics and Aesthetics in the State Department Exhibition, 1946–48* (Montgomery, AL: Montgomery Museum of Fine Arts, 1984), 20.

18 “Collection of American Art Held Unfair to U.S. Women,” *Washington Post*, 6 May 1947, 1, quoted in Ausfield, “*Circus Girl* Arrested,” 19.

19 Truman quoted in Drew Pearson, “The Washington Merry-Go-Round,” *Washington Post*, 18 February 1947, 9.

20 “Are These Men the Best Painters in America Today?” *Look* 12, no. 3 (February 3, 1948): 44–48.

21 Also see defenses in Magravite, “Freedom of Expression,” *American Artist* 11 (September 1947): 47; Boswell, “Artists Protest,” *Art Digest* 21 (15 May 1947): 16; Pearson, “State Department Exhibition for Foreign Tour,” *Art Digest* 21 (15 October 1946): 29.

22 In 1945 Sugimoto and his family, who had been interred in concentration camps during World War II, struggled to find grocers who would accept their War Relocation Authority ration tickets in New York City: “Because we were [looked at as] foreigners . . . they wouldn’t sell to us.” Kristine Kim, *Henry Sugimoto: Painting an American Experience* (Los Angeles: Japanese American National Museum; Berkeley: Heyday Books, 2000), 101–2. New York City landlords refused to rent to Chinese American watercolorist Dong Kingman, a draftee who served in the U.S. Office of Strategic Services during World War II in the 1950s, because he was “Oriental.” Gordon H. Chang, “America’s Dong Kingman—Dong Kingman’s America,” in *Dong Kingman in San Francisco* (San Francisco: Chinese Historical Society of America and Chinese American National Museum, 2001), 20.

23 Foujita made his reputation in Paris in the interwar era and reluctantly left after the outbreak of World War II. In 1940 he returned to Japan, where he made propaganda art for Japan’s government. Despite this record, the Brooklyn Museum of Art invited him to teach at its art school and he traveled to New York to take up the post in 1949. A year later, Foujita, who blamed Kuniyoshi for poisoning the

museum's and others' later opinion of him, left New York for France, where he died in 1968. See Phyllis Birnbaum, *Glory in a Line: A Life of Foujita—The Artist Caught between East and West* (New York: Faber and Faber, 2006).

24 In 1947 Tam, who was born in Kauai, Hawaii, joined the faculty of the Brooklyn Museum Art School, where he was an influential teacher until his retirement in 1979. "Reuben Tam," in *Asian-American Art: A History, 1850–1970*, ed. Gordon H. Chang, Mark Dean Johnson, and Paul J. Karlstrom (Stanford: Stanford University Press, 2008), 429–30.

25 "Art: Dashing Realist," *Time* 46, no. 10 (3 September 1945), available at http://www.time.com/time/magazine/article/0,9171,855245,00.html (accessed 14 July 2009).

26 "Gyo Fujikawa," *American Artist* 18, no. 5 (May 1954): 32–35. A decade earlier, Kingman had been pictured on the cover and profiled in the same magazine.

27 Yuji Ichioka, a historian of Asian American Studies, coined the term "Asian American" in 1968.

28 Gordon H. Chang, "Foreword: Emerging from the Shadows: The Visual Arts and Asian American History," in Chang, Johnson, and Karlstron, *Asian-American Art* (see note 24), x.

29 Meyer, *Whatever Happened to the Institutional Critique?* (New York: American Fine Arts, Colin De Land Fine Art, Paula Cooper Gallery, 1983), 28, 13.

30 Kalpana Seshadri-Crooks has arrived at the same conclusion, and has written, "We must develop a new adversarial aesthetics that will throw racial signification into disarray. . . . The idea is not to erase identity, even if such a preposterous act were possible. Rather, we must rethink identity in tension without our usual habits of visual categorization of images. Ideally, the practice I am advocating will deploy the visual against the visual." Seshadri-Crooks, *Desiring Whiteness: A Lacanian Analysis of Race* (New York: Routledge, 2000), 158–60.

BIBLIOGRAPHY

Adlow, Dorothy. "Art Exhibitions and Jazz Debuts at Brandeis Festival: Works Shown by Established and Young Contemporaries." *Christian Science Monitor* 49, no. 163 (7 June 1957): 5.

Advancing American Art: Politics and Aesthetics in the State Department Exhibition, 1946–48. Montgomery, AL: Montgomery Museum of Fine Arts, 1984.

Afri-Cobra III. Amherst: University of Massachusetts, 1973.

American Folk Art: The Exhibition of 1932. Williamsburg, VA: Abby Aldrich Rockefeller Folk Art Collection, 1932.

Anderson, Paul Allen. *Deep River: Music and Memory in Harlem Renaissance Thought*. Durham, NC: Duke University Press, 2001.

Anreus, Alejandro. *Orozco in Gringoland: The New York Years*. Albuquerque: University of New Mexico Press, 2001.

Antliff, Mark, and Patricia Leighten. "Primitive." In *Critical Terms for Art History*, edited by Robert S. Nelson and Richard Shiff, 170–84. Chicago: University of Chicago Press, 1996.

"Antwerp to See Foujioka's California Types." *Art News* 6, no. 20 (1 Sept. 1932): 11
Appiah, Kwame Anthony. *The Ethics of Identity.* Princeton, NJ: Princeton University Press, 2005.
———. "Identity, Authenticity, Survival." In Charles Taylor et al., *Multiculturalism: Examining the Politics of Recognition,* 149–63. Princeton, NJ: Princeton University Press, 1994.
Archer-Shaw, Petrine. *Negrophilia: Avant-Garde Paris and Black Culture in the 1920s.* New York: Thames and Hudson, 2000.
"Art: Dashing Realist." *Time* 46, no. 10 (3 Sept. 1945): 58.
"The Art Galleries: Nineteen Who Are Living." *New Yorker* 5 (21 Dec., 1929): 72
"Art—Harmon Awards." *Crisis: A Record of the Darker Races* 40 (May 1933): 111.
"Art in Review: Sargent Johnson Wins Chief Prize at Exhibition by Negro Artists, Sponsored by the Harmon Foundation." *New York Times,* 21 Feb. 1933, 22.
"Artists Protest Showing by 'Japanese Fascist.'" *Daily Compass,* 24 Nov. 1949, 20.
Asia/America: Identification in Contemporary Asian American Art. NY: Asia Society Galleries and New Press, 1994.
Auerbach-Levy, William. "Negro Painters Imitate Whites." *New York World,* 5 Jan. 1930, Metropolitan section 1M.
Bagley, Ralph L. "Question of Religion." Letter to the Editor. *Art Digest* 20, no. 10 (15 Feb. 1946): 4.
Baigell, Matthew. *A Concise History of American Painting and Sculpture.* New York: Harper and Row, 1984.
———. "From Hester Street to Fifty-Seventh Street: Jewish American Artists in New York." In *Painting a Place in America: Jewish Artists in New York, 1900–1945,* edited by Norman L. Kleeblatt and Susan Chevlowe, 28–71. New York: Jewish Museum; Bloomington: Indiana University Press, 1991.
———. *Jewish Art in America: An Introduction.* Lanham, MD: Rowman and Littlefield, 2007.
———. "Max Weber's Jewish Paintings." *American Jewish History* 88, no. 3 (Sept. 2000): 341–60.
Baigell, Matthew, and Julia Williams, eds. *Artists against War and Fascism: Papers of the First American Artists' Congress.* New Brunswick, NJ: Rutgers University Press, 1986.
Baigell, Matthew, and Milly Heyd, eds. *Complex Identities: Jewish Consciousness and Modern Art.* New Brunswick, NJ: Rutgers University Press, 2001.

Baltimore Museum of Art. *Six Living American Artists.* Baltimore, MD: Baltimore Museum of Art, 1939.

Barkan, Elazar. *The Retreat of Scientific Racism: Changing Concepts of Race in Britain and the United States between the World Wars.* New York: Cambridge University Press, 1992.

Barkan, Elazar, and Ronald Bush, eds. *Prehistories of the Future: The Primitivist Project and the Culture of Modernism.* Stanford: Stanford University Press, 1995.

Barnes, Albert. *The Art in Painting.* New York: Harcourt, Brace, 1925.

Baskind, Samantha. *Encyclopedia of Jewish American Artists: Artists of the American Mosaic.* Westport, CT: Greenwood Press, 2007.

———. *Raphael Soyer and the Search for Modern Jewish Art.* Chapel Hill: University of North Carolina Press, 2004.

Bearden, Romare, and Harry Henderson. *A History of African-American Artists from 1792 to the Present.* New York: Atherton, 1993.

Benjamin, Ruth L. "Japanese Painters in America." *Parnassus* 7, no. 5 (Oct. 1935): 12–15.

Benson, E. M. "Yasuo Kuniyoshi Exhibits at the Downtown Gallery." *American Magazine of Art* 29 (May 1936): 332.

Berger, Martin A. *Sight Unseen: Whiteness and American Visual Culture.* Berkeley: University of California Press, 2005.

Berger, Maurice, and Joan Rosenbaum. *Masterworks of the Jewish Museum.* New York: Jewish Museum; New Haven: Yale University Press, 2004.

Berlant, Lauren, and Michael Warner. "Introduction to 'Critical Multiculturalism.'" In *Multiculturalism: A Critical Reader,* edited by David Theo Goldberg, 107–39. Cambridge, MA: Basil Blackwell, 1994.

Bindman, David. *From Ape to Apollo: Aesthetics and the Idea of Race in the 18th Century.* Ithaca, NY: Cornell University Press, 2002.

Bird, Paul. "A Weber Profile." *Art Digest* 25, no. 18 (1 July 1951): 6.

Birnbaum, Phyllis. *Glory in a Line: A Life of Foujita—The Artist Caught between East and West.* New York: Faber and Faber, 2006.

Bloodgood, Josephine. *At Woodstock: Yasuo Kuniyoshi.* Woodstock, NY: Woodstock Artists Association, 2003.

Bohn, Willard. "In Pursuit of the Fourth Dimension: Guillaume Apollinaire and Max Weber." *Arts Magazine* 54 (June 1980): 166–69.

Bonnett, Alastair. *Anti-Racism.* New York: Routledge, 2000.

Boris, Stacy. *The New Authentics: Artists of the Post-Jewish Generation.* Chicago: Spertus Press, 2007.

Boswell, Peyton. "Artists Protest." *Art Digest* 21, no. 16 (15 May 1947): 16.

Boyarin, Daniel. *Unheroic Conduct: The Rise of Heterosexuality and the Invention of the Jewish Man*. Berkeley: University of California Press, 1997.

Brace, Ernest. "Henry Lee McFee." *American Magazine of Art* 27 (July 1934): 375–82.

——. "Yasuo Kuniyoshi." *Creative Art* 11 (Nov. 1932): 184–88.

Brandford, Edward J. "The Harmon Foundation Announces Awards to Negro Artists." *New York Age*, 25 Feb. 1933, 1, 7.

Braufman, Sheila B. "Max Weber's Judaic Themes." Master's thesis, San Jose State University, 1981.

Braunstein, Susan L., and Jenna Weissman Joselit, eds. *Getting Comfortable in New York: The American Jewish Home, 1880–1950*. New York: Jewish Museum, 1990.

Breuning, Margaret. "Art World Events." *New York Evening Post*, 27 Feb. 1933, 11.

——. "Metropolitan Shows Feininger, Kuhn, Kuniyoshi, Marin, and Nordfeldt." *Arts Magazine* 30 (Apr. 1956): 46.

Brilliant, Richard. *Facing the New World: Jewish Portraits in Colonial and Federal America*. New York: Jewish Museum; New York: Jewish Theological Seminary of America; Munich: Prestel, 1997.

——. *Portraiture*. Cambridge, MA: Harvard University Press, 1991.

Brodkin, Karen. *How Jews Became White Folks and What That Says About Race in America*. New Brunswick, NJ: Rutgers University Press, 2000.

Broun, Elizabeth. *Albert Pinkham Ryder*. Washington, D.C.: Smithsonian Institution Press, 1989.

Brown, Evelyn S. "The Harmon Awards." *Opportunity: Journal of Negro Life* 11 (Mar. 1933): 79.

Brown, Milton W. "Max Weber, 'Jewish Artist': The Painting of This Pioneer of Modern Art and Its Supposed 'Jewish' Nature." *The Jewish Survey* 1 (May 1941): 18–19.

Brown, Milton W., Sam Hunter, et al. *American Art*. New York: Harry N. Abrams, 1988.

Brubaker, Rogers, and Frederick Cooper. "Beyond 'Identity.'" *Theory and Policy* 29, no. 1 (Feb. 2000): 1–47.

Buermeyer, Laurence. "The Negro Spirituals and American Art." *Opportunity: Journal of Negro Life* 4 (1926): 158–59.

Bulliet, C. J. "On Trying to Smile in Front of Kuniyoshi's Babies: Kuniyoshi, Ganso Create Excitement." *Chicago Evening Post*, 3 May 1927, Magazine of the Art World section, 1, 6.

Buruma, Ian. "Between Two Worlds." Review of *The Orientalist: Solving the Mystery of a Strange and Dangerous Life*, by Tom Reiss, and *The Life of Isamu Noguchi:*

Journey without Borders, by Masayo Duus. *New York Review of Books* 52, no. 10 (9 June 2005): 40–43.

Bush, Ronald, and Eleazar Barkan, eds. *Claiming the Stones, Naming the Bones: Cultural Property and the Negotiation of National and Ethnic Identity*. Los Angeles: Getty Publications, 2002.

Cahill, Holger. *Max Weber*. New York: Downtown Gallery, 1930.

"California Artists [Sargent Johnson]." *San Francisco Chronicle*, 6 Oct. 1935, D3.

Calo, Mary Ann. "African American Art and Critical Discourse between World Wars." *American Quarterly* 51 (Sept. 1999): 580–621.

———. *Distinction and Denial: Race, Nation, and the Critical Construction of the African American Artist, 1920–40*. Ann Arbor: University of Michigan Press, 2007.

Camille, Michael. "Simulacrum." In *Critical Terms for Art Historians*, edited by Robert S. Nelson and Richard Shiff, 31–44. Chicago: University of Chicago Press, 1996.

Carter, Elmer A. "He Smashed the Color Line: A Sketch of Billy Pierce." *Opportunity: A Journal of Negro Life* 8, no. 5 (May 1930): 148–49.

Cassidy, Donna. *Marsden Hartley: Race, Region, and Nation*. Hanover, NH: University Press of New England, 2005.

Chandler, Hugh S. "Sources of Essence." *Midwest Studies in Philosophy* 11 (1986): 379–89.

Chang, Gordon H. "America's Dong Kingman—Dong Kingman's America." In Dong Kingman, Irene Poon, and Mark Johnson, *Dong Kingman in San Francisco*, 20–24. San Francisco: Chinese Historical Society of America and Chinese American National Museum, 2001.

Chang, Gordon H., Mark Dean Johnson, and Paul J. Karlstron, eds. *Asian-American Art: A History, 1850–1970*. Stanford: Stanford University Press, 2008.

Cheney, Martha Candler. *Modern Art in America*. New York: Whittlesey House, McGraw-Hill, 1939.

Chevlowe, Susan. *The Jewish Identity Project: New American Photography*. New York: Jewish Museum; New Haven: Yale University Press, 2005.

Cheyette, Bryan, and Laura Marcus, eds. *Modernity, Culture, and "The Jew."* Cambridge, England: Polity Press, 1998.

Cheyney, Sheldon. *Primer of Modern Art*. New York: Boni and Liveright, 1924.

Chipp, Herschel B., ed. *Theories of Modern Art*. Berkeley: University of California Press, 1968.

Chiu, Melissa, Karen Higa, and Susette S. Min. *One Way or Another: Asian American Art Now*. New York: Asia Society; New Haven: Yale University Press, 2001.

Ciolkowska, Muriel. "Absolutism in Modern American Art." *Artwork* 2 (Jan.–Mar. 1926): 94–95.
Clark, Eliot. *History of the National Academy of Design, 1825–1953*. New York: Columbia University Press, 1954.
Clifford, James. "Negrophilia." In *New History of French Literature*, edited by Denis Hollier, 901–8. Cambridge, MA: Harvard University Press, 1989.
Cohen, Richard I. *Jewish Icons: Art and Society in Modern Europe*. Berkeley: University of California Press, 1998.
Corn, Wanda M. *The Great American Thing: Modern Art and National Identity, 1915–1935*. Berkeley: University of California Press, 1999.
Cortissoz, Royal. *American Art*. New York: Charles Scribner's Sons, 1923.
Cotter, Holland. "Art in Review: Ellen Gallagher." *New York Times*, 1 Apr. 2005, national edition, section B, 32.
Craven, Thomas. *Men of Art*. New York: Simon and Schuster, 1931.
Crenshaw, Kimberlé, ed. *Critical Race Theory: The Key Writings That Formed the Movement*. New York: New Press, 2005.
Cunard, Nancy, ed. *Negro: An Anthology*. London: Cunard and Wishart, 1934.
Delgado, Richard, ed. *Critical Race Theory: The Cutting Edge*. Philadelphia: Temple University Press, 1995.
De Man, Paul. *The Rhetoric of Romanticism*. New York: Columbia University Press, 1984.
deSouza, Allan. "Name Calling." In *Tradeshow: New Currents in Asian American Art*, 2–5. Shanghai: c2 Gallery at the Pottery Workshop, 2003.
Dirlik, Arif. "Chinese History and the Question of Orientalism." *History and Theory* 35, no. 4 (Dec. 1996): 96–118.
Doss, Erika. *Benton, Pollock, and the Politics of Modernism: From Regionalism to Abstract Expressionism*. Chicago: University of Chicago Press, 1991.
"The Drop Sinister." *Crisis: A Record of the Darker Races* 10 (Oct. 1915): 286–87.
Du Bois, W. E. B. *The Gift of Black Folk: The Negro in the Making of America*. Boston: Stratford, 1924. Reprint, Millwood, NY: Kraus Thomson, 1975.
———. *The Souls of Black Folk*. Chicago: A. C. McClurg, 1903. Reprint, New York: Penguin, 1996.
DuCille, Anne. "Black Barbie and the Deep Play of Difference." In *The Feminism and Visual Culture Reader*, edited by Amelia Jones, 337–48. London: Routledge, 2003.
Dunning, Jennifer. *Alvin Ailey*. Reading, MA: Addison-Wesley, 1996.
Dyer, Richard. *White*. New York: Routledge, 1997.

Early, Gerald. "A Place of Our Own." *New York Times*, 14 Apr. 2002, national edition, "Educational Life," section D, 34–35, 40.

Ewen, Elizabeth, and Stuart Ewen. *Typecasting: On the Arts & Science of Human Inequality*. New York: Seven Stories Press, 2006.

"Exhibitions in New York: Yun Gee, Elliot Orr (Balzac Galleries)." *Art News* 30, no. 33 (May 1932): 12.

"Eyes to the Left: Modern Painting Dominates State Department and Pepsi-Cola Sections." *New York Times*, 6 Oct. 1942, section 2, 8.

Fabian, Johannes. *Time and the Other: How Anthropology Makes Its Object*. New York: Columbia University Press, 1983.

Favor, J. Martin. *Authentic Blackness: The Folk in the New Negro Renaissance*. Durham, NC: Duke University Press, 1999.

Ferguson, Roderick A. "Race-ing Homonormativity: Citizenship, Sociology, and Gay Identity." In *Black Queer Studies: A Critical Anthology*, edited by E. Patrick Johnson and Mae G. Henderson, 52–67. Durham, NC: Duke University Press, 2005.

Fleming, Tuliza N. *Breaking Racial Barriers: African Americans in the Harmon Foundation Collection*. Washington, D.C.: Smithsonian Institution; San Francisco: Pomegranate, 1997.

Flinn, Margaret C. "The Prescience of Élie Faure." *SubStance* 34, no. 3, issue 108 (2005): 47–61.

Forum Gallery. *Max Weber's Women*. New York: Forum Gallery, 1996.

Foster, Hal. *Prosthetic Gods*. Cambridge, MA: MIT Press, 2004.

Francis, Jacqueline. "Making History: Malvin Gray Johnson and Earle W. Richardson's Studies for *Negro Achievement*." In *The Social and the Real: Political Art of the 1930s in the Western Hemisphere*, edited by Diana Linden, Jonathan Weinberg, and Alejandro Anreus, 116–31, 302–13. State College: Pennsylvania State University Press, 2005.

———. "Modern Art, 'Racial Art': The Work of Malvin Gray Johnson and the Challenges of Painting, 1928–1934." PhD diss., Emory University, 2000.

———. "Painting the South with a Northern Eye." *Mississippi Quarterly* 56, no. 4 (Winter 2004): 597–617.

———. "'Trying to Do What Artists of All Races Do': Malvin Gray Johnson's Modernism." In *Climbing Up the Mountain: The Modern Art of Malvin Gray Johnson*, 52–84. Durham: North Carolina Central University Museum of Art, 2002.

———. "Writing African-American Art History." *American Art* 17, no. 1 (Spring 2003): 2–10.

Fusco, Coco. "Racial Time, Racial Marks, Racial Metaphors." In *Only Skin Deep: Changing Visions of the American Self*, edited by Coco Fusco and Brian Wallis, 13–48. New York: International Center of Photography; New York: Harry N. Abrams, 2003.

Gerber, David A. "Review: Caucasians Are Made and Not Born: How European Immigrants Became White People." *Reviews in American History* 27, no. 3 (Sept. 1999): 437–43.

Gibson, Ann Eden. *Abstract Expressionism: Other Politics*. New Haven: Yale University Press, 1997.

——. "Two Worlds: African-American Abstraction in New York at Mid-Century." In Kenekleba Gallery, *The Search for Freedom: African-American Abstract Painting, 1945–1975*, 11–53. New York: Kenkeleba Gallery, 1991.

——. "Universality and Difference in Women's Abstract Painting: Krasner, Ryan, Sekula, Piper, and Streat." *Yale Journal of Criticism* 8, no. 1 (Spring 1995): 103–32.

Glueck, Grace. "Art Review: European Influences on Americans' Views." *New York Times*, 3 Sept. 2004, national edition, section B, 27.

Goldwater, Robert J. *Primitivism in Modern Art*. Rev. ed. New York: Vintage Press, 1967.

Goodrich, Lloyd. *Max Weber: Retrospective Exhibition*. New York: Whitney Museum of American Art, 1949.

——. *Yasuo Kuniyoshi*. New York: Macmillan and Whitney Museum of American Art, 1948.

——. *Yasuo Kuniyoshi*. New York: Whitney Museum of American Art at Philip Morris, 1986.

Gornick, Vivian. "Radiant Poison: Saul Bellow, Philip Roth, and the End of Jew as Metaphor." *Harper's Magazine* 317, no. 1900 (Sept. 2008): 69–76.

Greenhalgh, Adam. "Yasuo Kuniyoshi's *Cows in Pastures*." *Gastronomica* 9, no. 3 (Summer 2009): 15–21.

Grimes, William. "A Metaphysics Starter Kit, and a Primer in Jewish Arcana." Review of *Kabbalah: A Very Short Introduction*, by Joseph Dan, and *Riddles of Existence: A Guided Tour of Metaphysics*, by Earl Conee and Theodore Sider. *New York Times*, 21 Dec. 2005, national edition, section B, 42.

Guggenheim Fellowship Archives, Guggenheim Foundation, New York.

"Gyo Fujikawa." *American Artist* 18, no. 5 (May 1954): 32–35.

Hall, Stuart. "New Ethnicities." In *Stuart Hall: Critical Dialogues in Cultural Studies*, edited by David Morley and Kuan-Hsing Chen, 441–49. New York: Routledge, 1996.

Hames-García, Michael. "'Who Are Our Own People?' Challenges for a Theory of Social Identity." In *Reclaiming Identity: Realist Theory and the Predicament of Postmodernism*, edited by Hames-García and Paula M. L. Moya, 102–29. Berkeley: University of California Press, 2000.

Handler, Richard. "Is 'Identity' a Useful Concept?" In *Commemorations: The Politics of National Identity*, edited by John R. Gillis, 27–40. Princeton, NJ: Princeton University Press, 1994.

"Harlem Library Shows Negro Art." *Art News* 31 (20 May 1933): 14.

Harmon Foundation. *Exhibition of the Work of Negro Artists*. New York: Harmon Foundation, 1931.

"Harmon Foundation Announces Awards to Negro Artists." *New York Age*, 25 Feb. 1933, 7.

Harmon Foundation Papers. Library of Congress, Washington, D.C.

Harris, Michael D. *Colored Pictures: Race and Visual Representation*. Chapel Hill: University of North Carolina Press, 2003.

Hartigan, John R. *Odd Tribes: Toward a Cultural Analysis of White People*. Durham, NC: Duke University Press, 2005.

Hartley, Marsden. "The Scientific Esthethic of the Redman, Part I." *Art and Archaeology* 13, no. 3 (Mar. 1922): 113–19.

Haskell, Barbara. *The American Century: Art and Culture, 1900–1950*. New York: Whitney Museum of American Art, 1999.

Hay, Jonathan, and Mimi Young, eds. *Why Asia? Contemporary Asian and Asian-American Art*. New York: New York University Press, 1998.

Hayward Gallery. *Rhapsodies in Black: Art of the Harlem Renaissance*. London: Hayward Gallery, 1997.

Henderson, Linda. *The Fourth Dimension and Non-Euclidean Geometry in Modern Art*. Princeton, NJ: Princeton University Press, 1983.

Henderson, Rose. "Negro Art Exhibit." *Southern Workman* 63 (July 1934): 215–17.

Hermand, Jost. "Artificial Atavism: German Expressionism and Blacks." In *Blacks and German Culture*, edited by Jost Hermand and Reinhold Grimm, 64–86. Madison: University of Wisconsin Press, 1986.

"Hotel Worker First Prize in Art Exhibition." *Amsterdam News* (New York), 5 Mar. 1930, 7.

Hughes, Langston. "The Negro Artist and the Racial Mountain." *Nation* 122 (23 June 1926): 692–94.

Hurston, Zora Neale. "Characteristics of Negro Expression." In *Negro: An Anthology*, edited by Nancy Cunard, 24–31. London: Cunard and Wishart, 1934. Reprint, New York: Frederick Unser Publishing, 1970.

Hutchinson, Elizabeth. "Modern Native American Art: Angel DeCora's Transcultural Aesthetics." *Art Bulletin* 83, no. 4 (Dec. 2001): 740–56.

Hutchinson, George B. *The Harlem Renaissance in Black and White.* Cambridge, MA: Belknap Press of Harvard University Press, 1995.

Ichikawa, Masanori. "A Study on Yasuo Kuniyoshi and the Problems of the Japanese-American Painters." In *Japanese Artists Who Studied in the U.S.A. and the American Scene*, 174–80. Tokyo: National Museum of Modern Art, 1982.

Ignatiev, Noel. *How the Irish Became White.* Cambridge, MA: Harvard University Press, 1995.

"In the Galleries: The Museum of Modern Art." *The Arts* 16, no. 8 (Apr. 1930): 568.

"Is William H. Johnson, Negro Prize Winner, Blazing a New Trail?" *Art Digest* 4, no. 13 (15 Jan. 1930).

"It's Striking, but Is It Art or Extravagance?" *Newsweek* 30, no. 8 (25 Aug. 1947): 17.

Jackson, George Pullen. "Genesis of the Negro Spiritual." *American Mercury* 26 (June 1932): 243–55.

Jacobson, Matthew Frye. *Special Sorrows: The Diasporic Imagination of Irish, Polish, and Jewish Immigrants in the United States.* Cambridge, MA: Harvard University Press, 1995.

———. *Whiteness of a Different Color: European Immigrants and the Alchemy of Race.* Cambridge, MA: Harvard University Press, 1998.

James, Clive. "Well-Versed." Review of *Break, Blow, Burn: Camille Paglia Reads Forty-Three of the World's Best Poems*, by Camille M. Paglia. *New York Times Book Review*, 27 Mar. 2005, section 7, 8–10.

Japanese Artists Who Studied in the U.S.A. and the American Scene. Tokyo: National Museums of Modern Art, 1982.

Japanese Artists Who Studied in the U.S.A., 1875–1970. Wakayama, Japan: Museum of Modern Art, 1987.

"Japan's Way." *Art Digest* 6 no. 4 (15 Nov. 1931): 2, 19.

Jewell, Edward Alden. "A Complex Art Fabric: Rich Melange in the Galleries Vibrates with Esthetic Urge of Races and Individuals." *New York Times*, 12 Feb. 1922, 122.

———. *Americans.* New York: Alfred A. Knopf, 1930.

———. "Art in Review: Kuniyoshi in New One-Man Exhibit at Downtown Galleries, Shows Considerable Progress." *New York Times*, 8 Feb. 1933, Arts and Books section, 15.

——. *Have We an American Art?* New York: Longmans, Green, 1939.

——. "Zorn, Weber, O'Keeffe and Others." *New York Times,* 16 Jan. 1944, x9.

Johnson, Barbara E. "Response" to Henry Louis Gates Jr., "Canon Formation, Literary History, and the Afro-American Tradition: From the Seen to the Told." In *Afro-American Literary Study in the 1990s,* edited by Houston A. Baker Jr. and Patricia Redmond, 39–44. Chicago: University of Chicago Press, 1989.

Johnson, Guy B. *Folk Culture on St. Helena Island, South Carolina.* Hatboro, PA: Folklore Associates, 1931.

Julien, Isaac, and Kobena Mercer. "De Margin and De Center." In *Black British Cultural Studies,* edited by Houston A. Baker Jr., Manthia Diawara, and Ruth H. Lindeborg, 194–209. Chicago: University of Chicago Press, 1997.

Kee, Joan. "Who's Afraid of Asian American Art?" In *Tradeshow: New Currents in Asian American Art,* 32–43. Shanghai: c2 Gallery at the Pottery Workshop, 2003.

Kemble, Edward. "Illustrating *Huckleberry Finn.*" *Colophon: A Book Collector's Quarterly* 1 (Feb. 1930): n.p.

Kenekleba Gallery. *The Search for Freedom: African-American Abstract Painting, 1945–1975.* New York: Kenkeleba Gallery, 1991.

Kennedy, R. Emmet. *Mellows: A Chronicle of Unknown Singers.* New York: Albert and Charles Boni, 1925.

K. G. S. "Exhibition at Church." *New York Times,* 6 July 1932, 22

Kim, Janine Young. "Are Asians Black? The Asian American Civil Rights Agenda and the Contemporary Significance of the Black/White Paradigm." In *Contemporary Asian America: A Multidisciplinary Reader,* edited by Min Zhou and J. V. Gatewood, 331–53. 2d ed. New York: New York University Press, 2007.

Kim, Kristine. *Henry Sugimoto: Painting an American Experience.* Los Angeles: Japanese American National Museum; Berkeley: Heyday Books, 2000.

Kleeblatt, Norman L., ed. *Mirroring Evil: Nazi Imagery/Recent Art.* New York: Jewish Museum; New Brunswick, NJ: Rutgers University Press, 2002.

——. *"Too Jewish"? Challenging Traditional Ideas.* New York : Jewish Museum; New Brunswick, NJ: Rutgers University Press, 1996.

Kleeblatt, Norman L., and Susan Chevlowe, eds. *Painting a Place in America: Jewish Artists in New York, 1900–1945.* New York: Jewish Museum; Bloomington: Indiana University Press, 1991.

Kootz, Samuel. *Modern American Painters.* New York: Brewer and Warren, 1930.

Kornweibel, Theodore, Jr. "Theophilus Lewis and the Theater of the Harlem Renaissance." In *The Harlem Renaissance Remembered*, edited by Arna Bontemps, 171–89. New York: Dodd, Mead, 1972.

Krane, Susan, and Percy North. *Max Weber: The Cubist Decade, 1910–1920*. Atlanta: High Museum of Art, 1991.

Krauss, Rosalind. *Cindy Sherman, 1975–1993*. New York: Rizzoli, 1993.

———. "In the Name of Picasso." *October* 16 (Spring 1981): 7–22

Kuniyoshi, Yasuo. "East to West." *Magazine of Art* 33, no. 2 (Feb. 1940): 75–84.

———. "Universality in Art." *League Quarterly* 20, no. 3 (Spring 1949): 6–7.

"Kuniyoshi Becoming Individual." *Art Digest* 7, no. 10 (15 Feb. 1933): 14.

"Kuniyoshi: One of America's Most Honored Artists Fuses East and West." *Look* 12, no. 25 (7 Dec. 1948): 94–96.

Kurzman, Dan. *No Greater Glory: The Four Immortal Chaplains and the Sinking of the Dorchester in World War II*. New York: Random House, 2004.

Lahr, John. "A Critic at Large: King Cole: The Not So Merry Soul of Cole Porter." *New Yorker*, 12 and 19 July 2004, 100–104.

———. "The Theater: Unnatural History: Studies in Psychology and Slickness." *New Yorker*, 19 and 26 Apr. 2004, 196–98.

Landsberger, Franz. *A History of Jewish Art* (1947). Reprint, Port Washington, NY: Kennikat Press, 1973.

Lears, T. J. Jackson. "Packaging the Folk: Tradition and Amnesia in American Advertising, 1880–1940." In *Folk Roots, New Roots: Folklore in American Life*, edited by Jane S. Becker and Barbara Franco, 103–40. Lexington, MA: Museum of Our Natural Heritage, 1989.

Lee, Anthony W. *Picturing Chinatown: Art and Orientalism in San Francisco*. Berkeley: University of California Press, 2001.

———. *Yun Gee: Poetry, Writings, Art, Memories*. Pasadena: Pasadena Museum of California Art; Seattle: University of Washington Press, 2003.

LeFalle-Collins, Lizzetta, and Judith Wilson. *Sargent Claude Johnson: American Modernist*. San Francisco: San Francisco Museum of Modern Art, 1998.

Leeming, David. *Amazing Grace: A Life of Beauford Delaney*. New York: Oxford University Press, 1998.

Leininger-Miller, Theresa. "African American Artists in Paris, 1922–1934." PhD diss., Yale University, 1995.

Levin, Gail. "Between Two Worlds: Folk Culture, Identity, and the American Art of Yasuo Kuniyoshi." *Archives of American Art Journal* 43, nos. 3–4 (2003): 2–17.

Levy, Jacob T. *The Multiculturalism of Fear*. New York: Oxford University Press, 2000.

Lewis, Theophilus. "The Harlem Sketch Book." *Amsterdam News* (New York), 22 Jan. 1930, 9.

Littleton, Taylor, and Maltby Sykes. *Advancing American Art: Painting, Politics, and the Cultural Confrontation*. 2d ed. Tuscaloosa: University of Alabama, 1996.

Locke, Alain. *Negro Art: Past and Present*. Washington, D.C.: Associated Publishers, 1936.

———. *The Negro in Art*. Washington, D.C.: Associates in Negro Folk Education, 1940. Reprint, New York: Hacker Art Books, 1979.

———, ed. *The New Negro: Voices of the Harlem Renaissance*. New York: Albert Boni and Sons, 1925. Reprint, New York: Atheneum, 1992.

———. "To Certain of Our Philistines." *Opportunity: Journal of Negro Art* 3 (May 1925): 155–56.

Loncheim, Aline B. "Yasuo Kunyoshi: Look at My Past." *Art News* 47 (Apr. 1948): 46–48.

Lowenthal, David. "Identity, Heritage, and History." In *Commemorations: The Politics of National Identity*, edited by John R. Gills, 41–57. Princeton, NJ: Princeton University Press, 1994.

Lozowick, Louis. "Jewish Artists of the Season." *Menorah Journal* 10, no. 3 (June–July 1924): 282–84.

———. *100 American Jewish Artists*. New York: YKUF Art Section, 1947.

———. "What, Then, Is Jewish Art?" *Menorah Journal* 35, no. 1 (Jan.–Mar. 1947): 110.

L. S. Alexander Gumby Papers. Amistad Research Center, New Orleans, Louisiana.

Lyford, Amy M. "Noguchi, Sculptural Abstraction, and the Politics of Japanese American Internment." *Art Bulletin* 85, no. 1 (Mar. 2003): 137–51.

Machida, Margo. *Unsettled Visions: Contemporary Asian American Artists and the Social Imaginary*. Durham, NC: Duke University Press, 2008.

Magravite, Peppino. "Freedom of Expression." *American Artist* 11 (Sept. 1947): 47.

Malvin Gray Johnson Papers. Harmon Foundation Papers, Library of Congress, Washington, D.C.

Marshall, Keith. *John McCready, 1911–1965*. New Orleans: New Orleans Museum of Art, 1931.

Martin, Robert K. "Painting and Primitivism: Hart Crane and the Development of an American Expressionist Esthetic." *Mosaic* 14, no. 3 (Summer 1981): 49–62.

Martin, Tony. *Literary Garveyism: Garvey, Black Arts and the Harlem Renaissance*. Dover, MA: Majority Press, 1983.

Max Weber Papers. Smithsonian Archives of American Art, Washington, D.C.

"Max Weber's Exhibition." *New York Times*, 18 Feb. 1923, x7.

McBride, Henry. "Joseph Stella and Max Weber." *Dial* 74 (Apr. 1923): 424–25.

——. "The Palette Knife." *Creative Art* 6, no. 1 (Jan. 1930): supplemental pages 9–11.

McBride, Henry, and Daniel Catton Rich. *The Flow of Art: Essays and Criticisms of Henry McBride*. New York: Atheneum, 1975.

McElroy, Elsie. "Yasuo Kuniyoshi—The Fist and the Shadow of the Fist." Typescript. Kuniyoshi Artist File, Archives of the Whitney Museum of American Art, New York.

Meier-Graefe, Julius. "A Few Conclusions on American Art." *Vanity Fair* 31, no. 3 (Nov. 1928): 83, 134, 136, 138.

Melquist, Jerome. *The Emergence of American Art*. New York: Charles Scribner's Sons, 1942.

Menand, Louis. "All That Glitters: Literature's Global Economy." *New Yorker*, 26 Dec. 2005, and 2 Jan. 2006, 136–40.

Mercer, Kobena. "Ethnicity and Internationality: New British Art and Diaspora-Based Blackness." *Third Text* 49 (Winter 1999–2000): 51–62.

——. *Welcome to the Jungle: New Positions in Black Cultural Studies*. New York: Routledge, 1994.

Meyer, James M. *Whatever Happened to the Institutional Critique?* New York: American Fine Arts, Colin De Land Fine Art, Paula Cooper Gallery, 1983.

Michaels, Walter Benn. "Autobiography of an Ex-White Man: Why Race Is Not a Social Construction." *Transition* 73, no. 1 (1998): 122–43.

Mooney, Amy J. "Representing Race: Disjunctures in the Work of Archibald J. Motley, Jr." *Art Institute of Chicago Museum Studies* 24 (1999): 162–79.

Morgan, David. *Visual Piety: A History and Theory of Popular Religious Images*. Berkeley: University of California Press, 1998.

Morgan, David, and Sally M. Promey. *Exhibiting the Culture of American Religions*. Valparaiso, IN: Brauer Museum of Art, Valparaiso University, 2000.

——. *The Visual Culture of American Religions*. Berkeley: University of California Press, 2001.

Mott, Christopher M. "The Art of Self-Promotion; or Which Self to Sell? The Proliferation and Disintegration of the Harlem Renaissance." In *Marketing Modernisms: Self-Promotion, Canonizing, and Rereading*, edited by Kevin Dettmar and Stephen Watt, 253–74. Ann Arbor: University of Michigan Press, 1996.

Mullen, M. *An Approach to Art*. Merion, PA: Barnes Foundation, 1923.

Mumford, Lewis. "The Art Galleries: The Rockerfeller Collection." *New Yorker* 8, no. 47 (7 Jan. 1933): 53, 56.
Munroe, Alexandra. *Japanese Art after 1945: Scream Against the Sky*. New York: Harry N. Abrams, 1994.
Museum of Modern Art. *Max Weber: Retrospective Exhibition, 1907–1930*. Text by Alfred H. Barr Jr. New York: Museum of Modern Art, 1930.
Myers, Jane, and Tom Wolf. *The Shores of a Dream: Yasuo Kuniyoshi's Early Work in America*. Fort Worth, TX: Amon Carter Museum, 1996.
"National Academy Makes Another Gesture Toward Liberalization." *Art Digest* 6, no. 13 (1 Apr. 1932): 3–4.
National Museum of Art. *Japanese Artists Who Studied in the U.S.A. and the American Scene*. Tokyo: National Museum of Modern Art, 1982.
The Negro Artist Comes of Age: A National Survey of Contemporary American Artists. Albany, NY: Albany Institute of History and Art, 1945.
"Negroes-Art" File. Schomburg Center for Research in Black Culture, New York City Public Library, New York.
"The Negro in Art: How Shall He Be Portrayed?" *Crisis: A Record of the Darker Races* 31, no. 5 (May 1926): 219–20.
"The Negro in Art: How Shall He Be Portrayed?" *Crisis: A Record of the Darker Races* 31, no. 6 (May 1926): 278–80.
"The Negro in Art: How Shall He Be Portrayed?" *Crisis: A Record of the Darker Races* 32, no. 1 (May 1926): 35–36.
"The Negro in Art: How Shall He Be Portrayed?" *Crisis: A Record of the Darker Races* 32, no. 2 (June 1926): 71–73.
"The Negro in Art: How Shall He Be Portrayed?" *Crisis: A Record of the Darker Races* 32, no. 4 (Aug. 1926): 193–94.
"The Negro in Art: How Shall He Be Portrayed?" *Crisis: A Record of the Darker Races* 32, no. 5 (Sept. 1926): 238–39.
"The Negro in Art: How Shall He Be Portrayed?" *Crisis: A Record of the Darker Races* 33, no. 1 (Nov. 1929): 28–29.
"Noguchi's Double Life." *Art Digest* 6, no. 11 (1 Mar. 1932): 19.
North, Percy. *Max Weber: American Modern*. New York: Jewish Museum, 1982.
Olin, Margaret. *The Nation without Art: Examining Modern Discourses on Jewish Art*. Lincoln: University of Nebraska Press, 2001.
100 *American Jewish Painters and Sculptors*. New York: Yiddisher Kultural Farband Art Section, 1947.

"One Hundred Important Paintings." *Creative Art* 4 (May 1929): supplemental pages 37–39.

"Originality in American Art." *American Architect and Building News* 3, no. 106 (5 Jan. 1878): 3.

Ozawa, Yoshio. *Critical Biography: Yasuo Kuniyoshi*. Tokyo: Shincho-Sha, 1975.

———. *Hisho to Kaiki: Kuniyoshi Yasuo no Seiyo to Toyo*. Okayama-Shi: Nihon Bukyo Shippan, Heisei 8 [1996].

———. *Kuniyoshi Yasuo: Hyoden*. Tokyo: Shinchosa, 1974.

Pearson, Drew. "The Washington Merry Go-Round." *Washington Post*, 18 Feb. 1947, 9.

Pearson, Ralph M. *The Modern Renaissance in American Art: Presenting the Work and Philosophy of 54 Distinguished Artists*. New York: Harper and Brothers, 1954.

———. "A Modern Viewpoint: State Department Exhibition for Foreign Tour." *Art Digest* 21 (15 Oct. 1946): 29.

Pemberton, Murdock. "Around the Galleries." *Creative Art* 6 (Jan. 1930): supplemental pages 12–14.

Petruck, Peninah R. Y. *American Art Criticism, 1910–1939*. New York: Garland, 1981.

Phillips, Duncan. *A Collection in the Making: A Survey of the Problems Involved in Collecting Pictures Together with Brief Estimates of the Painters in the Phillips Memorial Gallery*. New York: E. Weyhe; Washington, D.C.: Phillips Memorial Gallery, 1926.

———. "Personality in Art: III." *American Magazine of Art* 28 (Apr. 1935): 217–18.

Pieterse, Jan Nederveen. *White on Black: Images of Blacks in Western Popular Culture*. New Haven: Yale University Press, 1992.

Pina, Henry P. "Protest Against Weber." Letter to the editor. *Art Digest* 20, no. 9 (1 Feb. 1946): 4.

Pinder, Kymberly N., ed. "Black Representation and Western Survey Textbooks." *Art Bulletin* 81, no. 3 (Sept. 1999): 533–38.

———. *Race-ing Art History: Critical Readings in Race and Art History*. New York: Routledge, 2002.

Poore, Dudley. "Yasuo Kuniyoshi." *The Arts* 7, no. 2 (Feb. 1925): 113–14.

Porter, James A. "Malvin Gray Johnson, Artist." *Opportunity: Journal of Negro Life* (Apr. 1935): 117–18.

———. *Modern Negro Art*. New York: Dryden Press, 1943. Reprint, Washington, D.C.: Howard University Press, 1992.

———. "Roots of Culture." Letter to the editor. *New York Times*, 27 Dec. 1931, section 8, 12.

Portland Museum of Art. *European Muses, American Masters, 1870–1950*. Portland, ME: Portland Museum of Art, 2004.

Powell, Richard J. *Black Art and Culture in the Twentieth Century*. New York: Thames and Hudson, 1997.

———. *The Blues Aesthetic: Black Culture and Modernism*. Washington, D.C.: Washington Project for the Arts, 1989.

———. *Homecoming: The Art and Life of William H. Johnson*. Washington, D.C.: National Museum of American Art, Smithsonian Institution, 1991.

Price, Sally. *Primitive Art in Civilized Places*. Chicago: University of Chicago Press, 1989.

Rainey, Ada. "Negro Art Exhibit Has Merit." *Washington Post*, 19 May 1929, section 2, 9.

Reiss, Lionel. *My Models Were Jews: A Painter's Pilgrimage to Many Lands*. New York: Gordon Press, 1938.

Rewald, John. *Cézanne in America: Dealers, Collectors, Artists, and Critics, 1891–1921*. Princeton, NJ: Princeton University Press, 1989.

———. *The Paintings of Paul Cézanne*. Vol. 1. New York: Harry N. Abrams, 1996.

Reynolds, Gary A., Beryl J. Wright, and David C. Driskell. *Against the Odds: African-American Artists and the Harmon Foundation*. Newark, NJ: Newark Museum, 1989.

Riley, Denise. *The Words of Selves: Identification, Solidarity, Irony*. Stanford, CA: Stanford University Press, 2000.

Robinson, Jontyle T., Wendy Greenhouse, and Archibald John Motley. *The Art and Life of Archibald J. Motley, Jr.* Chicago: Chicago Historical Society, 1991.

Rodgers, Kenneth G. *Climbing Up the Mountain: The Modern Art of Malvin Gray Johnson*. Durham: North Carolina Central University Museum of Art, 2002.

Roediger, David R. *Working toward Whiteness: How America's Immigrants Became White; The Strange Journey from Ellis Island to the Suburbs*. New York: Basic Books, 2005.

Rosen, Jonathan. "Books: The Fabulist: How I. B. Singer Translated Himself into American Literature." *New Yorker*, 7 June 2004, 86–88, 90–93.

Rosenberg, Harold. "Is There a Jewish Art?" *Commentary* 42, no. 1 (July 1966): 57–60.

Rosenfeld, Paul. "American Painting." *Dial* 1 (Dec. 1921): 649–70.

———. *Port of New York: Essays on Fourteen American Moderns*. New York : Harcourt, Brace, and Co., 1924. Reprinted with introduction by Sherman Paul. Urbana: University of Illinois Press, 1961.

Ross, Marlon. *Manning the Race: Reforming Black Men in the Jim Crow*. New York: New York University Press, 2004.

Rubens, Alfred. *History of Jewish Costume*. London: Vallantine, Mitchell, 1967.

Rubinstein, Daryl R. *Max Weber: A Catalogue Raisonné of His Graphic Work*. Chicago: University of Chicago Press, 1980.

Rushing, W. Jackson. *Native American Art and the New York Avant-Garde: A History of Cultural Primitivism*. Austin: University of Texas Press, 1995.

Said, Edward. *Orientalism*. New York: Vintage Books/Random House, 1994.

Salpeter, Harry. "Yasuo Kuniyoshi: Artists' Artist." *Esquire* 7, no. 4 (Apr. 1937): 112–13, 214–16.

"San Francisco Artists." *San Francisco Chronicle*, 6 Oct. 1935, D3

Schapiro, Meyer. "Race, Nationality and Art." *Art Front* 2, no. 4 (Mar. 1936): 10–12.

Schomburg, Arturo. "The Negro Digs Up His Past." In *The New Negro*, edited by Alain Locke, 231–37. New York: Atheneum, 1925.

Schor, Naomi, and Elizabeth Weed, eds. *The Essential Difference*. Providence: Brown University Press, 1994.

Schuyler, George S. "The Negro-Art Hokum." *Nation* 122 (16 June 1926): 662–63.

Schwimmer, Suzanne. "The Four Chaplains Stamp: The Story of the Original First Design by Louis Schwimmer." Available at http://www.schwimmer.com/fourchaplains. Accessed 11 June 2007.

Seshadri-Crooks, Kalpana. *Desiring Whiteness: A Lacanian Analysis of Race*. New York: Routledge, 2000.

Shannon, Helen. "Toward the Harlem Museum of African Art: New Negroes, the Primitive, and the Folk." Unpublished paper, 1998.

Somerville, Siobhan. "Scientific Racism and the Emergence of the Homosexual Body." *Journal of the History of Sexuality* 5, no. 2 (Oct. 1994): 243–65.

Soussloff, Catherine M., ed. *Jewish Identity in Modern Art History*. Berkeley: University of California Press, 1999.

Stepto, Robert B. *From Beyond the Veil: A Study of Afro-American Narrative*. 2d ed. Urbana: University of Illinois Press, 1991.

Story, Ala. *First Comprehensive Retrospective in the West of Oils, Gouaches, Pastels, Drawings, and Graphic Works by Max Weber, 1881–1961*. Santa Barbara: Art Galleries, University of California, 1968.

Stott, William. *Documentary Expression and Thirties America*. New York: Oxford University Press, 1973.

Sweeney, James Johnson. "Art Chronicle." *Partisan Review* 11 (Spring 1944): 175–76.

"*Swing Low, Sweet Chariot* Will Be Popular." *Art Digest* 8 (mid-Jan. 1929): 1–2.

Taylor, Joshua C. "The Religious Impulse in American Art." *Papers on American Art*, edited by John C. Milley, 113–32. Maple Shade, NJ: Edinburgh Press for the Friends of Independence National Historical Park, 1976.

Teresi, Dick. "Eminent Victorian, Alas: Sir Francis Galton, Famous Polymath, Was in Reality a Blockhead." Review of Martin Brookes, *Extreme Measures: The Dark Visions and Bright Ideas of Francis Galton*. *New York Times Book Review*, 24 Oct. 2004, section 7, 34

Thurman, Wallace. "Negro Artists and the Negro." *New Republic* 52 (Aug. 1927): 37–39.

Tickner, Lisa. *Modern Life and Modern Subjects: British Art in the Early Twentieth Century*. New Haven: Yale University Press, 2000.

Tiresi, Dick. "Eminent Victorian, Alas: Sir Francis Galton, Famous Polymath, Was in Reality a Blockhead." Review of *Extreme Measures: The Dark Visions and Bright Ideas of Francis Galton*, by Martin Brookes. *New York Times Book Review*, 24 Oct. 2004, section 7, 34.

To Color America: Portraits by Winold Reiss. Washington, D.C.: Smithsonian Institution Press, 1989.

T. T. F. "Grotesque Exaggeration Dominates Art Sketches and Paintings and New Exhibit." *Amsterdam News* (New York), 14 May 1930, 11.

"Ugly or Beautiful, New York Sees the Art of Diego Rivera." *Art Digest* 6, no. 7 (1 Jan. 1932): 1, 12.

Vansina, Jan. *Art History in Africa*. London: Longman, 1984.

Wacquant, Loïc. "For an Analytic of Racial Domination." In *Political Power and Social Theory*, edited by Diane E. Davis, 221–34. Vol. 11. Greenwich, CT: Jai Press, 1997.

Walton, Lester A. "Art Not Racial, Negroes Tell Critic: Leaders Reply to Charge That Works Lack Individuality." *New York World*, 2 Feb. 1930, editorial section, 6.

Wang, Shi-Pu. "Becoming American? Asian Identity Negotiated through the Art of Yasuo Kuniyoshi." PhD diss., University of California at Irvine, 2006.

———. "Japan against Japan: U.S. Propaganda and Yasuo Kuniyoshi's Identity Crisis." *American Art* 22, no. 1 (Spring 2008): 28–51.

Watson, Forbes. "Max Weber." *Magazine of Art* 34, no. 2 (Feb. 1941): 78–83.

———. "The Universal Diplomat." *Parnassus* 5 (Jan. 1933): 2.

Watson, Steven, and Catherine J. Morris, eds. *An Eye on the Modern Century: Selected Letters of Henry McBride*. New Haven: Yale University Press, 2000.

Weber, Max. "Chinese Dolls and Modern Colorists." *Camera Work* 31 (July 1910): 51.

———. "Painting: A Note on the 'Talmudists.'" *Menorah Journal* 23 (Apr.–June 1935): 100.

—. "Whither American Art?" *Menorah Journal* 26 (Spring 1938): 244–51.

"Weber Show Strong, Varied." *American Art News* 21, no. 19, (17 Feb. 1923): 5.

Weinberg, Jonathan. *Speaking for Vice: Homosexuality in the Art of Charles Demuth, Marsden Hartley, and the First American Avant-Garde.* New Haven: Yale University Press, 1993.

Werner, Alfred. *Max Weber.* New York: Harry N. Abrams, 1975.

———. "Max Weber's Triumph." *Opinion: A Journal of Jewish Life and Letters* (May–June 1949): 12.

West, Shearer. *Portraiture.* New York: Oxford University Press, 2004.

Whiting, Cécile. *Antifascism in American Art.* New Haven: Yale University Press, 1989.

Whiting, F. A., Jr. "Argentine Artists at Richmond." *Magazine of Art* 33, no. 2 (Feb. 1940): 124.

Wilson, Judith. "Will the 'New Internationalism' Be the Same Old Story?" In *Global Visions: Towards a New Internationalism in the Visual Arts,* edited by Jean Fisher, 60–68. London: Kala Press; London: Institute of International Visual Arts,1994.

Wolf, Tom. *Yasuo Kuniyoshi's Women.* San Francisco: Pomegranate: 1993.

Wolff, Janet. *AngloModern: Painting and Modernity in Britain and the United States.* Ithaca, NY: Cornell University Press, 2003.

Woodall, Joanna, ed. *Portraiture: Facing the Subject.* Manchester England: Manchester University Press, 1997.

"The World of Art." *New York Times Book Review and Magazine,* 15 Jan. 1922, section 3, 18.

Yang, Alice. *Why Asia? Contemporary Asian and Asian American Art.* New York: New York University Press, 1998.

Yasuo Kuniyoshi. New York: Whitney Museum of American Art at Philip Morris, 1986.

Yasuo Kuniyoshi: 100th Anniversary of His Birth. Kyoto: National Museum of Modern Art, 1989.

Yasuo Kuniyoshi Papers. Smithsonian Archives of American Art, Washington, D.C.

"Your Money Bought These Paintings." *Look* 29 (18 Feb. 1947): 80–81.

Zhou, Min. "Are Asian Americans Becoming White?" In *Contemporary Asian America: A Multidisciplinary Reader,* edited by Zhou and J. V. Gatewood, 331–53. 2d ed. New York: New York University Press, 2007.

Zhou, Min, and James V. Gatewood, eds. *Contemporary Asian America: A Multidisciplinary Reader.* New York: New York University Press, 2000.

Zurier, Rebecca, Robert W. Snyder, and Virginia M. Mecklenburg. *Metropolitan Lives: The Ashcan Artists and Their New York.* New York: Norton, 1995.

INDEX

Page numbers in bold refer to figures.

www.ingramcontent.com/pod-product-compliance
Lightning Source LLC
LaVergne TN
LVHW050253080826
844660LV00012B/630
9780295996899